From Stanislavsky to Barrault

FROM
STANISLAVSKY
TO BARRAULT

REPRESENTATIVE DIRECTORS OF
THE EUROPEAN STAGE

Samuel L. Leiter

Contributions in Drama and Theatre Studies, Number 34

Greenwood Press
New York • Westport, Connecticut • London

Library of Congress Cataloging-in-Publication Data

Leiter, Samuel L.
    From Stanislavsky to Barrault / Samuel L. Leiter.
      p. cm.—(Contributions in drama and theatre studies, ISSN
0163–3821 ; no. 34)
    Includes bibliographical references and index.
    ISBN 0–313–27661–7 (alk. paper)
    1. Theatrical producers and directors—Europe—Biography.
2. Theater—Production and direction. 3. Theater—History—20th
century. I. Title. II. Series.
PN2570.L45 1991
792′.0233′09224—dc20
  [B]   90–45612

British Library Cataloguing in Publication Data is available.

Library of Congress Catalog Card Number: 90–45612
ISBN: 0–313–27661–7
ISSN: 0163–3821

First published in 1991

Greenwood Press, 88 Post Road West, Westport, CT 06881
An imprint of Greenwood Publishing Group, Inc.

Printed in the United States of America

The paper used in this book complies with the
Permanent Paper Standard issued by the National
Information Standards Organization (Z39.48–1984).

10 9 8 7 6 5 4 3 2 1

To Rose Lerner and Eddie Debowsky

Contents

Preface

When this book was first written, it was a rather novel offering in a field of theatrical research that was just then coming into its own as a matter of serious concern. Apart from Toby Cole and Helen Krich Chinoy's important collection of documents, *Directors on Directing* (rev. ed. 1963), only one prior book in English (Norman Marshall's excellent *The Producer and the Play,* rev. ed. 1975) had been published purporting to survey in some depth the careers of the most important stage directors. And Marshall's otherwise comprehensive book had not even ventured to look at American practitioners.

Meanwhile, as the present work languished in the hands of a succession of publishers (three to be exact), each of whom ran into catastrophic financial problems and had to scuttle the project (which as early as 1981 had been printed in galley form and was being advertised), a series of useful writings on directors began to appear. These ranged from such surveys as Edward Braun's *The Director and the Stage* (1982) to David Bradby and David Williams' *Directors' Theatre* (1988), along with a series of carefully researched monographs on specific directors, a number of whom are also discussed in the following pages.

At long last, the project found in Greenwood a publisher who had long been interested in it (Greenwood having published a considerable number of my other books), and the decision was made to divide what had become a rather unwieldy tome into two complementary books, *From Belasco to Brook: Representative Directors of the English-Speaking Stage* and *From Stanislavsky to Barrault: Representative Directors of the European Stage.*

Both books were thoroughly revised and updated through the years to take account of newly published materials and of new activity by the three directors who remained active (Abbott, Barrault, and Brook). The text represents all such developments through 1989.

For assistance in my research I would like to thank the staffs of the Lincoln Center Library for the Performing Arts and of the Gideonse Library, Brooklyn

College, City University of New York. I would also like to thank Ms. Erika Kralik, head of documentation at the Théâtre Renaud-Barrault, Paris, for her helpful responses to my inquiries.

For keeping me sane during these trying years, for helping me with numerous editorial details, and for compiling the indexes I must thank my wonderful wife, Marcia.

Introduction

Ever since Western theatre began in ancient Greece, there has been someone—an actor, playwright, producer, stage manager—to fulfill the basic functions of the stage director, although no particular term identified his role in the production process. In most cases, his responsibilities were primarily those of organization and traffic management; interpretation, albeit limited, must now and then have played a role as well. Still, for all its innate importance, it is generally agreed that stage direction was not accorded recognition as an independent theatrical art until the 1870s, when Georg II, Duke of Saxe-Meiningen, directed his court troupe and, through a series of international tours, showed Europe what could be done when a play was completely realized in performance through the application of a single, unified directorial vision.

The revolution in theatrical production effected by the Meiningen company was not accomplished overnight. It was necessary for a number of other distinguished members of this new breed of artists—men like André Antoine, Otto Brahm, Aurelian Lugné–Poë, and Augustin Daly—to make their mark before the need for directors became a theatrical commonplace. Even the terminology used to refer to directors and their art remained vague well into the present century. It is only in recent years, for instance, that the British have begun to lean toward the term ''director'' and away from ''producer,'' which, of course, has entirely different connotations in the American theatre. Nevertheless, by the end of the nineteenth century experienced theatregoers were, for the first time, talking about a growing number of individuals who were virtually transforming the nature of the theatre experience by the application of their personal touch to stage production, even when they were neither in the play nor credited with its writing. An age was dawning when audiences would increasingly attend the theatre not to see the work of some famous star or dramatist, but to confront the individualistic expressions of specific directors; this new period was to be called the ''age of the director.''

It is not difficult to identify who these directors are. What is problematic, however, is to select those who might be considered representative of this still young and continually evolving art. The choices made in *From Stanislavsky to Barrault* and its companion volume, *From Belasco to Brook,* will unquestionably differ from those others might have made. They have been selected to cover the broad spectrum of directorial art as it has developed during this century. It is not my intention to defend each of my selections. I would, however, like briefly to discuss all the directors in both books in aggregate and to identify some of the salient aspects of the director's art that they exemplify. These, I believe, are comprehensive enough to embrace a considerable range of available methodologies and, to a large extent, to be applied to those many outstanding directors not dealt with in these pages.

The first thing that identifies these directors is their diversity of taste and accomplishment. If we look, for example, at the matter of repertory, we see those like David Belasco and George Abbott, whose entire output was of the strictly commercial, escapist, entertainment-for-entertainment's-sake variety; the former concentrated on contemporary and historical melodramas, the latter on contemporary melodramas, comedies, farces, and musicals. Contrasting with them are directors like Bertolt Brecht and Vsevolod Meyerhold, who devoted much of their careers to making the theatre intellectually provocative and politically viable from a Marxist point of view. Some of these directors, like Harley Granville-Barker, Tyrone Guthrie, Margaret Webster, and Peter Brook can thank Shakespeare and other classics for the foundations of their reputations; while others, like Elia Kazan, David Belasco, George Abbott, and Bertolt Brecht rarely could be found within a stone's throw of a play older than themselves. Then again, Kazan could be cited as a director whose greatest successes come from the work of one or two specific modern playwrights (i.e., Tennessee Williams and Arthur Miller), while Konstantin Stanislavsky, for all his other accomplishments, is indelibly linked with the plays of Anton Chekhov. Several of the directors here were major playwrights. Brecht, for example—unquestionably the most outstanding German dramatist of the century—only staged someone else's plays on a handful of occasions, while Granville-Barker, Abbott, and Belasco directed plays written both by themselves and others. Max Reinhardt, Jean-Louis Barrault, Jacques Copeau, and Joan Littlewood directed new plays and old, classics and avant-garde, and consequently had rather eclectic repertories, with no single playwright or type of dramaturgy occupying an undue share of their credits.

The directors included here also represent a cross section of the modern theatre's stylistic attitudes toward production. Thus we have Belasco's use of minutely detailed naturalism in the service of each and every play; Stanislavsky's "spiritual naturalism" marked by a preoccupation with investigating the means for creating psychological truth in acting; the objective theatricalism of Meyerhold's biomechanics and constructivism; Reinhardt's never-ending search through every variety of style and environment for the perfect *gesamtkunstwerk*;

the flexible adaptability of a naked stage and the disciplined ensemble expressiveness of Copeau; the quiet naturalism and modern Elizabethanism (or Elizabethan-modernism) of Granville-Barker; the rapid-fire, door-slamming comedic techniques of Abbott; the estrangement devices of Brecht's anti-Aristotelian, Marxist-oriented epic theatre; Guthrie's "wouldn't-it-be-fun-if" interpretations of the classics; Webster's domestication and popularization of the Bard; Kazan's hard-hitting psychological theatricalism; Barrault's employment of mime and Artaudian "total theatre"; Littlewood's improvisational and anti-Establishment left-wing antics; and Brook's multifaceted concept of the "empty space" and his never-ending exploration of the essences and ritual structures of theatre.

Similarly varied is the approach of these directors to their work with actors; their own backgrounds, however, do not reveal such dissimilarity. Ten of them first established their careers as actors (Belasco, Stanislavsky, Meyerhold, Reinhardt, Granville-Barker, Abbott, Webster, Kazan, Barrault, and Littlewood); most continued to act—for varying lengths of time—either in their own productions, those of others, or both. Guthrie gave up acting very early on, Copeau began acting only when he also began directing, Brecht occasionally performed in cabarets but not on the legitimate stage, and Brook never acted at all.

In their rehearsal methods a number of these directors (Meyerhold, Belasco, Abbott, Reinhardt, and the early Stanislavsky, for example) were essentially autocratic, even dictatorial, using any method, foul or fair, to get desired results. Others (such as Brecht, Littlewood, and Brook, and the later Stanislavsky) gave their companies great freedom, allowing the actors to discover their own movement and behavior through the employment of a wide assortment of creative techniques, especially improvisation. Some brooked no interference from others who might have suggestions to offer; others were openly collaborative, often codirecting and even accepting critical comments from casual rehearsal visitors.

Some came to rehearsals with every move blocked out in advance, every vocal nuance preplanned; this could be in an extensive promptbook or it could be entirely in their head. Others followed the tabula rasa approach, and used the rehearsal process to discover what the play was about, what its theatrical possibilities were, and what the actors involved could bring to realizing it on stage. Then again, there were those who would accept a script and respect it implicitly (Granville-Barker, Copeau, and Webster are good examples), and there were those who could not direct a play without making extensive revisions in the text or having the playwright do so (see, especially, Meyerhold, Kazan, Abbott, and Littlewood).

On other fronts there is a surprising homogeneity in the approaches of these directors. An impressive statistic is the number who were devoted to the idea of working within the concept of a repertory company, with a band of permanent players who would appear in one play after another during one or more seasons. Even if they often had to work within the restrictions of the typical one-shot commercial milieu, they would return whenever possible to the less financially lucrative company idea where they could explore challenging plays with a fixed group of players under conditions which, more often than not, permitted relatively protracted rehearsal periods. Company directors, and some of the companies they headed, include Stanislavsky (Moscow Art Theatre), Meyerhold (Imperial Theatres, St. Petersburg; Meyerhold [State] Theatre, Moscow), Reinhardt (numerous theatres), Granville-Barker (the Court and Savoy Theatres, London), Copeau (Théâtre du Vieux Colombier, Paris), Brecht (Berliner Ensemble, East Berlin), Guthrie (Old Vic, London; Festival Theatre, Stratford, Ontario; Guthrie Theatre, Minneapolis), Webster (American Repertory Theatre, New York; Marweb Shakespeare Company, touring), Barrault (Compagnie Madeleine Renaud–Jean-Louis Barrault, Paris), Littlewood (Theatre Workshop, London), and Brook (Royal Shakespeare Company, London; Center for International Theatre Research, Paris). Kazan, after a successful career as a commercial director, fulfilled a dream when he took over the new Lincoln Center Repertory Company, but left the theatre when bureaucratic circumstances frustrated him. And if one looks at the careers of the two other commercially oriented directors in these books, it is clear that even Belasco and Abbott kept a ''company'' idea in mind when casting for their shows.

Another thing that ties many of these great directors together is the multiplicity of their theatre talents. Most of them are *hommes* and *femmes de théâtre*. For example, putting aside their directing abilities, we can point to such representative individuals as Belasco, who wrote popular plays, acted (in his early career), and was a master lighting designer; Meyerhold, who designed sets and acted; Granville-Barker, who was an important playwright and actor; Copeau, a critic turned playwright, actor, and theoretician; Abbott, a hit playwright, producer, and leading man; Brecht, the outstanding German playwright and theoretician of the century; and Brook, who not only designed many of his productions, but composed the music for them as well.

We see, moreover, in the careers of many of these directors a continuing fascination with the shape and function of the performance space. The traditional proscenium with its fourth-wall realism may have been the *sine qua non* for directors like Belasco, Stanislavsky, and Abbott, but most of the others were seriously alienated from the picture-frame stage. Meyerhold continuously sought to break through the ''fourth wall'' with aprons built over the orchestra pit, and Granville-Barker did likewise; the latter also discovered a suitable tripartite method of arranging the stage for Shakespeare so that Elizabethan conventions could be combined with contemporary styles of decor. Copeau reinvented the architectural stage on his *tréteau nu,* while Guthrie was almost single-handedly responsible for the reintroduction into contemporary theatre architecture of the three-quarters round stage combined with a permanent, but variable, scenic arrangement. Max Reinhardt made the revolving stage essential to the best-equipped theatres, and also showed what could be done by staging plays in circus arenas, on church steps, in wooded glades, on Venetian canals, in eighteenth-century ballrooms, in immense U-shaped indoor amphitheatres, and in tiny chamber theatres. Peter Brook regularly put on plays in the orchestra area of a burned-out nineteenth-century theatre, and in such natural environments as the awesome hills of Persepolis and the open, dusty, unadorned squares of African villages, with nothing but a carpet for a stage.

The majority of these great directors wrote about their theatre ideas, some of them extensively. Many of these works form the foundation for Western theatre thought in our times. A glance at some of the highlights of such writings (with reference to only those foreign works that have been translated into English)[1] would focus attention on Stanislavsky's books, from *My Life in Art* through his three major tomes on acting; Meyerhold's miscellaneous articles and treatises as translated by Edward Braun in *Meyerhold on Theatre*; Brecht's numerous theoretical works, including *The Messingkauf Dialogues* and *The Little Organon*; Granville-Barker's multiple *Prefaces to Shakespeare* and many other books, including *The Exemplary Theatre* and *The Study of Drama*; Tyrone Guthrie's *In Various Directions, A New Theatre,* and others; Webster's two-volume autobiography and her *Shakespeare without Tears*; Barrault's *The Theatre of Jean-Louis Barrault* and *Memories for Tomorrow*; and Brook's *The Empty Space* and *The Shifting Point.* It may not be too far-fetched to say not only that their productions have had a profound effect on the shape of the modern theatre, but that their ideas as communicated through the written word may have made an even more powerful impact because they were thus able to reach a far vaster audience than could ever have attended their productions.

Finally, the men and women of these volumes are linked by their each having contributed productions which may easily be seen as beacons charting the progress of the modern theatre. Hopefully, the capsule descriptions of many of these landmark works in the pages that follow will make apparent the changes that have marked the theatre of our times from such works as Stanislavsky's *The Seagull* to Barrault's *Rabelais.*

A few words are in order about the approach taken to the subjects of these volumes. Each chapter is organized into numerous subsections, but the essential pattern is to first discuss the individual's career, then his or her overarching conception of theatre art and directing, and finally his or her actual working methods. Each chapter includes a chronology that focuses on plays directed; apart from one or two exceptions, operas and films are not included, but, in some cases, musicals and operettas are. Because of the different natures of the careers involved, the listings vary slightly in format from one director to the other. Thus, almost every chapter has information on a director's repertory, major productions, theoretical concerns, techniques of working with actors, playwrights, designers, and composers, casting methods, production preparations, and rehearsal processes. There are as many approaches to directing as there are directors, and no one technique or ideology can be held up as an ideal. Each director must discover for himself or herself the best way of working; some of the greatest, such as Peter Brook, have gone from one method to another as experience taught them what was most appropriate to their own personalities and situations. One of the purposes in writing these volumes was to reveal this wide divergence of directorial styles and techniques and to thereby open the reader to the kaleidoscopic multiplicity of avenues open to exponents of the art. The treatment of the books' subjects then, is not critical, but descriptive. It implies that for some the paternalistic authoritarianism of a Belasco or Meyerhold may actually be appropriate, while for others the collaborative, investigative, and experimental methods of a Brook may be the route to travel.

It is a given that, in his or her own time, each of the directors described here was—despite obvious pockets of criticism—widely considered a master of the art. Today, some of these artists have been subjected to the whims of revisionist thinking which scorns techniques no longer in fashion. Occasionally, comment on negative contemporary criticism of various directors has been included, but just as it was never my intention to write hagiography, it was also not my aim to denigrate individuals selected because I deemed them representative of certain schools of directing.

The theatre is no longer the monolithic structure it was in pre modern times. Each new theatrical venture potentially expresses a new vision of the art; each new director has the option of following and expanding one of the many existing traditions or striking out on his own in search of some idiosyncratic notion of what the theatre's expressive potential might be. Every director discussed in these books has brought to the theatre a special viewpoint that has enriched its literary, architectural, decorative, and performance facets. These works are dedicated to all directors, conservatives and radicals, and every shade in between, for it is only through a healthy heterogeneity of styles and methods that the theatre of the future will survive and flourish.

NOTE

1. Much remains untranslated, both by those cited here and by Jacques Copeau, whose work has only appeared in English in scattered essays. Norman H. Paul is reported to be completing *Jacques Copeau: Texts on Theatre, an Anthology*.

From Stanislavsky to Barrault

Konstantin Stanislavsky

(1863–1938)

Konstantin Stanislavsky, whose career as an actor and director was a long and illustrious one, spent much of it in the often painful process of self-examination as he worked out a system of actor training which—in one form or another—is still the most widely practiced throughout the world. This system seeks for truthful onstage behavior with an organic connection between the internalization and externalization of a role. As a director, Stanislavsky sought to inspire his actors to perform with absolute conviction and to so enrapture his audiences by the lifelike acting and other production elements that they would even forget they were in a theatre. In everything he did, he aspired to the highest standards of artistry, and stood like a beacon of truth and sincerity to the legions he inspired and continues to inspire.

EARLY YEARS

Born Konstantin Sergeyevich Alexeyev near Moscow in 1863, he was the son of a wealthy manufacturer of gold and silver thread, Sergei Vladimirovich Alexeyevev, a full-blooded Russian, and Elisaveta Vasilievna Alexeyeva, of French and Russian parentage. Elisaveta's French mother (who bore her illegitimately) was an actress known as Marie Varley. Konstantin was one of a brood of ten siblings (nine of whom survived), and several of whom (two sisters and a brother) grew up to find employment in the theatre.

Shortly after Stanislavsky was born, his family moved to central Moscow, where he was raised in a large, comfortable home. His cultivated family often took him to the circus, opera, ballet, and theatre from the time he was six or eight. Amateur theatricals played an important part in his childhood and adolescence. In his youth he formed a troupe with his siblings, friends, and local residents to do plays and puppet shows for family gatherings. Known as the Alexeyev Circle, the group performed in a well-appointed little playhouse erected for them by Konstantin's father on the family estate at Lyubimovka. In 1883, his father turned two large rooms in his Moscow house into another theatre for the Circle; it seated 300 and was expensively decorated. Amateur theatricals were a widely practiced pastime among well-to-do Muscovites, but few could boast such splendid environments for their offerings.

Konstantin's first directing opportunity with the Circle came in 1881 when, at age eighteen, he staged four one-act comedies which he rehearsed assiduously in the hopes of creating a well-paced, carefully balanced presentation. The proper pace and proportion, however, remained elusive. He had staged the plays with his close friend Fedya Kashkadamov, and did not direct alone until 1882 when he did Molière's *The Forced Marriage*. He played the leading role in this and all other plays he directed during these years; this double task would occupy him for most of his professional career as well.

Vaudevilles (usually defined as a type of satirical French comedy with inter-polated songs) and operettas exerted a strong attraction for Konstantin, who had shown considerable promise as an opera singer before developing vocal problems in 1887. Music also played a crucial role in most of his straight productions, helping to establish tempo and keep the actors on their toes.

In 1883, Stanislavsky directed Victor A. Dyachenko's *The Practical Man*, a one-act comedy, at Lyubimovka. During the rehearsal period, the young director devised the then novel idea of requiring his company to live their offstage lives in the characters they were portraying, and to improvise dialogue and behavior suited to the circumstances of the comedy. Eventually this practice led Konstantin to realize how helpful finding the correct external behavior for a role could be in uncovering the proper internal state.

Among the French operettas he staged was Hervé's *Lili* (1886), which was then running in Paris. Even more impressive was his production of William Gilbert and Arthur Sullivan's *The Mikado* in 1887. It should be noted that these performances, amateur though they were, were rather lavishly done and attracted a distinguished audience, including critics for the Moscow newspapers; the re-views usually showered praise on the actors, whose social reputations were carefully protected by their being referred to via their initials. The help of a traveling company of Japanese acrobats was enlisted for *The Mikado* to teach the company numerous details of Japanese movement and behavior. The actors walked, bowed, danced, and gestured as if they were Japanese; they even mas-tered the art of using the fan as a means of theatrical expression. Both *Lili* and *The Mikado* were given unusually long rehearsal periods lasting the better part of a year. Lengthy periods of preparation later became a hallmark of Stanislavsky productions.

FROM ALEXEYEV TO STANISLAVSKY: THE SOCIETY OF ART AND LITERATURE

The Alexeyev Circle dispersed following its production of *The Mikado*. Kon-stantin Alexeyev was now a well-known Moscow amateur actor, having appeared in various other amateur theatres in addition to working with his family troupe. For the scion of a rich bourgeois family—the Alexeyevs were then as much a synonym for wealth as the Rockefellers are today—to spend all his spare time acting, even in amateur circles, was something that might have brought considerable embarrassment to his parents, who did not object to the performances when they were merely family events. To save his family any shame that might have accrued from his activities, Konstantin Alexeyev began to perform in 1884 under the name Konstantin Stanislavsky, taking the Polish surname from an amateur actor friend; the latter, in turn, had taken it from a ballerina named Stanislavskaya both he and Konstantin had admired years earlier. By this time Konstantin was an extremely tall, splendidly built, elegantly turned out young man; he would become prematurely gray, a family trait, and, with his black eyebrows and patrician features, come to be thought of as exceptionally handsome.

Konstantin, under the influence of the impressive Imperial theatre, the Maly, resolved to play in works of a more dignified nature and in a situation where he could have some control over the repertory. Furthermore, having played with poorly trained actors in the gorgeous amateur productions produced by the wealthy industrialist-aesthete Savva Mamontov, he began to understand that the actor is the heart of the theatre, and that without good acting all the most beautiful staging values are worthless.

In 1888 Stanislavsky, Alexandre Fedotov (a respected writer-director-actor, who was returning to Russia after many years in Paris), and the noted tenor Fyodor Komissarjevsky (father of the famous director of that name) founded a fashionable artists' club called the Society of Art and Literature; Stanislavsky himself provided the extensive funding necessary to set up the organization. Although its membership was open to artists from the worlds of painting, music, literature, and theatre, it was the latter to which Stanislavsky gave the bulk of his attention. The amateur acting company was run with professional goals and standards and attracted the attention of the entire Moscow intellectual and artistic world. Fedotov was the director (he also ran the club's acting school) and Stanislavsky the leading actor. Fedotov's devotion to the principles of artistic truth had a powerful effect on Stanislavsky.

Another director soon to have a strong influence on Stanislavsky was the German, Ludwig Chronegk, who staged plays for the famous company headed by the Duke of Saxe-Meiningen. The Meiningen company had visited Moscow in 1885, but it wasn't until their 1890 visit that Stanislavsky first visited them and woke to the powerful effects that could be created by a company that was perfectly drilled down to the last walk-on. They did plays in which every detail of production was expertly realized from a historical, archaeological, and aesthetic point of view. Only an autocrat-director could guarantee the visual perfection represented by the Meiningen troupe. Especially significant to Stanislavsky was Chronegk's ability to mask the inferiority of his actors by an inventive use of stage business.

Fedotov soon left his post as director, and following a period during which the job was filled by a director from the state-run Maly Theatre, Stanislavsky took it over. To meet expenses, the Society's theatre—set up in the Society's quarters, a rented mansion known as the Ginsburg House—was rented to the Moscow Hunting Club, and it was agreed that the Society would give a weekly performance for the families of club members. Later in the Society's history, productions were staged at other Moscow playhouses as well.

Stanislavsky staged his first production for the Society in 1889, A. F. Pisemsky's one-act *Burning Letters*. This first of his mountings outside the Alexeyev Circle was mounted in a manner influenced by the director's viewings of theatre in Paris during a recent sojourn there. Stanislavsky managed to produce a strikingly restrained and believable performance from his actors, one of whom even dared to turn his back to the audience. In addition, numerous realistic props were placed about the stage by Stanislavsky in order to help the actors believe in the actuality of their stage lives. No matter how flimsy the material, Stanislavsky consistently sought to establish the fundamental reality of the characters involved.

In 1891, as his first directorial job since taking over the artistic control of the theatre from Fedotov, he presented Leo Tolstoy's *The Fruits of Enlightenment,* a difficult play with many characters and the always sticky problem of handling large groups. During the then rather long rehearsal period of fourteen or fifteen sessions, Stanislavsky focused on achieving inner truth through careful attention to the details of external environment and activity; he even cast actors who matched the social class distinctions of the characters—upper-class society people as aristocrats and peasants as peasants. Each actor was instructed to base his role on real-life persons, a practice which Stanislavsky had begun to employ in *Burning Letters*. As would so often be the case in a Stanislavsky production, the ensemble effect in which each character was carefully etched as a three-dimensional individual was remarked upon by the critics, some of whom were finding that the young director's stagings—with their combination of psychological truth and integrated ensemble performances—were often superior to those of the Moscow professional theatre. In fact, there are those who date the rise of the "director's theatre" in Russia from this amateur production.

To help achieve his effects, Stanislavsky imposed a sharp, Meiningen-like rehearsal discipline on the company: lateness was punished, as were careless work habits, talking, leaving without permission, tasteless clothing, the wearing by the women of large hats, and flirting. It mattered little to the director that his actors were all amateurs who worked at other jobs all day (as did Stanislavsky himself) or attended classes and could rehearse only in the evenings, ending at midnight. Stanislavsky treated his dedicated company as professionals, and they tried to respond as such, giving him as much deference and respect as he could wish. Practically a fanatic over ethics in the theatre, he was preoccupied with making the theatre as respectable and cultured an occupation as that of any of the fine arts; the easy ways and undisciplined lives of many actors irritated him for reflecting unjustly on the entire profession. In this attitude, he was echoing the calls for reform made by the famous Russian playwright Alexander Ostrovsky. Stanislavsky, like Ostrovsky (many of whose plays he would one day stage), saw the theatre as a temple of art in which the noblest aspects of man's life were illuminated.

Stanislavsky's next major presentation was *Foma* (1891), his own successful adaptation of Fyodor Dostoyevsky's comic novel *The Village of Stepanchikovo*, in which he costarred with his talented wife, Maria Lilina, whom he had met and married during these fruitful years. The play (which had taken three years to pass the censors) attracted attention not only because of Stanislavsky's skilled acting in a principal role, but because of his masterful handling of the realistic, everyday atmosphere, including expressive pauses and offstage sound effects.

It was two years before Stanislavsky directed another play for the Society. In 1894 his mountings for the Society included Dyachenko's *The Governor* and Ostrovsky and Nikolai Soloviov's *Light without Heat,* but neither was as important as his staging in 1895 of Karl Gutzkow's well-known *Uriel Acosta,* set in the Jewish quarter of Amsterdam in the seventeenth century; with this initial attempt at a tragedy, Stanislavsky scored a tremendous hit as director and actor. Moscow theatre circles were greatly excited by the Meiningen-influenced documentary authenticity of costumes, sets, and manners. The crowd scenes, especially, were among the most effective ever seen in the city. Stanislavsky's brilliant handling of the crowds was an excellent way of covering up inept acting by the leading players while simultaneously delivering crucial dramatic points. Each crowd member was thoroughly rehearsed and made to develop a fully rounded and distinct personality; each was even given specific dialogue to speak so that the hubbub of voices would sound believable. Stanislavsky's inspired vision of precisely what effects he wanted was realized less by dictatorial demands than by a careful use of suggestions and explanations; thus, the production was unusually effective, and the climatic scene in which the mob murders the title figure had an unforgettably frightening emotional power.

Pisemsky's *Men above the Law* was mounted in 1895. A crowd scene in which a mob of peasants attack a country house was excellently conceived and executed. This was followed by *Othello* (1896), a presentation which revealed Stanislavsky's debt to the Meiningen principle of doing heavy research for a historical production. A trip to Venice was occupied with many hours in museums and antique shops. Stanislavsky even convinced an Arab he met in Paris, where he had gone to buy books and costume fabrics, to take off his robe so that he could study it and the way in which the man's body moved. The play was staged in an archaeologically realistic style, including the use of gondolas floating in Venetian canals. As had become his custom, the director prepared an extensively annotated production plan in which each moment of the play was enriched with realistic activity; the most minute pauses and transitions were noted as were the specifics of all the physical objects to be used in the staging.

Many novel ideas were developed. For example, taking a hint from two lines in Act II, scene iii, one mentioning a "mutiny" and the other the possibility that "the town will rise," Stanislavsky created an exciting scene of the native Cypriots rebelling against their Venetian conquerers. This gave Othello an opportunity to enter sword in hand and part the battling mob. Though he justified the scene in terms of its helping to elucidate the text, the regisseur also revealed that it was a device to shift attention from the weaker actors on the stage.[1] Apart from a strong beginning Stanislavsky himself was generally thought a failure in the title role, which he had wanted to do ever since being powerfully impressed by Italian tragedian Tommaso Salvini's epochal performance in it years before.

Stanislavsky next staged Gerhart Hauptmann's *Hannele* (1896), a strange blend of naturalism and fantasy. This was given under professional auspices and not for the Society. *Hannele*'s fantastical effects gave Stanislavsky another chance to create a startling mise-en-scène in the manner for which he had so much talent. He taxed his ingenuity in creating sensationally eerie moments. Suspenseful pauses, half-uttered words, whispers, moaning, the rise and fall of voices, slow and solemn movements, shadows, and frightening sound effects were combined to create an unforgettable phantasmagoria suggesting Hannele's delirium and death.

Stanislavsky was contemplating turning the Society into a professional company when he mounted his next offering, Emile Erckmann and Louis-Alexandre Chatrian's popular melodrama *The Polish Jew* (1896)—better known in English as *The Bells*. A burgomaster (played by the director), guilty of a Jew's murder, undergoes a series of guilt-inspired hallucinations that Stanislavsky staged with an impressive use of lighting, sound effects, and acting. In one hair-raising scene, the burgomaster's bedroom was transformed into a nightmare courtroom with ghostly figures, appearing as if from thin air, to try the murderer for his crime. Such trickery fascinated Stanislavsky, who revealed, "I like to create deviltry in the theatre."[2]

Following a production of Ostrovsky's *Girl without a Dowry* at the end of 1896, Stanislavsky returned to Shakespeare, directing *Much Ado about Nothing* (1897). He did the comedy not because he had a strong desire to stage the play for its poetry or ideas, but because he had become enchanted by the scenic and costume possibilities of a medieval background after visiting a castle in Turin. At the time he believed that an audience could only truly accept the actions performed onstage if they were part of an authentic-looking locale.

Another Shakespeare comedy, *Twelfth Night,* followed, at the end of 1897. Having played Benedick in *Much Ado,* Stanislavsky now tried Malvolio. This production made him aware of the need for an outstanding designer. Therefore, he hired the talented genre painter Victor Simov, who would be with him for many years to come. Simov soon designed Stanislavsky's last production for the Society, *The Sunken Bell* (1898), a poetic fantasy employing a range of bizarre creatures—including a toadlike water sprite and a cloven-hoofed wood goblin—and requiring a full panoply of special effects. Stanislavsky, who played Heinrich the bellwright, had come to recognize the importance of a three-dimensional scenic embodiment in place of the conventional two dimensions then in use at most theatres. The actor must harmonize with his environment and not contrast with it, as when flat painted scenery surrounded him. *The Sunken Bell* showed Simov's solution to the problem with his use of interesting levels made into hills with trees and rocks—natural obstacles placed in the actor's way—which forced the actor to climb, leap, and clamber rather than merely walk. The actor's consequent physicality was a distinguishing feature of the performance, and Stanislavsky thought this a great step forward in his progress as a director.

THE FOUNDING OF THE MOSCOW ART THEATRE

For some years Stanislavsky had been growing more and more dissatisfied with the conditions of the amateur stage. Most of the professional theatres in Moscow were upsettingly poor from an artistic standpoint. Their methods of acting and production were slovenly and stale. Stanislavsky had had several firsthand experiences directing professionals during his Society days; in one case he had undertaken Nikolai Gogol's *The Inspector-General* at a summer theatre near Moscow and surprised the smooth professionals by telling them that to play the real Gogol they would have to throw away all their old tricks and habits and start afresh from his point of view. Having made them insecure, he ruled them like a tyrant, though lack of time prevented him from getting the performances he sought.

Stanislavsky knew that a new theatre had to be established, but he needed someone to work with him in making it a reality. His Society actors had grown anxious to turn professional and form a company. They wanted a first-class theatre that would revolutionize the art of stage production in Russia and raise the theatre to a height worthy of respect. On June 22, 1897, the well-known playwright, critic, and acting teacher, Vladimir Nemirovich-Danchenko, who also wanted to establish such a theatre, met with Stanislavsky at the Slavic Bazaar Restaurant in a marathon eighteen-hour session that began at two in the afternoon and lasted until eight in the morning, ending at Stanislavsky's Lyubimovka estate. During this famous meeting, the two men laid the foundation for a new theatre of which they were to be codirectors. They called it the Open Art Theatre (another translation is Public Art Theatre, the original Russian word being intended as a euphemism for the politically suspect "popular") in the hope of attracting a middle- and lower-class audience; economic and political circumstances prevented this and, midway through its first season, the name was changed to the Moscow Art Theatre (MAT). Nemirovich-Danchenko was given full veto powers over all literary matters, especially choice of plays, and Stanislavsky was put in charge of all matters relating to production and direction; Nemirovich-Danchenko's powers, though, did extend to hiring actors and casting. The company was financed by shareholders, most of them small investors, but very little of its funding came from the prosperous Stanislavsky, who was afraid to risk his family's patrimony on the venture; he had been chastened by his economic losses on behalf of the Society theatre. The company was refinanced several years later so that the actors and other theatre workers could themselves become shareholders.

For two decades Stanislavsky had endeavored to provide Moscow with acting and productions which rivaled those of the professionals. He now embarked on the most significant period of his career, during which the MAT claimed world-wide attention for the excellence of its ensemble, the realism of its productions, and the effectiveness of its actor-training methods.

During the early MAT years, Stanislavsky gladly gave up to Nemirovich-Danchenko the theatre's administrative responsibilities. He had had his share of these in running the family business, where he still had to spend a good deal of his time. Additionally, Nemirovich-Danchenko proved to be a highly capable stage director; in fact, his and Stanislavsky's work for nearly a decade was more collaborative than not. Many of the productions for which Stanislavsky is famed, then, were also largely the products of input by Nemirovich-Danchenko. It was a stroke of enormous good luck that Nemirovich-Danchenko was a man who had been working toward the same goals of inner and outer stage truthfulness as Stanislavsky and that the two were able to coalesce in so dynamic a union. Their partnership was rarely smooth, however, and was marked by many dis-agreements, some of them quite wrenching. These quarrels were both artistic and bureaucratic, the latter stemming from Nemirovich-Danchenko's persistent attempt to maintain total control of the MAT's operations; he and many others perceived Stanislavsky as a gifted but naive artist with an excessively head-in-the-clouds approach to more mundane matters. Still, each retained great respect for the other, no matter what vicissitudes they faced or how many times Stan-islavsky threatened to quit and go to work somewhere else. By 1907 the artistic chasm between them had grown so wide that they decided to go their separate ways as directors, with each handling his own productions; Stanislavsky's first work staged under this arrangement was *The Drama of Life*. As technical head of the company, however, Nemirovich-Danchenko did appear at important Stan-islavsky rehearsals and, when he chose to or was asked for it, offered important advice.

The MAT was founded on the principles of a true repertory company—doing a series of plays in alternating performances using an ensemble system in which there are no stars; the actors' devotion to the art of theatre had to precede their desire for self-glorification. The group was composed mainly of Stanislavsky's best amateurs from the Society and the principal students of Nemirovich-Danchenko from the Moscow Philharmonic Society. There were also a number of older professionals whose experience was largely in the provincial theatres. Important actors in the original company, in addition to Stanislavsky, included his wife, Maria Lilina, Olga Knipper (who would marry Anton Chekhov), Vse-volod Meyerhold (who would become Stanislavsky's chief directorial rival),

Vladimir Gribunin, Vasily Luzhsky, and Ivan Moskvin. The great Vasily Ka-chalov joined the company in 1901.

In preparation for their first season, the company rehearsed on a farm in Pushkino, outside Moscow, in a barn rebuilt to their needs. They rehearsed a repertory of Aleksey Tolstoy's *Tsar Fyodor Ivanovich,* Sophocles' *Antigone* (directed by A. Sanin), Shakespeare's *The Merchant of Venice,* Hauptmann's *Hannele* (eventually banned before it opened because of church protests), and Anton Chekhov's *The Seagull,* working daily on one play from 11:00 A.M. to 5:00 P.M., and then resuming on another play from 8:00 to 11:00 P.M. Actors with principal roles would work privately with one of the directors, in addition to group rehearsals. Sultry days would see the troupe marching into the cool woods to rehearse in the open, while chillier weather saw them working in a caretaker's lodge. An atmosphere of strictest discipline was maintained. Actors were forbidden to quarrel at rehearsals, and one important actor who disobeyed this rule was dismissed for doing so. Everyone in the company was obliged to participate in whatever chores were necessary to keep rehearsal conditions clean and comfortable; the actors were even put to work sewing costumes and making props.

The MAT hoped to stage plays with total honesty, to remove all false the-atricality and unnecessary conventions from the stage. This was to apply to each area of artistic endeavor, from the direction and design areas to the acting. Many of the actors, especially the experienced professionals, found the new lessons hard to learn. Although quarreling at rehearsals was forbidden, some of the actors made it clear to Stanislavsky that they were unhappy with his methods. These actors wanted to continue their old habits of being theatrically effective in the manner to which they had become accustomed, i.e., big voices, dramatic gestures, rapid pacing, and the like. One way Stanislavsky got them to obey was by going onstage and acting scenes out with Nemirovich-Danchenko (whom he says was a talented actor), thereby displaying the success of his ideas. Another way was to ignore the recalcitrant actor while concentrating on his stage partner, making the latter's performance as interesting as possible. Stanislavsky might even go so far as to encourage the obstinate actor in his exaggerated ways, while teaching his partner to play with simplicity and sincerity. The object was to embarrass the former actor by making his appearance seem ridiculous when contrasted with the newer ways. Finally, when other methods failed, Stanislavsky simply ordered the actors about in Chronegk's dictatorial manner. He had no time for a slower, more organic approach. As in the past, moreover, acting problems which could not easily be solved in rehearsal were glossed over by imaginative staging, costumes, sets, and properties.

SCENIC STYLE

Simov was the chief scene designer who worked in close collaboration with Stanislavsky. A man of advanced ideas, Simov did not settle for stock solutions, but strove instead to discover original answers to the company's scenic needs. The striking realism of his sets soon set them apart from others on the Russian stage. Simov was also impressive because, unlike his contemporaries, he sought not merely designs that were visually attractive, but ones that made a statement about the play and were also in tune with the requirements of the acting and direction. Other major designers would later make important contributions to MAT productions as well, among them Vladimir Egorov, Mstislav Dobuzhinsky, Alexandre Benois, and Alexandre Golovin.

The total physical aspect of any production was based on painstaking historical research. Expensive shopping trips to the locales depicted were often undertaken to find authentic items for stage use. Although visual authenticity had its exponents in Germany, France, England, and America at the time, such attention to scenic realism was practically unheard of in the Russian theatre, which typically resorted to stock costumes and scenery for new and old plays alike. For *Tsar Fyodor,* the first of the new company's presentations, trips were taken to various cities—to libraries, to museums, to secondhand stores and antiquaries—resulting in the purchase of a great pile of old materials, props, and garments. In addition to the authentic costumes and materials, many visual elements were created out of more artful means, using imitation goods to pass for real ones. Stanislavsky credits his actress-wife, Maria Lilina, with many of the innovations that the MAT made in historical costuming. Interestingly, pedants noted some anachronisms in the costumes, although it was agreed that the proper atmosphere had been achieved despite such un-Meiningen-like errors.

The MAT scenery was built according to the new principles of creating a three-dimensional environment for the actors; the old conventional two-dimensional wing and drop backgrounds (in which doors were usually set up between the wings with the area over the doorframe left completely open) were abandoned in favor of sets that looked as solid and substantial as the world offstage. Two-dimensional units, painted in perspective, were not totally rejected, however. A number of sets continued to have two-dimensional backdrops, much as they do today.

A characteristic of Simov's interiors was the depiction of offstage rooms, seen through open doors and archways, where simple masking would have been placed by other contemporary designers. The world onstage seemed to extend beyond the boundaries of the stage, so minutely had the decorative and architectural arrangements been observed and reproduced. In addition, floors were designed to look like real ones, various levels were introduced to add picturesqueness to the staging, chairs were often placed with their backs to the audience, scenes that might formerly have been played on a brightly lit stage were now done on a realistically darkened one, and so on.

Toward the end of his career, Stanislavsky rejected the use of preplanned sets and had the designer attend rehearsals while working out plans that evolved from the needs of the action as it was developed by the actors. This idea was ahead of its time. He also rejected elaborate decors and costumes as being distractions from what he gradually had come to see as the essence of theatre, the actor. Near the close of his autobiography, *My Life in Art,* Stanislavsky complained of his failure to find a truly effective background for the acting style he had helped create. As the actor is the ruler of the stage, he needs scenery that will support him, not hinder or distract. Something of infinite simplicity is required, but it must not in its own ingenuity be distracting. In the absence of an artist to match his aspirations, all Stanislavsky could envision was a performance on a bare stage, with nothing to assist the actor but his naked talents, "like a singer or musician,"[3] to perform his roles from the interior of his being. But in these beginning years, Stanislavsky's faith in the actor's abilities was not yet secure, and he felt that anything that could help make his productions successful was worth using.

THE MOSCOW ART THEATRE OPENS

The first home of the MAT was a rundown theatre called the Hermitage, in Karetny (Carriage) Row. One of its innovative features was the replacement of the conventional drop curtain with a simple traveler curtain that opened to the sides. The Hermitage had been refurbished for the new company, but remained theirs for only four years. In 1902 an old operetta and cabaret theatre, the Omon, in Kamergersky Lane, was leased; after it was thoroughly renovated it became the troupe's permanent home. Its interior was redesigned to rid it of any ostentatious decor that might draw attention from the stage, its orchestra pit was eliminated, and it included comfortable, heated dressing rooms; the stage was completely rebuilt with modern equipment, including a revolve; and the electrical system was entirely done over. The theatre also had a traveler curtain like that at the Hermitage; on it was depicted the stylized figure of a sea gull, which, because of the impact of Chekhov's play of that name, henceforth became the symbol of the MAT.

On October 14, 1898, *Tsar Fyodor Ivanovich* was opened, and the MAT immediately became the most talked about subject among Moscow's artists and intellectuals. The realism of the production seemed to transport its audiences back to the time of the title figure. No one onstage seemed even slightly aware of the spectators' presence, so convincingly did they go about their business as if in natural surroundings. Often actors turned their backs on the audience, either because the action demanded it or because the realistic disposition of the furniture forced them to do so. The tiniest walk-ons were given unusually vivid individualization; for example, Stanislavsky's production book contains fourteen minutely detailed paragraphs describing each person passing across a scenic bridge and the closely observed dramatic behavior in which they engage.

Sound effects and lighting, two of the regisseur's favorite production elements, contributed to the feeling that the audience was present, not at a play, but at a real event. With *Tsar Fyodor Ivanovich*, the MAT revealed the style which was to remain its signature no matter how hard it tried to move in other directions.

Stanislavsky wanted his productions to exist as if no audience were present; the opening formed by the proscenium arch was considered a fourth wall, and the actors were instructed to think of it as such. The historically accurate sets, props, and costumes helped the actors believe in the verity of their environment so that they could practically live their characters' lives onstage. All excessively artificial behavior was eliminated so the audience had the feeling it was over-hearing the characters rather than being the target for their performances.

Over the years, Stanislavsky introduced various practices to preserve and enhance the representational quality of his work. Audiences were not allowed to clap during the play, curtain calls were prohibited except for the final curtain, and there were no warning chimes to announce the performance's commence-ment. Moreover, the use of music before the play and during the intermissions was rejected as being too destructive of the illusion created. Stanislavsky elim-inated whatever would remind the audience that it was in a theatre watching a show. He hoped that the audience would come to see his productions not as if going to see a play, but as if visiting old friends. They would go to see not *Uncle Vanya* or *The Three Sisters* but the Prozorof sisters or Vanya himself. Stanislavsky noted in 1933 that the spectator "is an accidental witness" to the play; the actor should "speak up so that he can hear you, place yourself in the right parts of the stage so that he can see you, but for the rest, forget entirely about the audience and put your mind solely on the characters in the play."[4]

THE SEAGULL AND OTHER CHEKHOV PLAYS

After *Tsar Fyodor*'s success, the first season suffered one box-office failure after the other. In addition to the repertory mentioned earlier, this first season included a revival of Stanislavsky's Society production of *The Sunken Bell*, his new staging of Pisemsky's *Men above the Law*, his production of Carlo Goldoni's *La Locandiera* (or *The Mistress of the Inn*), in which he played Ripafratta, and Henrik Ibsen's *Hedda Gabler,* which opened in February 1899 with an outstand-ing Lovborg from the director. The company might not have survived into the new year, however, had it not been for the great success of Chekhov's *The Seagull,* produced in December 1898, which pulled the troupe out of a deep economic hole and permanently changed the course of the MAT's history.

Stanislavsky had not wanted to do Chekhov's play. He felt uncomfortable with its novel style and did not know how to handle it. The play had been selected by Nemirovich-Danchenko, even though its one previous production, in St. Petersburg in 1896, had been a failure. Chekhov was so upset by the jeering of the first-nighters that he was resolved never again to write a play. To Stanislavsky, who admits that his literary tastes were then undeveloped, the play had none of the theatrical excitement of which he was so fond; it seemed colorless and flat. One had to look very closely simply to learn what its plot was. As Stanislavsky began to study the play, while preparing a promptbook for rehearsals, it gradually wove a web of magic over him and drew him into what he perceived as its heart.

The Seagull was directed by Stanislavsky and Nemirovich-Danchenko. Instructed in the overall interpretation of the play by his partner, Stanislavsky, who also played Trigorin, prepared a detailed production plan in which almost every move and inflection was set down, and in which his written comments were accompanied by detailed drawings. Nemirovich-Danchenko, working at Pushkino in the summer of 1898, rehearsed the actors according to the plan, with Stanislavsky joining the company for its final rehearsals. A total of eighty hours (not an unusual amount of time by today's standards but considerable for 1898) was given to rehearsals, with fifteen of the twenty-six sessions led by Nemirovich-Danchenko and nine by Stanislavsky; the others were taken by assistants.

After the St. Petersburg debacle, Chekhov was wary of a new production, especially one in Moscow. Nemirovich-Danchenko had to rely on his close friendship with Chekhov to convince the latter to agree to its revival. The play required a sensitivity to its atmospheric and lyric moods, with an awareness of its abundant humor and profound, though subtle, depiction of character. Stanislavsky may not have fully comprehended the nature of the play, but his intuitive sensibilities—informed by the careful instructions of his partner—led him to create a remarkable production that convincingly grasped the drama's soul.

Stanislavsky's approach was in the basic mode of naturalism, though his evocation of a melancholy mood and feeling lifted the play to a higher sphere. The psychological and physical milieu of Chekhov's characters was suggested believably through a well-observed arrangement of props and scenery. The stage looked as much like an authentic environment as was technically possible. Sound effects played their usual crucial role. Stanislavsky's fame stemmed to a considerable degree from his ability to paint aural pictures of offstage reality. The editor of his notes on *The Seagull* observed:

He introduces sounds taken from human surroundings and sounds imitating various natural phenomena, as he does the sounds made by inanimate things; the clatter of plates, or the fall of a chair, ringing of doorbells and jingling of harness-bells, the whistling of the wind and the patter of the rain, the songs of birds, and so on, are all used by him as indications of the "actual," real life which takes place on the stage as well as means for intensification of some definite mood.[5]

Also in the naturalistic mode was Stanislavsky's use of lighting, which was especially effective in establishing an exact time of day, conditions of weather, and the darkness of evening (in these scenes the dim lighting seems to have made it difficult to see the action).

A study of Stanislavsky's published promptbook for *The Seagull* gives a clear picture of the detailed ways in which he created stage business based on slight textual hints.[6] For instance, characters are seen to enter when not specifically called for in the script, so as to motivate other characters' lines. One such instance is Yakhov's appearance in Act IV, when he whispers in Arkadina's ear; this motivates her request to the others that they go in to dinner. Everything onstage had to happen for a reason, and the myriad of minute motivational activities gave birth to an astonishing lifelikeness in the performance.

Sometimes Stanislavsky felt compelled to alter Chekhov's stage directions to follow through with a particular line of action. He would put in pauses where none were called for and remove them where explicitly requested. Tenses were revised to suit his needs so that, among various examples, "I'll put a chair against it" became "I have put a chair against it."

Chekhov was disturbed by the overly literal methods of staging used by Stanislavsky, complaining that neither *The Seagull* nor his other plays were works of naturalism. He felt that audiences did not desire a reproduction of life but a presentation of a selective and heightened reality, and that they would gladly accept suggestive means for filling in the details not shown onstage. He told the young Meyerhold, for example, that just as one would not put a real nose on a two-dimensional portrait, one should not fill the artificial realm of the stage with the minutia of everyday existence. At the same time, Meyerhold would later express his belief that the naturalism in Stanislavsky's *Seagull* was peripheral, and that the director's genius had captured "the poetic nerve-centre, the hidden poetry of Chekhov's prose."[7]

As his work on Chekhov matured and he came to appreciate the writer's unique manner, Stanislavsky departed from his overly naturalistic staging and moved into a style usually called selective or spiritual realism. In this style the emphasis was not so much on the multitude of closely observed details as it was on the total picture, an orchestration of moods, sounds, pauses, feelings, and character relationships. Internal life gradually took precedence over the external. Actualism was suggested by the realistic environment, but the playing was tied together by subtle rhythmic principles that seemed to come forth effortlessly from the actors. The surface qualities of conventional realism were enhanced by an ability to seek out the inherent truth of each character and to perform this with a sense of conviction that made the fictional personages seem real.

Stanislavsky claimed that the more overt examples of his early naturalism were the only way he could hide his actors' inability to fully internalize their roles. As in the fantastical productions of his amateur days, the ingenious realistic staging was a mask for acting problems. These external veracities were marvelously appealing and served, in a very short time, to make the MAT Russia's most successful theatre. Eventually he learned the lesson that what occurs onstage can never be a mirror of life itself, that stage life of necessity is artistically selective and not a duplicate of reality. Once, as an experiment, he enacted a scene from *A Month in the Country* in an actual outdoor environment resembling that in the play's second act. He ended the experiment, however, when he realized how false he was, acting in natural surroundings. The truth and beauty of nature were ideals toward which the theatre could only struggle; God's artistry was unattainable by man.

The Seagull was actually the least successful Chekhov play produced by the

MAT. After three seasons in the repertory, totaling seventy-nine performances, it was removed and not produced again until 1960. Nevertheless, Stanislavsky realized that with its production, he had found the touchstone for the kind of theatrical truth he would perpetually be seeking.

Possibly because, among other reasons, he thought that the results would be more lucrative, Chekhov almost gave his next work, *Uncle Vanya,* to the Maly Theatre. This was a shock to the MAT, but when the Maly demanded certain textual revisions, the playwright grew angry and removed the script from its possession. Nemirovich-Danchenko, desperate for another hit, persuaded Chekhov to give the play to the MAT. It should be observed that Chekhov, recuperating from illness in Yalta, had not seen the MAT staging of *The Seagull* at this time, although he had read and heard favorable accounts of it. Soon after he gave the company permission to stage *Uncle Vanya,* he viewed a special performance of the earlier work, done *sans* sets but in makeup and costume; his reaction was approving, although he didn't care for Stanislavsky's Trigorin or for the actress playing Nina.

In October 1899, following codirected productions of Aleksey Tolstoy's *The Death of Ivan the Terrible* (staged with brilliant historical pageantry and verisimilitude), *Twelfth Night,* and Hauptmann's *Drayman Henschel,* came *Uncle Vanya,* with an outstanding Dr. Astrov from Stanislavsky; it eclipsed even *The Seagull* in the effective depiction of the dramatic environment.

One persistent activity that Stanislavsky introduced in rehearsals was the constant swatting at mosquitoes by most of the characters. Nemirovich-Danchenko was annoyed by this, but even more so by the business of people placing handkerchiefs over their heads and faces as further insect protection; he demanded that these touches be removed, but Stanislavsky appears to have resisted his partner. Other effects, like the offstage sound of horses' hooves clattering over a bridge to emphasize the departure of the characters in Act IV, were organically integrated with the text and had nothing intrusive about them. The ailing Chekhov saw the play in Yalta, to which the MAT brought it with four other plays in April 1900. Unlike *The Seagull,* the production gradually earned a permanent position in the repertory.

Seen between *Uncle Vanya* and the MAT's next Chekhov play, *The Three Sisters,* were Hauptmann's *Lonely People* (1899), Ostrovsky's *Snow Maiden* (with Stanislavsky again plunging ingeniously into the world of fantasy; 1900), and Ibsen's *An Enemy of the People* (1900), in which Stanislavsky's acting as Dr. Stockmann was acclaimed as one of his greatest achievements. *The Three Sisters* appeared in January 1901, with the codirector giving perhaps his greatest Chekhov performance as Vershinin. This was the first Chekhov play specifically written for the MAT. Unfortunately, Chekhov became upset over Stanislavsky's insistence that the play was a pessimistic drama, not a comedy as the playwright claimed.[8] The same argument would break out when *The Cherry Orchard* was being staged a couple of years later. However, Stanislavsky did come to acknowledge *The Three Sisters,* despite its many darker passages, as essentially affirmative and positive. Among the methods he used to underline this new vision was his revision of the potentially gloomy ending by having Olga speak her lines with great ebullience. Tusenbach's body was not carried across the stage, as indicated in the text, because to do so would add an unwanted tragic note in addition to various staging problems it presented.

Stanislavsky founded his overall production approach on a musical view of the structure, seeing each scene in terms that might have been used to describe a symphony. His interpretation, for all its emphasis on the positive elements of the characters and events, underlined the conflict between the characters' aspirations and the deadening influence of their environment. All the production devices of lights, sound, props, sets, and blocking were expressively used to heighten and explore emotional and psychological values. For example, in Act II, the director ironically undercut the pretensions of several characters by having others play with some of the children's toys scattered over the stage; thus, Vershinin manipulated a clown with cymbals as Irina spoke of going to Moscow.

Chekhov's *Ivanov* was successfully staged by Nemirovich-Danchenko in October 1904, apparently with minimal input from his partner, who played Shabelski, seventeen years after its premiere at Moscow's Korsh Theatre. It was the last of Chekhov's major works to be done by the MAT. However, in January of that same year, Stanislavsky had been largely responsible for the final play of Chekhov's great career, *The Cherry Orchard*. When they saw it years afterwards, the American critic and producer Kenneth Macgowan and designer Robert Edmond Jones found it realistic, but unlike any other form of realism in the theatre. "It carries us through life and out on the other side. It drenches us with a mystic sense of existence." The performance reached heights of symbolical expression, "fused by playwright and players into what seems a work of the most perfect resemblance, but what is actually only the appearance of appearance."[9]

Stanislavsky felt particularly close to this play, as it had been conceived at his country estate and included several characters based on people well known to him. He played Gayev, although the dramatist had written Lopakhin for him. Moreover, as mentioned before, the two artists disagreed over the temperament of the work, Stanislavsky declaring it a tragedy, for all its expression of hope for a better future, and Chekhov demanding it be played as a comedy sometimes bordering on farce. For the most part, however, Chekhov acceded to the director's vision, attended many rehearsals, and did numerous rewrites during the process. Stanislavsky felt inspired by this masterpiece; his production book includes a welter of annotations on motivations for each moment in the action, far more detailed than in any of his previous production books. Nevertheless, the under-rehearsed play, to Chekhov's despair, was only a mild success at its opening; although it continued to improve over time, it was never seen in its later stages by Chekhov, who heard of it through the reports of others. He died the year of its premiere, going to his grave certain that Stanislavsky had irreparably harmed the play by directing it too ponderously, dragging out what should have been acted three times faster than it was; by having characters perpetually in tears; and by burdening the performance with an unnecessary accumulation of naturalistic offstage sounds. To the latter charge, which was leveled by others as well, Stanislavsky was quick to respond that he was only providing what Chekhov requested in numerous stage directions.

The Cherry Orchard may indeed have been too lugubrious for Chekhov's tastes, and it is surely incorrect to label the play as either comedy or tragedy, it being a brilliant blend of the joy and sadness one associates with these genres; still, the comedic elements appear, over time at least, to have been given their due, as demonstrated by the reactions of the New York press to the production they saw in 1923 when Stanislavsky and the MAT visited America. Although none of the regular critics understood Russian, the majority agreed that the abundant humor of the material was conveyed so clearly that words were not needed to understand it. As Heywood Broun reported, the company "never had the least temerity about introducing the broadest strokes into this subtle and poignantly tender comedy."[10]

Chekhov was the most important dramatist discovered by the MAT. Through his plays, Stanislavsky was given an ideal springboard for the evolution of his ideas on playing the character's inner life. It took many years for Stanislavsky to cultivate his system to a satisfactory end result, and Chekhov's plays—combined with the lessons learned from such great actors as Tommaso Salvini and Mikhail Schepkin—continued to act as an inspiration and incentive during this period. More than any dramas of their time, these plays demanded a dismissal of the old stock acting and staging conventions. The MAT played Chekhov with extraordinary subtleness and restraint, and with a stirring combination of lyricism and psychological verity.

Stanislavsky's directorial work during the MAT's first seven years, in addition to the Chekhov plays, was largely devoted to Ibsen (*Hedda Gabler; An Enemy of the People; The Wild Duck,* 1901; *Ghosts,* 1905) and Hauptmann (*The Sunken Bell; Drayman Henschel; Lonely People; Michael Kramer,* 1901), with an occasional play by major Russian writers such as Ostrovsky, one of the Tolstoys, or Nemirovich-Danchenko himself. However, he and Nemirovich-Danchenko also codirected the earliest plays of a new Russian author, the short story writer and political rebel Maxim Gorky, during these years, beginning with *Petty Bourgeois* (also known as *Smug Citizens, Small People,* and by other titles) in 1902. Although his plays were in no way as significant in the theatre's history as Chekhov's, the post-1917 revolutionary period saw the MAT officially renamed in his honor; to the world at large, however, it remains the Moscow Art Theatre.

Most outstanding among Gorky's plays was the controversial *The Lower Depths* (1902), produced in the spirit of romantic naturalism. To portray the drama's milieu of lower-class social outcasts, Stanislavsky and his actors took a research jaunt to Moscow's notorious Khitrov market so they could observe firsthand the type of "skid row" creatures Gorky had portrayed. Based on the people he had seen in the market, Stanislavsky created a "biography" of each for use by the actors in investing their roles with complete truth; the idea of having a full biography of each character, whether composed by the director or the actors themselves was a vital feature of most of Stanislavsky's productions. Simov made numerous sketches and photographs of the people and locales. He and Stanislavsky were thus able to describe each character to the actors in total physical and psychological detail. Stanislavsky, who also played Satin, handled the early portions of the rehearsal period, but Nemirovich-Danchenko stepped in to apply the finishing touches and to give it the antitragic tone it needed to avoid overemphasizing the heaviness of the material. The staging concentrated on the authenticity of the props, costumes, and environment, but employed a more straightforward and sharply outlined acting style, quite unlike the gentle ambivalence with which Chekhov's characters were presented.

Gorky's *Children of the Sun* (1905), which was being produced when the 1905 Revolution broke out, was subsequently staged by Stanislavsky, but the playwright believed the director erred in burying the play's anti-intelligentsia theme under a blanket of extraneous naturalistic details.

SYMBOLISM

While Stanislavsky was perfecting his style, the European theatre was enthusiastically encouraging a more presentational mode, then generally known as symbolism. Here the spiritual longings, soulful agonies, and lyrical expressiveness which Stanislavsky had come to recognize as inherent in Chekhov's seemingly realistic style were divorced from conventional characters and environments and placed in symbolical settings where mystical emotions and moods predominated. Stanislavsky saw in these plays a chance to move beyond the confines of corporeal reality into a theatrical manner that would evoke man's subconscious spirit through an artful employment of suggestive techniques. In 1905, obsessed with a desire to realize this manner, and dissatisfied with his own first attempts at directing symbolist plays, he put the young actor-director Vsevolod Meyerhold in charge of an experimental Theatre-Studio setup for the purpose of producing such works. Although the Studio was formally connected to the MAT, its costs were entirely paid for out of Stanislavsky's own pocket. The venture (described in the chapter on Meyerhold) soon ended when Stanislavsky grew upset by Meyerhold's inability to find an approach which would make use of the actor's inner reality within a matrix of artificially imposed directorial ideas.

Stanislavsky was unwilling to part from his dream of the organic relation of an inner-outer acting method, no matter how ethereal or abstract the play in question. He undertook to direct a series of plays of fantasy and symbolism, and in all of them maintained his in-depth procedures toward character and environment. The spirit of realism prevailed in these plays of dreamlike fantasy and spirituality, despite what he termed their "irrealistic" nature.

Most famous of Stanislavsky's experiments in the symbolic-psychological style were Knut Hamsun's *The Drama of Life* (1907), Leonid Andreyev's *The Life of Man* (1907), and Maurice Maeterlinck's *The Blue Bird* (1908).

The Drama of Life—the central work in a trilogy written by the Norwegian dramatist between 1895 and 1898—was the first play Stanislavsky directed on the basis of the new insights he had made into the actor's creative tasks, especially the need for complete concentration on a character's inner life, and he tried to do nothing in his staging to contradict this. For the first time he began rehearsals with improvisational exercises, skipping the usual extensive table discussions of the play and its problems. Nemirovich-Danchenko, the archpriest of literary discussion at the start of rehearsals, was revolted. Stanislavsky soon returned to "at the table" procedures, but would again abandon them near the very end of his career.

Rejecting suggestions that the play be staged realistically, Stanislavsky—who played the leading role of Kareno—chose to direct the play by focusing entirely on its psychological content. He actually denied trying to do the play in a "symbolist" style, claiming that there was no such thing, and that anything poetic was *ipso facto* symbolic. To capture the interior life of the play, he had his actors rely principally on vocal and facial expressions, with barely any physicalization, so that the slightest movement would thereby seem greatly intensified.

An interesting feature of the production was the bas-relief setting, then currently in fashion because of the experiments of Georg Fuchs in Munich. Special lighting effects also contributed an important share. Stanislavsky describes the scene:

Gigantic figures of workmen with shovels and pickaxes in poses that were reminiscent of the sculptures of Meunier were placed along a stone wall. A fine effect was made by the scenery and *mise-en-scène* of the fair with a mob of Chinese shadows. The tents of the tradesmen, made of oiled linen, were a fine screen for the silhouettes of the actors in the mob scenes, who moved behind the linen in the light of a reflector that threw their shadows on a screen, or who walked in front of a screen.[11]

The critics and public rejected the production as neither fish nor fowl. Stanislavsky believed that the actors had been unable to rid themselves of their overtly realistic methods, and he determined to continue his investigations into the problems of creating a fusion of theatricalist staging and profoundly truthful acting.

With *The Life of Man* Stanislavsky dealt with the problem of making human feelings seem true for schematic characters within a highly abstract environment. No matter how stylized the visual effects or how bizarre the actor's behavior he demanded that everything acted onstage be rooted in clearcut motivations. His unusual Beardsleyesque scenic conception consisted of a black velvet background in which all locales—even the furniture—were suggested by outlines of varicolored ropes. A timeless, mysterious quality was elicited on a stage whose depths seemed endless. The special effect of using black velvet against black velvet was called into play to make objects and people come forth suddenly from the darkness and vanish just as quickly. The final scene was a brilliant piece of phantasmagorical staging in the nightmare manner Stanislavsky had employed in *Hannele* and *The Polish Jew*. Through it all an offbeat musical score by Ilya Sats helped to underscore the otherworldliness of the dramatic atmosphere.

Set in an inn where the "man" of the title is seeking the solace of drink, the scene employed actors in long, trailing, black coats moving like vermin slowly across the stage. Frightful vocal rumblings emerged from their throats as they went by. A strange crowd of drunkards arose in the shadows of the downstage area, vocalizing and gesticulating in a carefully composed vision of despairing souls. As death came to the central figure, enormous human shadows reaching to the highest parts of the set appeared, and a climactic sound effect crashed down on the ears of the auditors to signal the departure of life. All scenic effects now vanished to be replaced by the gigantic figure of the symbolic "Some One in Gray" whose eerie, fateful voice pronounced the sentence of death on mankind.

Once again, despite Stanislavsky's fascinating inspirations, there was an uncomfortable clash between the two-dimensions of the symbolist characters and the three of Stanislavsky's actors. Actually, the play was not one he had any taste for, and he only directed it on the insistence of Nemirovich-Danchenko, who by now had attained the powerful position of chairman of the MAT board. Stanislavsky looked on the production as a failure in that it did not help to advance his swelling concerns with the problems of the actor.

Maeterlinck was the ruling master of symbolism. It was, in fact, with three one-acters by this Belgian playwright that, in 1904, Stanislavsky made his very first symbolist experiments in directing. The production flopped, largely because the actors were completely at sea in the highly allusive style, but the opposite was true of Maeterlinck's *The Blue Bird*.

With this production Stanislavsky (who codirected with Leopold Sulerzhitsky) enjoyed the leisure of a truly extended rehearsal period of 150 sessions during which he concentrated on various problems associated with bringing this allegorical fantasy to life. He explored the use of improvisations in which the actors imitated animals (Nemirovich-Danchenko thought this ridiculous); he avoided all the traditional gauzy and painted effects of fantasy as evoked in traditional ballets; and he insisted that actors apply the carefully worked out motivations he had prepared for them, although such an approach was better suited to Ibsen, Chekhov, or Gorky. The cast was instructed to carefully observe life, to seek out and befriend children in order to see things through their eyes. Despite the resistance initially displayed to many of his ideas by the actors, each character was performed with emotional sincerity and truth; unlike *The Drama of Life* and *The Life of Man*, *The Blue Bird* profited from this approach, helping to make the production one of the most popular in the repertory, where it remained for many years, even influencing several important foreign versions. *The Blue Bird* was a masterpiece of fantastical staging that Stanislavsky produced as if it were life seen through a child's eyes, with love and wonderment at the strangeness of existence. The play was done with captivating charm and simplicity, avoiding extremes of spectacle and show business trickery and using sets that were fundamentally lifelike and capable of instilling belief. The acting and mise-en-scène blended with Sats' music in a vision of unearthly transformations, golden hues, and a suggestion of vastness that belied the stage's limited dimensions.

EVOLUTION OF THE SYSTEM

Leaving symbolism behind, Stanislavsky returned to the immobile style he had used for *The Drama of Life* when he experimented with Ivan Turgenev's *A Month in the Country* in 1909. This comedy, a realistic depiction of nineteenth-century landed gentry, was directed purely to bring out the finely tuned psychological nuances of the characters. The lovely set was, for its time, minimalist, and the actors, (including Stanislavsky as Rakitin) were given few props with which to occupy themselves, forcing them to concentrate on communicating the subtleties of character relationships through their eyes, faces, voices, and barely perceptible physical adjustments. Long speeches that were cut were spoken in full during rehearsals, with the excised passages spoken in subtextual tones. The play marked several firsts, it being the first time that the director broke the text down into units of action and introduced such units into the rehearsal process; the first time Stanislavsky insisted that rehearsals be closed to outsiders; and the first time he commenced rehearsals without a preplanned production book. The success of the experiment was very helpful in gaining for Stanislavsky the attention he required to establish his rapidly developing acting ideas. He looked on *A Month in the Country* as the first proof that his system could work.

Stanislavsky had begun to make serious progress toward what became his famous "system" while on a summer vacation in Finland in 1906. He was at a point of physical and emotional exhaustion, and had come to feel dried up creatively. He began to study his accumulated notebook jottings on acting and theatre art and to organize them into a systematic approach to the actor's problems. What he was working toward was a method by which the actor could learn to relax physically and mentally, thereby invoking the appropriate "creative state" that would allow him to concentrate on the inner and outer life of his role so that he could almost live the part onstage. Everything done by the actor had to grow out of an internal motivation; nothing could be done merely for its theatrical effectiveness. All such motivations had to be suitable to the circumstances of the play and its characters as conceived by the playwright. Stanislavsky searched for years to find the proper internal keys to stimulating truthful behavior and feelings; his system was a succession of specific, psychological exercises and techniques through which the actor could bring forth from his subconscious proper emotional responses. For example, an important element in the system was the "magic if." The actor was to imagine that the circumstances in which his character existed (his age, health, relationships, job, environment, social position, wealth, etc.) were real by acting "as if" they were so. To determine his character's behavior, the actor would ask himself "What would I do if I were this character in this situation" and other similar questions. Even the most barefaced lie had to become truth in order to become art. The actor had to cultivate a childlike naïveté and trustfulness to fully invoke the "magic if" and other such psychological aids.

Another vital technique, was "emotion memory," a method by which the actor could evoke feelings like those of the character; this was accomplished by recalling situations in his own life when he had felt similar emotions. The technique first began to be developed during Stanislavsky's work on his 1908 staging of *The Inspector-General*, and its acceptance by the company marked one of his earliest breakthroughs in getting the actors to acquiesce in his experimental ideas. After arriving at the concept independently, he was overjoyed soon after to discover that a Frenchman named Théodule Armand Ribot had earlier published two books, *Illnesses of the Memory* and *Illnesses of the Will*, that vindicated his own findings. Emotion memory (also known by other terms such as "affective memory" and "emotional recall") has become one of the most controversial features of the system as it is taught today, especially in America, despite Stanislavsky's ultimate repudiation of it in the 1930s in favor of what he called the "method of physical actions."

As a director, Stanislavsky's problem was learning when to transfer the responsibility for the creation of this truthful behavior to the actors. He had to restrain his impulse to interfere in creating all the stage business himself. The MAT actors often bitterly opposed his attempts to have them practice his ideas; this opposition continued even after Nemirovich-Danchenko accepted the system (after considerable resistance) and, during rehearsals for their production of Leo Tolstoy's *Redemption* (or *The Living Corpse*; 1911), made it a requirement for all MAT actors to study it. Still, Nemirovich-Danchenko continued to harbor serious doubts about the system for years, believing it too mechanistic an approach to an essentially mysterious process. His reasons for accepting the system were purely political, a means of conciliating Stanislavsky, whom he feared the MAT would lose if his demands were not met. At this point in the MAT's history, it should be remembered, Nemirovich-Danchenko was technically the most powerful figure in the theatre's management.

From 1906 to 1917, when the Revolution broke out and completely reversed the pattern of Russian history, with serious implications for the theatre, Stanislavsky experimented on advancing his system, using each play as a laboratory for his ideas, often being more of a teacher than a director. Frequently, he was accused of wasting valuable rehearsal time because of his preoccupation with using the actors to experiment on his system. He had several notable successes, such as the previously mentioned *The Blue Bird, The Inspector-General,* and *A*

Month in the Country; he also made lasting impressions with his mountings of Alexandre Sergeyevich Griboyedov's nineteenth-century verse classic, *Woe from Wit* (1906), Ostrovsky's *Enough Stupidity in Every Wise Man* (1910), Leo Tolstoy's *Redemption,* Turgenev's short play, *The Provincial Lady* (1912), Molière's *The Imaginary Invalid* (1913), a new version of *La Locandiera* (1914), and Antonio Salieri's opera, *The Siege during the Plague* given on a bill with Alexandre Pushkin's *Mozart and Salieri* (1915). In most of these works Stanislavsky played leading roles.

Also during these years was his collaboration with England's Gordon Craig on the controversial *Hamlet* of 1911, a production that, for all of Stanislavsky's efforts on it (he believed it vindicated the applicability of his system for the classics), is indelibly linked with Craig's name. Craig, the brilliant but impractical British theorist-director-designer, disdaining the actual process of working with actors, allowed Stanislavsky or the latter's assistants (especially Sulerzhitsky) to carry out most of his directorial ideas. The production process took two years to complete, with Craig arriving in Moscow and leaving at his convenience; during it considerable friction developed between Craig and Stanislavsky despite their mutual admiration of one another. One factor in their divergence was Craig's lack of respect for the actor's creative powers and Stanislavsky's enormous respect for them. The well-rounded characterizations Stanislavsky helped to evolve were in striking contrast to the schematic, puppetlike figures Craig hoped to produce. The famous production, despite its unusual modernistic sets and costumes, split audiences and critics, but Stanislavsky deemed it a success.

Many of the older actors in the company were too set in their ways and too resistant to new ideas to provide Stanislavsky with the inspiration he required to make headway with his system, so he progressively turned to the younger actors as they gradually joined the MAT ranks. To work with such young actors in an atmosphere as free of the MAT's pressures as possible, he founded a school, the First Studio, in 1912, putting his most capable assistant, Sulerzhitsky, in charge of it to teach his system. With the young actors and directors at his disposal there, Stanislavsky saw many of his burgeoning ideas tried and refined. In succeeding years he founded several studios (and often grew alienated from them as they went off in their own directions and became independent entities), such as the Second Studio (1916), the Third Studio (1920), the Fourth Studio (1921), and the Opera Studio (1918), later the Stanislavsky Opera Studio. The studios gradually created unfortunate divisions among the available MAT talent, including Stanislavsky, whose work became more and more bound up with them while slackening off with the MAT's main production activities.

THE POST-REVOLUTIONARY YEARS

The Revolution and the new government it put in power begot many problems, artistic, economic, and administrative, for the MAT. Stanislavsky's personal finances suffered a crushing blow when his family's enterprises were nationalized and converted from thread manufacturing to the making of steel cables. The MAT itself came under continuing attack from more experimental, left-wing theatre artists and critics, who now began to flourish, and who viewed it as an outward relic of the decadent bourgeois culture. It was fortunate indeed that the MAT was not liquidated, but rather preserved by the minister of education, Anatoly Lunacharsky, as an example of the best of the old culture's artistic achievements. Lenin, too, was a strong defender of the MAT, and in 1919 the company was granted acceptance as an officially subsidized state theatre. Finding plays appropriate to the new regime's political viewpoint, however, was extremely difficult. To a considerable extent the theatre was reduced to reviving its old productions but with their intrinsic social commentary underlined in new interpretations.

New audiences drawn from the masses now began to attend the MAT's performances, but these were people who had never seen a first-class theatre production before. Stanislavsky personally favored the expansion and popularization of the theatre's audience, but he was gravely offended by the post-Revolutionary spectators' lack of proper theatre manners; on more than one occasion he found himself having to stop a performance to chastise the audience for their noisiness and to demand quiet attention from them.

Stanislavsky continued to direct on a regular basis; in each successive work he pursued answers to new problems of acting and production. In addition the MAT spent two years touring abroad, from 1922 to 1924 (their first foreign tour had been in 1906), including two seasons in New York which had an immense impact on the course of American actor training. Two Stanislavsky-trained actors in particular, Richard Boleslavsky and Maria Ouspenskaya, soon set up shop in New York and laid the foundations for the Stanislavsky system's eventual domination of American actor training. This would eventually create a problem, as these actors, disheartened by the new political realities, had departed Soviet Russia not long after the Revolution, and were trained in the emotion memory technique, having little knowledge of Stanislavsky's gradual shift to the method of physical actions. Thus, their teaching emphasized the earlier phase of the master's system; this, in turn, was learned by Lee Strasberg, who became the American guru of the emotion memory approach to the Stanislavsky system in contrast to the physical action approach advocated by such American teachers as Stella Adler, who studied briefly with Stanislavsky late in his life. This essential split still divides many adherents of the system as it is taught in America.

Stanislavsky's productions during the post-Revolutionary period were *Twelfth Night* (1917) at the First Studio, Lord Byron's *Cain* (1920), a new production of *The Inspector-General* (1921), Ostrovsky's *The Burning Heart* (1926), A. Kugel's *Nicholas I and the Decembrists* (1926), Marcel Pagnol and Paul Nivoix's *Merchants of Glory* (1926), Mikhail Bulgakov's *The Days of the Turbins* (1926), Pierre Caron de Beaumarchais' *The Marriage of Figaro* (1927), Adolph d'Ennery and Eugène Cormon's *The Two Orphans*, L. M. Leonov's *Untilovsk* (1928),

Valentin Katayev's *The Embezzlers* (1928), Bulgakov's adaptation of Gogol's *Dead Souls* (1932), Ostrovsky's *Artists and Admirers* (1933), Bulgakov's *Molière* (1936), and the posthumous staging of Molière's *Tartuffe* (1939). There were also nearly a dozen operas, some of outstanding quality, and an abortive version of *Othello* (1930). Stanislavsky was not always the director in charge of these plays. After suffering a heart attack in 1928, followed by various other ailments, he restricted his directorial work to supervising the productions of his pupils and disciples. His occasional appearances at rehearsals came to be dreaded by some, since plays that had been in rehearsal for lengthy periods, the smooth progress of which had bred complacency in both actors and director, could be ruthlessly shredded by the master's unusually sensitive eye for the meretricious and insincere.

Most of the directing at the MAT during the 1920s was in the hands of Ilya Sudakov, although Nemirovich-Danchenko and Stanislavsky oversaw all productions before allowing them to be shown to the public. Stanislavsky's directorial contributions were largely eclipsed during the decade by the more spectacular presentationalism of directors like Meyerhold and Tairov. Stanislavsky's own protégé, Evgeni Vakhtangov, revealed directorial powers of great dimensions, too, but cancer killed him at age thirty-nine in 1922.

TWELFTH NIGHT AGAIN

Stanislavsky's third attempt at *Twelfth Night* came when he assumed control of B. M. Sushkevitch's First Studio production during the rehearsal period. Discarding his early attempts at historical realism in an Elizabethan atmosphere, he succeeded in turning Sushkevitch's dreary staging into a lightly skipping one that avoided tiresome waits for scene shifting, and used a cleverly variable decor of curtains and suggestive scenic elements to create the necessary locales. Among his then rather bold inventions was the casting of both Viola and Sebastian with the same performer, with an obvious trick of doubling in the final scene when both characters appear together, and the deployment of the tiny studio auditorium itself for action that spilled over from the stage. Although some questioned Stanislavsky's neglect of the inner techniques of his system for this exercise in overt presentationalism, the production was a hit that was allowed onto the main MAT stage; when the First Studio evolved into the Second Moscow Art Theatre, *Twelfth Night* was an integral part of its repertory.

CAIN AND RHYTHM

In 1907 Stanislavsky's wish to stage *Cain* had been denied by the religious censorship, but the play had no problems being approved for production in the post-Revolutionary years. *Cain*—the only new play at the MAT from 1917 to 1923—was staged with a full assortment of those scenic and auditory effects at which the director was a master. The play, however, with its theological probing into the conflict between good and evil as represented by God and Lucifer, was of little interest to an audience caugth up in the turmoil of building a new society. Despite the regisseur's attempt to translate its themes into political terms, Byron's mystical religious drama, which had 160 rehearsals, lasted only eight performances. Originally intended as a spectacular production in which the theatre would be transformed into a cathedral, *Cain*, because of a lack of money, had to settle for the black velvet effects that Stanislavsky had deployed in his symbolist period. Since not enough black velvet could be procured at the time, the effects were often marred by the substitution of black canvas, which lacks the light-absorbing properties of velvet.

Cain ran into several other major technical difficulties as well as serious problems in its acting, when the cast found it impossible to achieve the kind of style Stanislavsky had envisioned. He sought from them performances of artless, even childlike, simplicity, avoiding the use of subtextual thinking, with all the characters, no matter how superhuman, behaving in a fundamentally realistic way, including the use of definite objectives. An attempt was made to relate the characters to contemporary political concerns, such as Lucifer being considered a radical, God a conservative, and Cain a Bolshevik, but the piece failed to cohere with a unified point of view. Nevertheless, this failure had a positive outcome in that it began to lead Stanislavsky to explore the rhythmic possibilities of an actor's performance. Rhythmic problems became increasingly important to Stanislavsky in the years following *Cain*; much of his work in this area grew out of his activities in directing opera.

Stanislavsky's treatment of rhythm was of particular interest to Vasily Osopovich Toporkov, an important actor who joined the MAT in mid-career. In *Stanislavski in Rehearsal,* he explains how the director, through his creative use of rhythm, was able to transform "long, drawn-out rehearsals . . . into full-blooded conflicts of great intensity."[12] Vasily Osopovich Toporkov, baffled at first, watched with fascination as Stanislavsky taught his actors not only how to move rhythmically, but to behave rhythmically even when sitting or standing still.

Stanislavski admirably demonstrated his own skill in using different rhythms. He would take the simplest episode from everyday life—for example, buying a newspaper at a stand in the station—and play it in completely different rhythms. He would buy a paper when there is a whole hour before the departure of the train and he doesn't know how to kill the time, or when the first or second bell has run, or when the train has already started. The actions are all the same but in completely different rhythms, and Konstantin Sergeyivich was able to carry out these exercises in any order: by increasing the rhythm, by diminishing the rhythm, by sudden change.[13]

The demonstration revealed to Toporkov how rhythm is integral to all human behavior, no matter how simple, and how great interest can be created through its effective employment.

Nikolai Gorchakov, an MAT director, describes how the regisseur worked on a scene's rhythm in *The Two Orphans*. First, the rhythm to be aimed for was established in a discussion with the actors, and then its variations were analyzed. Stanislavsky stressed that ''The scenic rhythm is not the acceleration or diminishing of the tempo, but the acceleration or diminishing of the *inner intensity*— the desire to realize the problem and to execute the inner or outer physical action.''[14] The scene's inner rhythm may be the opposite of the external rhythm, so that a growing urgency in the feelings of the scene may be revealed through a slowing of speech and movement, not quickening.

In the scene from *The Two Orphans*, he had the actors work for the proper rhythm by rehearsing the scene with each ''conducting'' his own rhythm, using hand movements to mark the tempo. In addition to clarifying rhythmic problems, the exercise also led to a greater understanding by the actors of the relative emotional values of their roles to the scene.

FINAL PRODUCTIONS

Stanislavsky's new production of *The Inspector-General*, in 1921, starring Michael Chekhov in the role of Khlestakov, was performed in the then much discussed ''grotesque'' style, which Stanislavsky viewed as the vivid and boldly exaggerated externalization of dynamic inner content; the performances were enormously enriched by the director's development of a deep inner reality that served to justify what might otherwise have seemed empty formalism in performance. The production, which united the audience with the performance by keeping the houselights on, was filled with one novel but fully justified moment after another.

In 1926 Stanislavsky directed Ostrovsky's *The Burning Heart* (taking it over from Sudakov) and succeeded so well that it remained in the repertory for many years. In contrast to the expressionistic style of Meyerhold's recent highly unconventional production of Ostrovsky's *The Forest* (1924), Stanislavsky presented *The Burning Heart* with a reverence for its author's style. He sought out Ostrovsky's satirical quality, and even managed to produce the effect of psychologically justified grotesquerie he had achieved with Gogol's masterpiece. Meyerhold himself, a master at the formal elements of the grotesque style, made a public announcement congratulating his former mentor on the brilliance of his achievement.

The same year that saw *The Burning Heart* also witnessed Stanislavsky's staging of Kugel's historical play *Nicholas I and the Decembrists*, and Pagnol and Paul Nivoix's *Merchants of Glory*, a quite recent satire on postwar political shenanigans in a French provincial town. This was followed by his work on Bulgakov's *The White Guard*, a play about the 1917 Revolution that took a controversially unsympathetic view of the revolutionaries. A number of factors led to the play's running into trouble with the censors, including the use of the word ''white'' in its title, and it eventually had to be retitled *The Days of the*

Turbins, after the tsarist family at its core. Before it could open, it was closed by the authorities. Stanislavsky continued to work on the play, getting Bulgakov to revise it extensively to remove anything that might seem offensive. Finally, it was permitted to open, and it became a great success with audiences among whom it struck a powerfully responsive chord; it did suffer extreme critical hostility, however. Opposition grew so strong in certain quarters that the play was taken from the repertory in 1929, but was put back in when, in 1932, was learned that Stalin liked it enough to have seen it fifteen times.

Beaumarchais' *The Marriage of Figaro* was done in 1927, after 300 rehearsals of which Stanislavsky led eighty-two. The play, often considered a factor in the atmosphere leading up to the French Revolution, clearly had political relevance for post-Revolutionary Russia. As a production, it was a masterpiece of pre-Revolutionary aesthetics. The expertly individualized crowd scenes, the careful re-creation of period decor (moved from Spain to pre-Revolutionary France), and the use of a revolving stage in full view of the spectators helped make this one of Stanislavsky's finest classic revivals. The sets were by Meyerhold's pre-Revolution designer, Alexandre Golovin, and resembled those of the great Meyerhold–Golovin St. Petersburg period. "Here," said Norris Houghton, "was fantasy, lightness, music, dancing."[15] The characters were all conceived as specific individuals, not types; the action moved as rapidly as possible, and many revisions were made to the text to speed it up; the staging progressed breathlessly from scene to scene by means of the revolve.

Most important, this work marked a shift in Stanislavsky's theory of acting that was to occupy him during the remaining years of his life. All the actors were asked to study their roles so thoroughly that they could account for everything they would have done throughout the day. Not one deed or thought onstage could be dissociated from its place within that imaginary day. This gave all the actions that transpired a sense of absolute believability. The actor's behavior was linked to a full comprehension of his character's "given circumstances." By concentrating on the truth of his actions, each of which was tied to a specific objective, the actor was to find that the emotions suited to the scene would arise naturally, without resorting to psychological techniques like emotion memory. Correct physical activities led naturally to truthful psychological responses. This was a vital step forward for what came to be known as the "method of physical actions."

Toporkov observed of this method, "*The importance of the transference of the actor's attention from the search for feelings inside himself [as in the use of emotion memory] to the fulfillment of the stage task which actively influences his partners* is one of Stanislavsky's greatest discoveries."[16] (His italics.) The system did not, however, spring full-blown into life with this production; in fact, an embryonic form of it had begun to emerge in 1916 when the director was engaged in preparations for what turned out to be an aborted revival of *The Village of Stepanchikovo*. Furthermore, the many difficulties it held for actors as Stanislavsky struggled to develop it were often a source of considerable despair.

Related to his emphasis on physical actions—which he actually preferred to think of as "psycho-physical actions"—was Stanislavsky's concern with images. Toporkov's discussion of rehearsals of *Tartuffe* offers many instances in which the director sought to have the actor realize the importance of always having vivid images in his mind related to the circumstances of the action. If, for example, Orgon was to speak rapturously of Tartuffe, then the actor would have to employ his fantasy to conjure up an image of just the sort of man Orgon takes Tartuffe to be. Stanislavsky suggested that this saintly individual might be someone known personally to the actor or someone he worshipped; he would then use his concrete image when trying to convince the actor with whom he was playing of Tartuffe's saintliness.

The year 1927 saw Stanislavsky's involvement in staging the popular old French tearjerker *The Two Orphans,* and a production of *Armored Train 14-69* by Vsevolod Ivanov, this being the first overtly pro-Communist Soviet play done by the MAT. It was Stanislavsky's idea to have the play adapted from its original form as a short story; the play was in rehearsal under another director when Stanislavsky assumed command, but the needs of the repertory forced it to go on after only seventy-six rehearsals, which to the MAT at that time was no time at all. Stanislavsky handled only eleven rehearsals, although the success of the production was attributed to the work he did during them. One of his new rehearsal devices emerged here to unplug blocked emotions; eventually called the "Here, Today, Now" exercise, it involved the asking of the actors to imagine what they themselves would do if a particular situation occurred. For example, hoping to prevent them from overgeneralizing the acting of a crowd scene, he asked them what they would do if Lunacharsky, the important government bureaucrat, were to show up at rehearsal and demand that the company march immediately to the radio station to denounce those capitalist enemies who were claiming that the MAT was going to abandon its production of *Armored Train 14-69*. The exercise immediately brought a rush of excitement and enthusiasm to the playing of the scene.

Following these productions in 1928 came Leonov's *Untilovsk,* set in an imaginary Siberian town and concerned with the rather depressing post-Revolutionary life there, and Valentin Katayev's dramatization of his novel *The Embezzlers*, a comedy about the spending spree of a humble clerk who absconds with his bank's funds. Both plays were considered politically and artistically deficient; despite lengthy rehearsal periods they were quickly withdrawn.

Ever since his production of *Othello* for the Society of Art and Literature, Stanislavsky had wanted to revive the play, thinking it a perfect vehicle for the exhibition of his system as it had thus far evolved. Following his 1928 heart attack, he was often forced to leave Moscow for more recuperative climates. He nevertheless began to work toward a production, and wrote up a detailed

production book so that his ideas could be carried out by someone else; this
production book has been published in English and displays more of a preoccupation with character analysis than with staging problems. His concern with
the method of physical actions led him to place more emphasis on objectives
and motivations than on the specifics of the mise-en-scène. The play went into
rehearsal with Stanislavsky recuperating on the Mediterranean, in Nice; in a
sense, he directed the play by mail, sending his notes to Moscow where they
were put into practice by his proxy, Sudakov, as well as by Leonid Leonidov,
who also played Othello. He also wrote long, analytical letters to the latter.
However, his notes were still arriving in Moscow when, unknown to him, the
play opened and turned out to be a great failure. Sudakov had been able to
transmit only the letter but not the spirit of Stanislavsky's plans. Among other
reasons for the flop was the serious illness of Leonidov. Stanislavsky was irate
to learn that, with his name on the posters as the director, the production, still
far from ready, had been opened to the public. His name was swiftly taken off.

In addition to several operas, four more plays were to occupy Stanislavsky
before his death. His productions of Bulgakov's adaptation of Gogol's *Dead
Souls* and of Ostrovsky's *Artists and Admirers*, for all their worthwhile qualities,
suffered from his having to work with the actors in the cramped quarters at his
home, his physical condition allowing him to attend full-scale rehearsals at the
theatre—where he was likely to be dismayed by the way his ideas for the sets
were realized—only rarely. Still, the former was a popular—if not critical—
success, while the latter made little impression.

Stanislavsky first became involved in the staging of Bulgakov's *Molière* after
it already had been in rehearsal under Gorchakov for a year. At the time,
Bulgakov had been working on the play for close to five years, making many
revisions to satisfy the MAT leaders, and was not happy with some of the new
ideas on which Stanislavsky sought to have him work. Stanislavsky's fiddling
eventually so disturbed the author that he stopped attending rehearsals. After
286 rehearsals, *Molière* opened, and was an instant failure. In the Soviet Union
of 1936 it was not a wise idea to produce a play whose ostensible theme was
the oppression of a sensitive artist by a cabal of bureaucrats carrying out the
wishes of an autocratic leader.

Finally, there was *Tartuffe*, undertaken by Stanislavsky, not with production
in mind, but as a means for further explorations of his ever-developing acting
system. He died after two years of working on it, having only gotten through
four of its five acts and never having had a single run-through; however, what
he had accomplished proved to be so valuable that the MAT agreed to complete
its preparation, and it was eventually staged with much success under the direction
of Mikhail Kedrov, who also played the title role. The production's achievement
is said to have been the feelings it evoked of Molière's contemporaneity and
universality; the characters all seemed recognizable and the treatment completely
human and three-dimensional.

Stanislavsky's last decade as a director, while not unusually prolific, does show him hard at work on fourteen plays and operas, in addition to several that were abandoned before their openings. All this was done while he was fighting one serious illness after another and simultaneously composing the books on acting that were to make his name familiar to theatre lovers around the world. His own acting career, however, had ended in October 1928.

DIRECTORIAL ACHIEVEMENTS

Stanislavsky's directing achievements spanned a broad range of dramatic styles, from the Meiningen-like archaeological exactitude of the historical plays, through the subtle lyricism and psychological penetration of the Chekhov works, to the politically sensitive works of Ivanov and Bulgakov. Phantasmagorical theatricalism, abstract symbolism, and satirical grotesquerie also share a large part of Stanislavsky's successful output. No matter what the genre, though, he endeavored always to reveal the reality of his characters and their fictive worlds.

He was never addicted to naturalism in his work, despite his success with it; instead, he had a personal vision of reality and truth which he transferred to every play he directed. As Nemirovich-Danchenko explained, "He was never in the least interested in nature. He created it such as he wanted it in his theatrical imagination."[17] Stanislavsky himself often asserted his antagonism to naturalism, insisting that his goal was "realism." Gorchakov explains that to Stanislavsky naturalism meant resorting to an accumulation of external details, which were not relevant to the style and meaning of a play. Naturalism was unable to discriminate between the main and the secondary elements. By realism he meant a selective approach which emphasized the typical, not the accidental.

Politics in drama did not appeal to Stanislavsky, although the plays he staged often carried themes of vital social significance. His pre-Revolutionary plays were rarely committed to a particular ideology, aside from the expression of values which could be interpreted as liberal or humanist in intention. Social commitment was more obvious in his post-Revolutionary years, particularly in the occasional attempt to depict the evil conditions of life under the old system.

His perspective on art was an emotional one. To him a good play was one with fully rounded characters, closely observed and deeply understood by the author. He looked at a play primarily for the originality and perception of its characters, and not for any statement its creator was making. Therefore, he saw each play through an actor's eyes, and insisted time and again that his was an actor's, not a director's, theatre.

Stanislavsky rejected a theatre of directorial ingenuity and intellectuality because of its imposition on the actor of a conception not organic to him. Only a theatre founded on the actor's own emotional life is valid, he declared. Very infrequently does the actor's emotional creativity coincide with the imaginative conceptions of a strong director, and this is usually by accident, not intention. Norris Houghton observed in the 1930s that Stanislavsky's method and that of the other MAT directors was "that of a combination wet-nurse and doctor. Their presence and assistance at the birth of the play is essential, but the play is actually given birth to by the actors; the pangs are his—or hers!''[18]

The MAT stagings were so carefully done and required so much in terms of money and rehearsal time that, not surprisingly, relatively few plays were staged over the years and those that succeeded became permanent parts of the repertory. Actors often played the roles they had originated for a quarter of a century or more. Stanislavsky, for example, was still playing Vershinin in *The Three Sisters* in 1928, though he had created the part in 1901.

By the late 1930s audiences came to the MAT as if to a museum, for an evening of quiet, subdued culture, much as if they were stepping back into a world of pre-Revolutionary bourgeois surroundings. Although Stanislavsky endeavored to the day he died to further his investigations into the wellsprings of truthful acting, audiences accepted his theatre as a bastion of long and meaningful traditions with acting and directing that rarely surprised but rather comforted with a solidified technique, which demanded attention and respect.

MAT REHEARSALS

Rehearsals at the MAT were workshops in perfectionism. Productions were rehearsed for many months, sometimes for considerably more than a year, as Stanislavsky was constantly seeking to improve and perfect his creations before showing them to the public. Naturally, lengthy rehearsal periods were never a guarantee of success; some plays receiving well over a hundred rehearsals lasted only a week or two in performance.

In the post-Revolutionary period, he would often begin the rehearsal process, turn the work over to his well-informed assistants, and return weeks later to take over the final stages. In other cases he might entrust the production to a disciple, but, unhappy with the results, assume control and redirect it himself. A chill must have gone through the company when, after months of rehearsing, they had to present a run-through before Stanislavsky. No matter how smoothly and creatively they may have thought their work on a play was going, there were always major objections that occurred to the supersensitive regisseur, who had an uncanny ability to spot insincerity in a performance. Following such a rehearsal, the play—despite the theatre's need for a new production—might have to return to square one and undergo many additional months of preparation before Stanislavsky would deem it ready to face the public.

Before beginning a rehearsal, Stanislavsky insisted that certain conditions be met. Everything on the stage or in the rehearsal room had to be clean and well-disposed—all unneeded props and scenery placed out of sight. The actors had to be neatly dressed, as did the technical crew, the ventilation had to be adequate, and an enthusiastic state of mind was expected from all concerned.

Stanislavsky engaged in extremely close collaboration with his designers. Sketches were drawn and redrawn; models were built and rebuilt until he was happy with the results. He had a vivid pictorial imagination and made many sketches of the costumes, sets, and action while preparing his production plan. He was also quite capable to telling a designer precisely what he sought in the ground plan, furnishings, colors, moods, and acting areas. The process of his collaboration with Simov on the 1905 *Ghosts* has been preserved in his notes. They reveal Stanislavsky's tireless attention to detail, especially in searching for the appropriate Norwegian architectural features that he thought imperative for capturing the drama's mood. When, after days of building and rebuilding models, a workable solution was found, a makeshift version was immediately put onstage for the actors to rehearse in.[19]

Rehearsals were planned with care, so that no time would be wasted. A staff of assistants saw to it that the well-organized rehearsals did not get sidetracked on nonessentials. This practice did not hold true, however, for those rehearsals that Stanislavsky undertook on plays that already had been given extensive rehearsal by other directors. Stanislavsky was now more concerned with his role as a teacher and would spend many hours working on the smallest details, hoping to make a breakthrough in getting an actor to provide a moment of truth where Stanislavsky had seen insincerity. The actor might have to repeat the same small action over and over and over until Stanislavsky was satisfied. Often, especially in his last years, he would allow himself to be swept up in anecdotal ruminations, talking of his past experiences and acquaintances, and would forget about the time passing, so that the actors were in danger of being late for their arrival at the theatre to get into costume for the evening's performance.

Visitors were usually permitted to attend rehearsals only once the actors felt secure in their parts, and never in the early stages of rehearsal. Both the director and the actors needed an atmosphere of privacy in which they could work unhampered by the stares of outsiders. Even actors not in a scene had to wait in the wings, rather than in the auditorium, so that the director could work unimpeded by their presence.

Rehearsals were a time when the actors could realize their potentials as artists, as people striving for the highest ideals of beauty and truth; they were not a time when personal egotism had any opportunity for expression or growth. The ensemble sought to work in selfless harmony, the immediate problems of the play rising above individual pettiness. Any infraction which tended to hinder the harmonious atmosphere was likely to be dealt with by a sharp fine. Lateness particularly irked Stanislavsky, and he made a point of embarrassing actors for being tardy.

Stanislavsky's own manner at rehearsals is said by David Magarshack, one of his biographers, to have been pleasant, polite and shy. He behaved with childlike sincerity, bright and cheerful, despite an aloofness cultivated to maintain his authority. Although Magarshack says that Stanislavsky neither shouted nor spoke contemptuously to his actors,[20] evidence points to a furious temper, which he tried valiantly to control though it often got the better of him—especially when he was faced with insincerity or lack of effort. Moreover, if a matter of artistic import was disturbing him, he was prone to psychologically flog his actors with increased severity. Once, according to Toporkov, when Stanislavsky had been informed of a local director's allegedly perverse handling of *Hamlet,* he came to rehearsal with an "especially critical" attitude, "attacking the smallest blunder or show of bad taste. He was sometimes cruel and unjust. We were paying for those who had outraged the genius of Shakespeare."[21] Younger actors were most likely to bear the weight of his outbursts. Sometimes he hurt an actor to incite an emotional reaction. He once spoke severely to a young actress and then told her that the tears his words provoked should be used in her scene. He cautioned her, however, that in the future she should be able to produce them, not by being insulted but through her technique.

Stanislavsky's ire could easily be invoked by actors in crowd scenes. He was proud of his aphorism that "there are no small parts, there are just small actors," and crowd scenes gave him a chance to put this philosophy into practice. He wanted every crowd member to play his role with complete conviction; if he saw evidence of boredom or empty acting, he would grow angry and rebuke the offender, reminding him that crowd scenes were the pride of the MAT and that anyone who could not create a three-dimensional character in one did not belong in the company. So offended was he by the indifferent acting in one crowd scene that he warned the cast: "You shall not do it! If you did I would demand that the theatre be closed down and I am convinced that I would be understood by those on whom the authority to do so rests."[22]

From the available transcripts of his rehearsals in the 1930s, one gets the impression of an autocrat, who, for all his courtliness of manner, expected everyone to defer to his greater age, experience, wisdom, and talent. His attitude remained extremely patriarchal, even though his more despotic methods had been dropped years before.

DISCIPLINE AND PERFECTION

Stanislavsky expected a great deal from his actors, in return for the opportunities he offered them. His stringent requirements extended to talent, vocal and physical expressiveness, education, appearance, personality, and imagination; many actors were frightened away by his high standards. He demanded that actors continually study and perfect their instruments. To him, an actor's calling should be like a priest's in its constant devotion to self-sacrifice and self-improvement. Above all, an actor had to be master of his own self, one who had purged himself of all personal vanities and petty feelings, in order to concentrate all his energies on his art. He urged his actors to live nobly, to cleanse themselves of base emotions, to seek out the best features in everyone, and to transfer this selfless attitude to their acting. In every part they were to find the sources of goodness, kindness, and courage, and not dwell on more morbid characteristics. No matter how villainous the character, the actor had to find that which was honest and true in it. Further, he wanted his actors to obey their director not by his enforced authority, but by the respect he engenders through providing an example for emulation.

Stanislavsky lived a disciplined life and demanded discipline from all his coworkers, from actor to cloakroom attendant. He believed that only a disciplined environment could produce the atmosphere in which the best theatre art is created.

Stanislavsky's requirements for a director were as demanding as those for actors. He felt the role of the director "comprises an aesthete, a poet, a psychologist, a teacher and theorist, a critic, an administrator, a man with creative initiative, and so on."[23] In addition to the various technical abilities needed for staging a play, he felt a director should be thoroughly well informed in all fields, not only in theatre. (He was himself ashamed of the weak classical education he received, and was always uncomfortable in the presence of famous writers.) Sharply perceptive powers of observation and continual practice at improving them were also called for. The director must bring an original point of view to a play, making it pertinent to the times. Finally, the director must be a master of those acting techniques with which he requires his actors to be familiar.

DIRECTING THE DIRECTOR

As one of Russia's leading actors, Stanislavsky had the doubly difficult job of acting in most of the plays he directed. Like most other actor-directors, he admitted to the enormous burden of concentrating on his role while being concerned for the presentation as a whole. By itself directing can make one a nervous wreck, he acknowledged; this nervousness is compounded when the director also plays a major role. "A role which demands the whole being of the actor will not tolerate this double identity and takes its revenge,"[24] he said. It may require up to ten performances before the director can relax and let his actor-persona take over. It was too bad, he noted, that by this time the critics had already written about his performances.

In directing himself he would work privately on his own part before acting it with others. He would learn his lines swiftly, so as not to represent an impediment to rehearsing. It was necessary for him to draw out criticisms on his acting from Nemirovich-Danchenko and senior MAT players to give him an objective view of his work.

One trial Stanislavsky faced during the formative years of the MAT was the practice of codirecting plays with Nemirovich-Danchenko. Confusion often developed when the two men clashed over ideas. Rambling arguments were frequent. Nemirovich-Danchenko could easily disturb Stanislavsky's tenuous equilibrium by showing up at a late stage of rehearsals, when Stanislavsky was suffering doubts about the work, and then offering painful criticism. (Stanislavsky would himself do the same to other directors toward the end of his career.) As previously mentioned, they decided in 1907 to direct on their own or in collaboration with others.

Nemirovich-Danchenko's forte was in verbally elucidating a text, whereas

Stanislavsky could best explain it by demonstrating. "When I mounted the stage and showed what I was talking about," Stanislavsky wrote, "I became understandable and eloquent."[25] His penchant for demonstrating continued up to his final years, although he knew that this approach was more geared toward results than the process-oriented method he preferred.

During the years of his collaboration with Nemirovich-Danchenko, they agreed on character interpretation, general mood and atmosphere, textual cuts, and dialogue alterations. An arrangement was worked out whereby Stanislavsky would prepare a detailed plan of the production, handle the actors in the earliest stages of rehearsal, and then allow his partner to take over the more detailed stages of working with the company. Stanislavsky would then move on to the next scheduled play, and the same process would continue for each successive play. He found this a congenial system and admitted to a distaste for working intensively with the individual actors (a distaste he would one day overcome); Nemirovich-Danchenko, he then thought, was better suited for this task. As Stanislavsky's workload grew, with him preparing several productions simultaneously while also playing leading roles, this system—or variations of it—proved useful, although a number of assistant directors eventually had to be engaged to handle one or more stages in the rehearsal process.

Nemirovich-Danchenko liked to begin the rehearsal process with a very detailed, moment-by-moment breakdown and exploration of the script with the actors, going into particular depth from his literary perspective. Stanislavsky, however, thought this overburdened them and confused them with too much detail. He preferred to start from a broader base. "When the actor has gained control of his image, characters, and mood in general outline, then he can be given various details and fine touches," he noted in 1905 during the preparations for *Ghosts*. In his opinion, the approach "*à la Nemirovich*" so disoriented actors "that they can produce only vague images even when perfectly simple and straightforward feelings are involved."[26] Of course, Stanislavsky himself practiced "at the table" rehearsals; he may have had reservations about them, but, as Toporkov notes, he "never disclaimed the value of such rehearsals in principle." At these sessions, "future performers of the play, with the director at the head [of the table], subjected the separate units of the work to careful analysis, with much searching and even more experiments in embodiment."[27] The difference appears to be that Stanislavsky objected to the excessively literary analysis practiced by Nemirovich-Danchenko, and himself preferred to examine a script "at table" in terms of its theatrical dynamics. Apart from some early exceptions, it was not until his work on a new staging of *The Three Sisters* in 1934 (never completed) that Stanislavsky decided to give up such rehearsals for good and plunge right into putting the play on its feet.

FROM AUTOCRAT TO COLLABORATOR

Stanislavsky's methods during his period of codirecting with Nemirovich-Danchenko were rather limited compared to those he developed later. In addition to imposing definite conceptions on the actors as to characterization, movement, vocalization, and business, he would also resort to artificial means to overcome bad acting habits or to prompt desired responses. Insulting an actress to make her cry was only one such measure. Disturbed by another performer's excessive gesturing, for instance, Stanislavsky tied his arms down; when this led to too much finger movement, the fingers were restrained. At another time he would use psychological pressure to bring actors into line. Once he convinced a group of actors to obey him by making a secret arrangement with an old veteran who agreed to be berated at a rehearsal before the others. Seeing the old actor's compliance, the younger actors thereupon began listening seriously to everything their director said.

Many such techniques were eventually discarded as Stanislavsky learned to trust his actors' creative instincts. His career shows a gradual transition from giving the actor most of the details about his performance to allowing him to find these for himself. In preparing a production he would thoroughly annotate a promptbook or production plan in which every production element from acting to sets and lighting was described. A classic example from his early years is his promptbook for *The Seagull*. Reading it, one can easily envision the performance. Since Nemirovich-Danchenko read the notes to the actors in Stanislavsky's absence, the promptbook had to be especially clear and detailed. It tells not only what the actors were to do, but why. Stanislavsky suggested characteristic props for each role, and described each character's look and typical behavior (one would always smoke, another would crack nuts, etc.). All the staging evolved from an understanding of the characters' social positions, the way such people would act given the circumstances provided by the playwright. Expressive stage business was set down, with even the desired emotional tones indicated. Poses and attitudes were defined so that each character would immediately register his relationship to the scene in nonverbal terms. Even vocal inflections, words to stress, and tone of voice were prescribed by the director.

At the time, such minute planning was new in Russia. All the actors had to do was follow the instructions to achieve a satisfactory performance. Such autocratic control led to a total unity of production, but it was a unity inspired almost solely by the director, with a very diminished contribution from the actors. As Stanislavsky learned to depend on the actor's creativity, he began to rely less on such diligent preparations. In the final stages of his work, he ceased using the promptbook entirely. He came to rehearsal with only an outline in his head, willing to see where his actors would take him and where his suggestions could lead them. Lines did not have to be learned early in the rehearsal process, as formerly, but could be memorized during the rehearsal period as the actors first discovered their characters. As each actor became familiar with his character's actions and behavior, the words and movements remained in his mind, not because they had been studied mechanically, but because they were understood within an organic context.

SUBTEXT AND OBJECTIVES

An important element in rehearsals was the actor's understanding of his subtext or "inner monologue," the thoughts which lie behind the character's words. Identifying the subtext was one of Stanislavsky's most profound contributions to modern acting technique.

Subtext was to be understood by every actor, no matter how small his part. Exercises were often played at rehearsals to guarantee that the subtext was employed in the performance. In one such exercise, the actors would do an improvisation based on a scene from the play, saying both the text and subtext. Then the scene would be repeated with the subtext whispered, and finally, without saying it at all.

When an actor had grasped the subtext, he reframed it in terms of specific objectives or "I wants." These provided the actor with a concrete psychological context within which to carry out his actions. Every moment bore a particular and specific objective, but the actor also had to locate an ultimate objective, or the "superobjective." This allowed him to see the role in a total perspective, as well as in individual units. The superobjective is vital to the continuity and style of a production. Stanislavsky once staged and acted in Molière's *The Imaginary Invalid*; he played the leading role with the superobjective "I want to be sick," but this made the farce into a tragedy; he thereupon rephrased the superobjective as "I want to be thought sick," and this helped establish the proper comic mood. By this means the whole play was affected, although not all superobjectives play so crucial a role in the total production.

Stanislavsky considered it dangerous for the superobjective to be defined too early in the rehearsal process, as it could lead to mechanical results. It is better, he felt, for the actor to determine it over time under the director's guidance. The superobjective of the play itself encompasses every element in the production, including each actor's interpretation; to reach this superobjective, everything must follow along a single "through-line" leading to it. Anything which fails to accord with the integrity of the through-line must be avoided, for it will cause distortion by introducing elements in discord with the play's true nature. Among such discordant ingredients, for example, would be an inappropriately tendentious interpretation by the director. It was Stanislavsky's long-standing practice, before determining the play's superobjective, to break the play down into its component parts, called "units" or "beats." In each unit he would help the actors determine what their characters did and why they did it. Units could be as short as a line or two, or they could extend for several pages. Actors were to phrase their unit objectives in action terms: " 'I wish to conquer the heart of this woman,' 'I wish to penetrate into her home,' 'I wish to get rid of the servants guarding her,' etc."[28]

One way that Stanislavsky helped the actor discover his strongest actions and objectives was to question him intently on the reason for his choices. He wanted to be sure the actor saw the relation between what he did and why he did it. If the actor knew the biography of his character (even crowd actors had to write a biography of their parts) as well as the plot and theme of the play, and was conversant with human behavior and emotions as expressed under many circumstances, he would be able to respond with valid answers. Stanislavsky tried to get the actors to reply in terms of what they would do if they were the characters in the circumstances of the play. Based on his perceptions, the actor was to see how his own behavior and that of his role were different, thus helping him to perceive what the character does and why. He could then proceed to combine his own behavior patterns with those of the character.

A good example of the way in which Stanislavsky spoke to an actor is contained in this passage from the rehearsals for *Dead Souls* (the actor is Toporkov):

"Why, after all, does Chichikov buy the dead? . . . "

"What might one answer? It is evident to everyone, but. . . . "

"Well, for what purpose?"

"Gogol writes that he will mortgage the dead serfs as living and receive money for them."

"And what for?"

"What do you mean, 'what for'?"

"Why is this advantageous to him; what does he need the money for? What will he do with it? Have you thought of that?"

"No, I haven't thought about it in such detail."

"Well, think about it."[29]

This sort of questioning was typical of Stanislavsky's method of getting the actor to dig deeply into the background and circumstances of every aspect of his role so as to produce continuously truthful behavior. Numerous examples of it can be found in Toporkov's *Stanislavski in Rehearsal*.

When displeased with an actor's answers to his probing, Stanislavsky would often say, "I don't believe it," or "I don't understand you," and continue to drive the actor, possibly mimicking him or demonstrating for him, until the latter arrived at a truthful perception. His well-known use of "I don't believe it" signalled an illogical facet in the actor's interpretation. Stanislavsky put himself in the place of the audience when asking his questions so that no seams would be evident in the presentation. He asked his actors to "Accept my 'I don't believe you' calmly, seriously, and trustfully."[30]

IMPROVISATION

Stanislavsky's most interesting and unusual rehearsal techniques were those he developed in his final period, when he came to depend on the use of improvisations to stimulate creativity. Maxim Gorky had once interested him in founding a theatre of improvisations, like the *commedia dell'arte*, but rehearsal "improvs" were about as far as the idea ever went. Few directors have been so consistently imaginative in their use of this method. Analytical discussions came to play a secondary role to the technique of improvs as Stanislavsky gradually became aware of how effective they were. An actor's truthful behavior could be evoked through a variety of spontaneous rehearsal situations.

Scenery and costumes began to lose their former significance as Stanislavsky grew increasingly fascinated by the potentialities of a theatre which focused almost exclusively on human beings and their interrelationships. What was happening became more worthy of attention than concerns for the reality of the environment.

Stanislavsky used various improvisations in rehearsing *The Two Orphans* (retitled *The Sisters Gerard*), the nineteenth-century French melodrama which Gorchakov and another young director had been working on before Stanislavsky took control. In one, he wanted the actress playing a blind girl to feel what being sightless and alone in a strange Paris street felt like; he unexpectedly turned off all the lights and forced the actress to move about searching for him, with all the room's furnishings providing difficult obstacles for her. In another improvisation, developed to increase attentiveness to one's partners and personal expressiveness, he had the actors play a scene silently, using only their eyes. As they improvised, the actors felt more and more compelled to speak until, by the end of the scene, they did just that, but with a far greater variety and sense of color than before. Stanislavsky then had them underline each sentence's key words, beginning with special stress on the noun, then the verb, and then other emphatic parts of speech. Such a difficult exercise, acknowledged the regisseur, could only be done by actors who had been rehearsing for a long time and were thoroughly familiar with the given circumstances.

Following this exercise was one in which only the selected key words of a scene were spoken; as before, communication via the eyes was made vital, especially during the silent passages. The result was a scene filled with meaningful pauses, a heightened focus on the relationships and action, and a tremendous sense of contact between the players.

Stanislavsky's improvisations were based on the actions of a specific scene. The actors would slip in and out of the dialogue, adding their own words when needed, and playing the action as if it were really occurring. If an obstacle arose, Stanislavsky would invite a more experienced actor to do an improvisation with him as a demonstration for the younger players, even though the actor was not doing that particular role in the play.

After creating a number of improvs, Stanislavsky would select the best discoveries from each, so that a scene requiring fifteen minutes to improvise might last only a moment or two in production; those moments, though, would be exceptionally expressive ones. This method was not so effective with the introspective dramas of writers like Chekhov, Ibsen, and Dostoyevsky, he pointed out, but was excellent for plays reliant upon the type of dynamic stage action that such improvisations evoked.

Stanislavsky's method grew increasingly experimental as he came to the end of his career. In *Tartuffe* he allowed the actors to hold a number of rehearsals with no director present so they could try out ideas with total freedom. Real props were given up in favor of imaginary ones, and floor plans changed from rehearsal to rehearsal. He began to think that giving the actor the script before he understood the dramatic actions was a mistake. Afraid that incorrect vocal inflections would develop, he made up exercises in which meaning was expressed through intonation and rhythm, using arbitrary syllables rather than dialogue. The words when introduced would fill an organic need for communication established through the preliminary exercises.

CONCLUSION

His productions in the 1920s and 1930s may not have been as inspired as those of Meyerhold or Reinhardt, but that is because Stanislavsky did not seek to be an "inspired" director. Had he continued in the vein of his late nineteenth- and early twentieth-century work he might have staged plays as revolutionary as those of any other director, but he chose not to put the director at the center of the theatre. For him, the actor was the artist who counted most and for whom all the theatre's other arts were to be of service. He strenuously altered the course of his own ego-supportive tendencies, and turned his directing interests toward seeking ways of getting actors to act—no matter what the play—with honesty, simplicity, sincerity, and believability. The director was a stimulating guide and the actor had only to be receptive to imaginative suggestions and exercises to find his own way (provided, of course, that he had mastered all the preliminary facets of the master's system). Stanislavsky's writings are largely concerned with the actor's problems, not the director's; it is because of his total devotion to the actor's art that few acting schools in the modern world are unfamiliar with, if not dedicated to, some variant of the Stanislavsky system. Some of these variants have aroused considerable controversy, in particular the one developed by Lee Strasberg and popularly called "the Method"; as mentioned before, its major variation is the emphasis it places on emotion memory, which Stanislavsky eventually abandoned in favor of the method of physical actions.

No matter what the permutations undergone by his ideas, Stanislavsky's spirit continues to guide the world of theatre; even his principal theoretical adversaries, Meyerhold and Brecht, acknowledged the force and significance of his contributions. These contributions will be debated and examined as long as there is theatre.

NOTES

1. A detailed examination of Stanislavsky's achievement with Shakespeare is presented in Joyce Vining Morgan's *Stanislavski's Encounter with Shakespeare* (Ann Arbor, Mich.: UMI Research Press, 1984). Morgan includes extensive descriptions of the na-

turalistic 1903 *Julius Caesar,* staged by Nemirovich-Danchenko with Stanislavsky as Brutus, and the Gordon Craig *Hamlet,* in addition to those Shakespeare productions more properly considered Stanislavsky's work. The most thorough account of the Craig *Hamlet* is in Laurence Senelick's *Gordon Craig's Moscow "Hamlet": A Reconstruction* (Westport, Conn.: Greenwood Press, 1982).

2. Constantin Stanislavski, *My Life in Art,* trans. J. J. Robbins (New York: Meridian Books, 1956), p. 207.

3. Ibid., p. 570.

4. Constantin Stanislavski, *Stanislavski's Legacy: A Collection of Comments on a Variety of Aspects of an Actor's Life and Art,* ed. and trans. Elizabeth Reynolds Hapgood (New York: Theatre Arts Books, 1958), p. 134.

5. S. D. Balukhaty, ed., *"The Seagull" Produced by Stanislavsky,* trans. David Magarshack (New York: Theatre Arts Books, 1952), p. 110.

6. David Richard Jones provides a detailed analysis and evaluation of Stanislavsky's accomplishment with *The Seagull* promptbook in *Great Directors at Work* (Berkeley: University of California Press, 1986), pp. 15 ff.

7. Jones presents a reasonable rebuttal of this standard assessment of the Chekhov-Stanislavsky artistic relationship in ibid., pp. 56–61. A good account of this relationship from the traditional point of view may be found in Edward Braun, *The Director and the Stage: From Naturalism to Grotowski* (London: Methuen, 1982). Braun points out a number of ways in which Stanislavsky may be considered to have misinterpreted Chekhov's intentions in *The Seagull, Uncle Vanya, The Three Sisters,* and *The Cherry Orchard.*

8. Quoted in Jean Benedetti, *Stanislavski: A Biography* (New York: Routledge, 1988), p. 76.

9. Kenneth Macgowan and Robert Edmond Jones, *Continental Stagecraft* (New York: Benjamin Blom, 1964), p. 9.

10. Heywood Broun, *New York World,* 23 January 1923.

11. Stanislavski, *My Life in Art,* p. 477.

12. Vasily Osopivich Toporkov, *Stanislavski in Rehearsal: The Final Years,* trans. Christine Edwards (New York: Theatre Arts Books, 1979), p. 60.

13. Ibid., p. 63.

14. Nikolai A. Gorchakov, *The Theater in Soviet Russia,* trans. Edgar Lehrman (New York: Columbia University Press, 1957), p. 323.

15. Norris Houghton, *Moscow Rehearsals* (New York: Harcourt Brace, 1936), p. 28.

16. Toporkov, *Stanislavski in Rehearsal,* p. 58.

17. Quoted in Sergei Melik-Zakharov and Soel Bogatryev, eds. and comps., *Konstantin Stanislavsky 1863–1963: Man and Actor,* trans. Vic Schneirson (Moscow: Iskustvo Publishers, 1963), p. 50.

18. Houghton, *Moscow Rehearsals,* p. 66.

19. Konstantin Stanislavski, "Director's Diary, 1905: The MAT Production of Ibsen's *Ghosts,*" trans. Elizabeth Reynolds Hapgood, in *Stanislavski and America,* ed. Erika Munk (Greenwich, Conn.: Fawcett, 1967), pp. 40–42.

20. David Magarshack, *Stanislavsky, A Life* (New York: Chanticleer Press), p. 25.

21. Toporkov, *Stanislavski in Rehearsal,* p. 119.

22. Stanislavski, *Stanislavski's Legacy,* p. 64.

23. Quoted in Magarshack, *Stanislavsky,* p. 284.

24. Stanislavski, *Stanislavski's Legacy,* p. 64.

25. Stanislavski, *My Life in Art,* p. 353.

26. Stanislavski, "Director's Diary, 1905: The MAT Production of Ibsen's *Ghosts,*" p. 41.

27. Toporkov, *Stanislavski in Rehearsal,* p. 81.

28. Stanislavski, *Stanislavski's Legacy,* p. 181.

29. Toporkov, *Stanislavski in Rehearsal,* p. 81.

30. Nikolai M. Gorchakov, *Stanislavsky Directs,* trans. Miriam Goldina (New York: Grosset and Dunlap, 1962), p. 183.

CHRONOLOGY

Only representative productions of Stanislavsky's from his Alexeyev Circle period are given. Most of the plays he staged for the Moscow Art Theatre were codirected; operas and most other musical events are not listed.

1863   born near Moscow

1881   begins to codirect amateur group, the Alexeyev Circle

1882   first solo directing effort, Alexeyev Circle: *The Forced Marriage*

1883   Alexeyev Circle: *The Practical Man*

1884   begins to use stage name, Konstantin Stanislavsky

1886   Alexeyev Circle: *Lili*

1887   Alexeyev Circle: *The Mikado*

1888   Alexeyev Circle ends; cofounds artists' club, the Society of Art and Literature; all subsequent listings through 1898 for the Society of Art and Literature (SAL), except where noted

1889   *Burning Letters*

1891   *The Fruits of Enlightenment; Foma*

1894   *The Governor; Light without Heat*

1895   *Uriel Acosta; Men above the Law; The Inspector-General,* latter for a professional company

1896   *Othello; Hannele; The Polish Jew; Girl without a Dowry*

1897   *Much Ado about Nothing; Twelfth Night*; famous meeting with Nemirovich-Danchenko to plan Moscow Art Theatre (MAT)

1898   *The Sunken Bell,* final production for SAL; cofounds MAT; opens with *Tsar Fyodor Ivanovich* (all subsequent productions for MAT); *The Sunken Bell* (revival); *The Merchant of Venice; Men above the Law; La Locandiera; The Seagull*

1899   *Hedda Gabler; Death of Ivan the Terrible; Twelfth Night; Drayman Henschel; Uncle Vanya; Lonely People*

1900   *The Snow Maiden; An Enemy of the People*

1901   *The Three Sisters; The Wild Duck; Michael Kramer; In Dreams*

1902   *Small People; The Power of Darkness; The Lower Depths*

1904   *The Cherry Orchard*

1905   *Ghosts; Children of the Sun*; sets up Studio for Meyerhold

1906   tours to central European cities; Finnish vacation sees breakthroughs in his understanding of the actor's creative process; *Woe from Wit*

1907   ends codirecting period with Nemirovich-Danchenko; *The Drama of Life; The Life of Man*

1908   *The Blue Bird; The Inspector-General*

1909   *A Month in the Country*

1910   *Enough Stupidity in Every Wise Man*

1911   *Redemption* (or *The Living Corpse*); Gordon Craig's *Hamlet*

1912   *A Provincial Lady*; founds First Studio of MAT

1913   *The Imaginary Invalid*

1914   *La Locandiera* (revival)

1916   founds Second Studio

1917   First Studio: *Twelfth Night*; Russian Revolution

1920   *Cain*

1921   *The Inspector-General*

1922–24   foreign tours; two seasons in New York, Fifty-ninth Street Theatre: *Tsar Fyodor Ivanovich; The Lower Depths; The Cherry Orchard; The Brothers Karamazov; A Provincial Lady; La Locandiera; Uncle Vanya*

1924   autobiography, *My Life in Art*, published in USA

1926   *The Burning Heart; Nicholas I and the Decembrists; Merchants of Glory; Days of the Turbins*

1927   *The Marriage of Figaro; The Two Orphans; Armored Train 14-69*

1928   *Untilovsk; The Embezzlers*; suffers heart attack and leaves USSR to recuperate

1930   *Othello*, directed in absentia

1932   *Dead Souls*

1933   *Artists and Admirers*

1936   *Molière; An Actor Prepares* published in USA

1938   dies in Moscow

1939   *Tartuffe*, completed posthumously

Vsevolod Meyerhold

(1873–1940)

Early in 1938 the *New York Times* ran the following dispatch:

> Moscow, January 8—The long expected axe fell today on Ysevolod E.
> Meyerhold, whose eccentric stage productions once caused him to be revered
> as the prophet of the revolutionary theatre. The arts committee of the Council
> of People's Commissars ordered his theatres dissolved and members of his
> acting company transferred to other theatres and directed that the question
> of whether Mr. Meyerhold be permitted to continue in the theatrical field
> be discussed separately.[1]

The Soviet Government charged Meyerhold with adherence to bourgeois, for-
malistic ideas, of having produced distortions of the classics, of failing to discover
worthwhile new Soviet plays, of being unable to retain good actors or attract
good writers, and of misusing state funds in one of his productions. A year and
a half later, another *New York Times* article announced, "Soviet Police Arrest
Meyerhold."[2] Meyerhold died in a prison camp, on a date now generally accepted
as February 2, 1940.

   In the nation ruled by Joseph Stalin, the name of Russia's greatest director
was erased from public discourse for a decade and a half. On August 1, 1956,
however, the *Times* disclosed that Vsevolod Meyerhold's name was being "resurrected" by the post-Stalinist regime.[3] In the years since then, Meyerhold's
accomplishments have been expounded and his reputation as a pillar of the
modern theatre firmly established. A "Meyerhold Centennial," marking the
hundredth year of his birth, was held throughout the USSR in 1974. Meyerhold's
death in tragic circumstances only serves to emphasize his stature as one who
refused to permit the stifling of the artist's vision by the forces of tyranny. Today
Meyerhold's revolutionary ideas continue to inspire and intrigue theatre artists
all over the world.

EARLY YEARS

Karl Theodore Kazimir Meyergold was born 550 miles from Moscow, in the provincial city of Penza, where his German father owned a prosperous vodka distillery. When young Meyergold became a naturalized Russian citizen (and a convert to Orthodoxy) in 1895, he took the name of Vsevolod Emilovich Meyerhold. His well-off Lutheran parents had provided him with a rich cultural education, and childhood theatricals at home had played their share in his youthful upbringing. An attempt at law studies at Moscow University proved abortive; in 1896, at the end of a year, he transferred to the Moscow Philharmonic Society to study his true interest, theatre. As an acting student of Vladimir Nemirovich-Danchenko's, he was outstanding and even won a medal for his work. When Nemirovich-Danchenko joined up with Konstantin Stanislavsky in 1898 to create the Moscow Art Theatre (MAT), the former took along his best students, including Meyerhold, who acted with the MAT until 1902. Although he played several major roles, including Trepleff in *The Seagull*, his acting promise appears not to have been fulfilled; besides, directing had become his major goal and he left the MAT to cofound, with A. S. Kosheverov, a company called a Troupe of Russian Dramatic Artists, which played a prolific repertory in Kherson, the Ukraine, in 1902–3. Most of these productions were of the best new European plays of the time—works by Anton Chekhov, Henrik Ibsen, Gerhart Hauptmann, Arthur Schnitzler, and Maurice Maeterlinck—but production methods mainly resembled those of the MAT. Meyerhold was still learning his trade and, apart from one or two symbolist plays, was not yet ready to delve into the truly unconventional.

Tiflis was the scene of the 1903–4 season for the Fellowship of the New Drama, as the troupe now called itself. At the season's end Meyerhold found himself in Moscow working once more for Stanislavsky in a daring new enterprise.

THE 1905 THEATRE-STUDIO

Stanislavsky, fearing that naturalism was an artistic dead end, was seeking an effective approach to theatrical symbolism. Having failed with some Maeterlinck one-acts in 1904, he felt he was not equipped for the style but that young Meyerhold, whose ideas he knew to be advanced, might hold the key. Meyerhold was set up as director of the new Theatre-Studio in 1905 and here he planned many productions, although only two came anywhere near completion. Working with the designers Nikolai Sapunov, Sergei Sudeikin, and Nikolai Ulynav, he helped create impressionistic designs which captured the essence of historical styles without the minutiae of naturalistic details. Models were dispensed with in favor of painted sketches which would allow the designer to transfer his ideas immediately to the stage. Meyerhold found his actors less receptive to his ideas, however, and recognized that their MAT training did not prepare them for the nonrepresentational physical style he demanded.

The two plays that almost reached performance were Maeterlinck's *The Death of Tintagiles* and Hauptmann's *Schluck and Jau*. Stanislavsky had viewed a run-through of *Tintagiles* and was very excited about Meyerhold's work. But soon he came to feel that the experimental director's approach deprived the actors of human truth and turned them into robots.

Meyerhold's production methods revealed ingredients soon to reappear in other plays. *Schluck and Jau,* for example, had an unusual scene in which a group of court ladies, stripped of individuality by being dressed identically and moving in rhythmic unison, embroidered a single long ribbon. Scenic elements of enormous size, such as huge castle gates, were employed for symbolic effect. Period motifs in costumes, sets, and music retained the proper historical style despite the modernism of interpretation.

Tintagiles likewise revealed strongly formalized methods. Dialogue was spoken with overt musical values, sound effects and background music were provided by a chorus of a cappella singers, and all movement was carefully planned and executed to definite rhythmic patterns. A shallow, flat, painted background threw the movements into sharp relief, a technique then being promulgated by the bas-relief stagings of Georg Fuchs in Munich. The dim lighting so upset Stanislavsky that, at a dress rehearsal, he forced Meyerhold to turn up the lights so he could see the actors' faces. When the abortive revolution of 1905 erupted, all Moscow theatres, including the Studio, were closed. Busy now with other matters, Stanislavsky chose not to reopen it.

VERA KOMISSARJEVSKAYA

After a short period in Kherson in 1906 with his old theatre company, Meyerhold became a director with the St. Petersburg company of the leading Russian actress, Vera Komissarjevskaya. Komissarjevskaya was a tragic star of great charm and power; she had a mystical quality that made her unsuited for the typically realistic plays of the day. Seeking an art which would employ her unique abilities, she felt the symbolist theatre (already losing strength in Western Europe) would provide an appropriate outlet. Meyerhold, given total directorial freedom, created for her some of the most controversial productions of the day.

His first production for Komissarjevskaya was *Hedda Gabler* (1906). Fuchs' influence was very evident in the bas-relief staging, which used an acting area a dozen feet deep and thirty-three feet wide. The two-dimensional background served to ''project'' the three-dimensional actor forward so that his gestures and facial expressions were clearly heightened by the aesthetic contrast. Symbolic colors, movements, and postures further emphasized the actor's presence by signaling at once the most essential facts about a character—his feelings, his thoughts, his relationships.

Sister Beatrice (1906), by Maeterlinck, was the greatest success for the director and actress during their period of collaboration. Again the bas-relief style was employed; in this case, the decor was based on careful research into the relief sculptures of Gothic cathedrals. Only seven feet of space stood between the audience and the neutral panel background, and the movements were choreographed in hieroglyphic patterns based on those found in old church sculptures and in pre-Raphaelite and Renaissance paintings.

Meyerhold tried to create for Maeterlinck's plays a form of static action which would evince the power of Greek tragedy through a minimum of physical activity and a concentration on the psychological subtext. Restrained and economical gestures had to be developed to illustrate the interior meanings. From his receptivity to the slightest pause or moistened eye, the attentive spectator could deduce a great deal more than less simple means would have afforded.

Meyerhold staged over a dozen other plays for Komissarjevskaya, including works by Leonid Andreyev, Alexander Blok, F. Sologub, Frank Wedekind, and two more by Maeterlinck. Blok's *The Fairground Booth* (1906) was one of the most successful and controversial of these. The acting style associated with the relief stage was abandoned in favor of a distinctively nonillusionistic *commedia dell'arte* style, employing the energy of grotesque tragic farce. Meyerhold acted the role of Pierrot in this unusual play about the triangular love affair of Pierrot, Harlequin, and Columbine. No attempt was made to disguise the fact that the audience was viewing a play; all the workings of the production were exposed to view, even the prompter crawling to his box to light a candle there. Among the innovative ideas was the satirizing of the play's five mystics by presenting them as headless cardboard cutouts with places for the actors to rest their own heads and holes through which to put their hands.

Meyerhold's innovations were wide-ranging, including the effective use of highly selective area lighting on simultaneous scenic arrangements in Andreyev's allegorical *The Life of Man* (1907) and Wedekind's proto-expressionist *Spring's Awakening* (1907).

After failing miserably in Meyerhold's staging of Maeterlinck's *Pelléas and Mélisande* (1907), Komissarjevskaya seriously began to consider firing the director. Sologub's *Victory of Death* (1907), a critical success, was his thirteenth and final production for the star; shortly after it opened she dismissed him. She respected Meyerhold's brilliance, but saw that his methods were a threat to hers and that his directorial ingenuity made her role as actress a secondary one.

THEATRICALISM OVER ILLUSIONISM

By this time Meyerhold had abandoned naturalism; instead, he strove in each production to reveal the heart of the play through imaginative, nonillusionistic means. From both his personal acquaintance with Chekhov and his knowledge of his plays, he had learned that the theatre must be a place for essences, allusiveness, restraint, and selectivity, not for the detailed reproduction of offstage reality.

Meyerhold discerned that the proscenium had erected a barrier between the auditorium and the stage and began to seek ways to bring them together, as they had been in the theatres of the past. He experimented with various psychological and atmospheric techniques of joining the actor and the spectator in a shared experience. And while his architectural innovations were still tentative and, aside from his relief stages, limited to some experimentation with the apron stage, by 1907 he was nonetheless sure that the modern theatre required a modified version of the classical Greek theatre with its acting space surrounded by an audience on three sides. A nonrepresentational architectural background, he thought, was the ideal scenic solution.

Acting had to be plastic, thoroughly expressive, and iconographic in order to stimulate the audience's imagination and communicate more than the words could alone. What went on onstage was never to deceive the audience into accepting it as a reproduction of life. Audience and actor were always to be conscious that they were engaged in an act of artistic creation, that they were present in a theatre, and that no deception was intended. Whereas Stanislavsky virtually ignored the audience in his realistic productions—the life onstage theoretically existing apart from the audience—Meyerhold's audience was itself the core of his presentations.

ST. PETERSBURG'S IMPERIAL THEATRES

In September of 1908, Meyerhold took up residence as director of the conservative Imperial Theatres of St. Petersburg, a surprising appointment considering his reputation as an upstart innovator. The controversial choice was a wise one: Meyerhold remained until the end of the Russian Revolution of 1917. He staged a series of outstanding works at two imperial playhouses, doing plays at the Alexandrinsky and operas at the Marinsky. Aware that he could not go too far in his theatricalist innovations at these theatres, he chose to explore his more experimental ideas in a variety of unconventional private playing spaces. To cloak his involvement in these ventures, he used the name of a character from a tale by E. T. A. Hoffmann, Dr. Dapertutto.

From 1908 to 1918 Meyerhold staged fourteen plays at the Alexandrinsky, in addition to the many works he staged elsewhere, both in St. Petersburg and in other cities. His Alexandrinsky productions included plays by Knut Hamsun (*At the Gates of the Kingdom,* 1908), Nikolai Gogol (*A Lawsuit,* 1909), Molière (*Don Juan,* 1910), Sir Arthur Wing Pinero (*Mid-Channel,* 1914), Pedro Calderon de la Barca (*The Constant Prince,* 1915), George Bernard Shaw (*Pygmalion,* 1915), Alexander Ostrovsky (*The Storm,* 1916), Mikhail Lermontov (*Masquerade,* 1917), and Henrik Ibsen (*The Lady from the Sea,* 1917). The emphasis was on well-known plays, old and new; most of the selections, however, were less familiar than those found in the typical Continental repertory of the time. There were no Shakespeare productions, for example. In fact, though Meyerhold carried with him the dream of a *Hamlet* throughout his career, he never once staged a play by the great English dramatist.[4]

A schedule requiring about two new productions a year allowed Meyerhold the time to plan his work with extreme thoroughness. The Alexandrinsky productions, by and large, were elaborately conceived and executed, and employed all the excellent resources of this state-funded playhouse. Meyerhold's developing ideas on moving out beyond the proscenium arch were actively incorporated in many of these shows. He also employed a wide range of theatricalist inventions in his staging, and worked with Russia's leading set designers, especially Alexandre Golovin, who designed almost all of his productions. Their collaboration is especially remembered for *Don Juan* and *Masquerade*.

The set for *Don Juan* was a re-creation of the spirit of luxury that prevailed when the play was produced in the seventeenth century at Versailles. A nonillusionistic decor reminiscent of Gobelin tapestries was lit by beautiful hanging and standing candelabra, and the houselights were kept on during the acting. No curtain or footlights were used. Removing the curtain allowed the spectators to fruitfully occupy their time while waiting for the play to start by carefully examining the scenery, thus preventing the background from distracting them during the performance. Also during the preshow period, two boys, dressed in fancy eighteenth-century livery and made up as blackamoors, set the stage with props and furniture. These boys acted throughout as stage assistants much like those used in the Kabuki theatre, though in the Japanese theatre they would normally be dressed in black and considered invisible. Meyerhold also had them do acrobatics, light and snuff candles, and ring a silver bell to call the audience after the intermission. He used similar "proscenium servants," as he called them, in several other works of this period. An apron stage broke through the proscenium arch and covered up the orchestra pit, bringing the action far downstage. Actors spoke directly to the spectators, whom, with the houselights on, they could clearly see, thereby granting them the feedback the regisseur felt essential to a good performance. Visible onstage were two well-costumed and wigged prompters, seated behind decorative screens with apertures in them. Meyerhold chose to use the prompters in order to ease the problems presented by the poor memory of Konstantin Varlamov, the great actor who played Sganarelle. Varlamov was also permitted free improvisation and frequently took the opportunity to throw amusing comments to friends he spotted in the audience.

Meyerhold claimed that a period play should not be revived with a stage that archaeologically reproduced the one used by the play's original production, but should capture the spirit of that stage within the framework of contemporary design. *Don Juan* attempted, first of all, to suggest the quality of the seventeenth-century court stage; secondly, it sought to introduce those popular theatre innovations Meyerhold felt Molière was trying to effect in bringing drama closer to the audience. He therefore used the apron to move the actor closer to the spectator. Here, he felt, every aspect of the action could be seen, clear of the encumbrances of scenery and props.

In a different vein was the mystical-symbolical style of *Masquerade*. This drama has a story in some ways like that of *Othello*. The debauched nobleman, Arbenin, reforms his ways upon marrying young Nina; when vicious rumors convince him of her unfaithfulness, he kills her. Unlike Othello, proof of his wife's innocence leads Arbenin not to suicide but to madness. One of the regisseur's most richly decorative productions, *Masquerade* used the painted sets of Golovin in a strictly conventional manner.

The apron had a bannister at its downstage end and was buttressed at either side by extensions of the setting placed before the box-seats situated there. Doorways in these sculptured portals allowed for exits and entrances. Mirrors on the portals allowed the audience to see its own reflection. The acting was mainly located far downstage, the upstage painted backdrop providing atmosphere more than environment. A cast of over two hundred was used magnificently for compositional effects.

Meyerhold placed the focus for the production on the mysterious, frightening figure of the Unknown Man, a seemingly supernatural character garbed in black and a tricornered hat and wearing a full-faced, white, birdlike, lantern-jawed mask. The play's central role, that of the conventional hero and raissonneur, was reinterpreted so that he seemed a passionate tragic figure. Employing Lermontov's own notes on the play to substantiate his interpretation, Meyerhold reversed the conventional view of the play as romantic tragedy and underlined its satirical nature as an attack on St. Petersburg society.

DR. DAPERTUTTO, THE COMMEDIA, AND THE GROTESQUE

Meyerhold's Dr. Dapertutto doppelganger emerged briefly in 1910 when he opened a small old theatre he called the House of Interludes. He had been interested in cabaret-style theatre for several years because of the intimacy it afforded. Now he had a theatre with a low stage whose steps led into the audience area, with spectators seated around small tables. He hoped to put on light comedies here, straight and musical, in an attempt to create a popular style reminiscent of the folk traditions of the fairground theatres. His favorite form of popular theatre, *commedia dell'arte,* to which he kept returning for inspiration, played a significant role in these endeavors. Among the pieces on the opening bill was a short musical pantomime by Arthur Schnitzler, retitled *Columbine's Scarf,* which was set to music by Ernö Dohnányi and designed by Sapunov. Its fourteen sharply contrasting episodes (based on the three scenes of the original) epitomized a theme often found in his work, that of the grotesque. His use of commedia style in *Columbine's Scarf* was, as in Blok's *The Fairground Booth*, in the mystical-symbolic vein associated with the work of E. T. A. Hoffmann, though in other plays he held more closely to the old street-fair traditions of this popular theatre art. The actors mingled with the audience during part of the action, effecting a decidedly intimate atmosphere.

Meyerhold's second and last House of Interludes production, *The Transformed Prince* (1910), also employed vivid theatrical *jeux* to underline the play's make-believe existence.

Meyerhold considered the style exemplified by these productions of great significance. He had come to believe that the theatre must revive the spirit of the medieval strolling player, wherein a single actor, using improvisational techniques, could be a director, writer, and actor all in one. This versatile "cabotin" would be akin to the old marketplace jugglers and acrobats, with the additional talents of the commedia actor. His art would be an essentially nonverbal one of pantomimic expression.

Meyerhold claimed the actor's face should not reflect the nuances of psychological reactions. Although he spoke of "masks," he did not mean actual masks such as commedia actors had worn. Instead he meant a kind of masklike acting in which the actor's physicality conveyed the essence of a stereotypical character type. (In this sense, the *characters* of the commedia could be considered masks.) As he shifted from one aspect of his role to another, revealing the various elements of which it was composed, the actor's movements and gestures were to dispel all vagueness.[5]

These contrasting elements of character were fundamental to Meyerhold's conception of the grotesque, a style composed of exaggeration, jarring transitions, and seeming illogicalities; properly combined, these elements were to lead to a humorous or tragic effect of mocking irony. Meyerhold felt that the grotesque afforded him a distinctly individualistic method of expressing his artistic vision, which was impossible in a more representational style. Rejecting the harmony and unity of the typical "stylized" approach to production, where all is subordinated to a specific scheme, he desired disunity and shocking contradictions.

Implicit in this approach was Meyerhold's long-held belief that the audience must never be hypnotized into accepting the dramatic world as everyday reality. The cabotin-actor should always strive to remember his existence as a performer: "every time the actor leads the spectators too far into the land of make-believe he immediately resorts to some unexpected sally or lengthy address *a parti* to remind them that what is being performed is only a *play*."[6]

The last of the Dr. Dapertutto productions was in 1916 when Meyerhold unsuccessfully revived *Columbine's Scarf* at a cellar theatre called the The Comedians' Rest.

STUDENT WORK

In addition, these years were occupied with the training of student actors by Meyerhold and his staff. Throughout his career he devoted energy and time to the creation and management of workshops and studios. No single method of teaching can be attributed to him, as he changed his ideas frequently. Essentially, his training prepared the actor to work effectively in an overtly physical manner, using his body as a means for creating visual imagery rather than psychological byplay. Pantomime and commedia techniques were core features of the training. Classes in vocal techniques were not ignored. Choral reading and verse reading, taught by experts, were fundamental to the curriculum.

Public presentations of the students' work charmed all by their delightfully fast-paced, rhythmic, and acrobatic quality. The two finished productions shown by the students to the public were Blok's *The Unknown Woman* (1914) and a revival of the same author's *The Fairground Booth* (1914). In these shows, which were built on a stylistic framework of the grotesque, the audience surrounded an apron on three sides and masklike makeup was used.

THE REVOLUTIONARY MEYERHOLD:
ACTIVIST THEATRE

Despite the breadth of Meyerhold's pre-Revolutionary ideas, his concerns were primarily aesthetic. He had held strong pro-proletarian political feelings since the late 1890s, and his outspokenness may have been behind the MAT decision of 1902 not to offer him a share in the company. Published correspondence between Meyerhold and Stanislavsky reveals that relations between the two were seriously strained; as early as 1899 Meyerhold was complaining to Nemirovich-Danchenko that the "director-in-chief" (Stanislavsky) completely ignored the "social significance" of the works he directed.[7] Yet politics played an almost nonexistent role in his own imperial theatre work and in that of Dr. Dapertutto. The same apolitical stance was true of a number of famous Russian directors on whom he had a great influence, among them Alexandre Tairov, Fyodor Komissarjevsky, and Nikolai Evreinov. Unlike these artists, Meyerhold's artistic spirit was fired by the outbreak of the Russian Revolution, which seemed to channel his multifarious activities of the earlier years into a definite direction with a precise goal; he quickly became one of the most rabidly political artists in the new Bolshevist state. It is his contributions in this post-Revolution era for which he is best remembered.

Meyerhold wasted little time in joining the Communist party and taking an active role in making his theatre a vital tool in the process of educating the populace about Soviet ideas. Although he was not the first to use the post-Revolutionary stage for agitational theatre, he was the first to gain widespread attention and appreciation for such uses. Before long his politically oriented mountings thrust him to the top of the nation's revolutionary artists; he even dressed as a revolutionary, wearing semimilitary clothing, including a cap with a red star and a shoulder holster which he wore even to rehearsals. His enthusiasm was soon rewarded when he was made head of the Theatre Division of the Education Commissariat in 1918. Had he had his way, all the old "bourgeois" theatres (soon to be labeled "academic theatres"), beginning with the MAT, would immediately have been liquidated; fortunately, more moderate views prevailed.

An enormous number of theatres, professional and amateur, sprang up through-

out the Soviet Union in the decade following the revolution. Many were concerned with the new staging ideas then bursting forth like fireworks in Europe
and America. However, Vladimir Ilyich Lenin's government was less interested
in aesthetics than in the use of theatre as a platform for effective communist
propaganda. For such purposes, they believed, the traditional means were sufficient. Meyerhold and others may have thought they had complete freedom to
work as they saw fit, since government attention was too distracted by more
pressing problems to sit heavily on the artistic experimenters. The toleration
accorded Meyerhold in the early through mid-1920s gradually dissolved as Lenin's successor, Stalin, turned against the artistic radicals and pummeled them
into party-line submission.

The post-Revolutionary decade was the most active and creative one Russian
artists had ever known. The liberal New Economic Policy (NEP) was instituted
as a stopgap measure to help strengthen the economy while the government
attended to the business of converting the country to socialist programs. Meyerhold, as the leading avant-garde director, called for "October in the Theatre,"
a slogan by which he hoped to inspire use of the theatre in keeping with the
spirit of the October Revolution. He was elevated to head of the Theatre Division
of the People's Commissariat of Enlightenment in 1920, but resigned a year
later. Although he agreed with Lenin about using the theatre as a political tool,
he could not bring himself to do so in any way but one he found artistically
valid.

To celebrate the first anniversary of the October Revolution, Meyerhold directed the first Soviet play to be done under the new government, Vladimir
Mayakovsky's *Mystery-Bouffe* (1918). This futurist work was staged in Petrograd
(formerly St. Petersburg; later, Leningrad) and was a broad anticapitalist farce
based on the story of Noah and the Ark. The settings, by Kasimir Malevich,
were in the abstract geometrical style called suprematism, a mode considered
highly progressive at the time. Meyerhold's production vividly caricatured the
bourgeoisie. All the proletarian characters were dressed identically in factory
uniforms, an idea soon to resurface in several of his other presentations. An
unusual element was the use of circus acrobatics, the most spectacular feat being
performed by Mayakovsky himself when he leaped into sight from within the
proscenium arch, suspended by wires, and spoke his lines in mid-air.

Meyerhold directed no plays in 1919. He nearly lost his life that year when,
recuperating from tuberculosis in the south, he was arrested by the White Army
and threatened with execution. He managed to evade this fate through some
fortunate personal contacts; after his release he directed *A Doll's House* (which
he called *Nora,* 1920) at Novorossiysk.

Meyerhold's great Moscow period began in November 1920 when he staged
Belgian playwright Emile Verhaeren's *The Dawns* at the New Theatre RSFSR
1 (RSFSR = Russian Socialist Federated Soviet Republic). This playhouse,
previously known as the Zon (or Sohn), was unheated and in poor condition,
but Meyerhold made it his home for many years, eventually refurbishing it,

though never converting it to a place of luxury. The huge theatre, more like a meeting hall than a playhouse, was well suited to his needs. "He wanted a harsh, open, rugged theatre that was clearly established to serve a much different clientele than the quietly comfortable interiors of the Maly, the Bolshoy, the Kamerny, and the MAT."[8]

The Dawns was an 1898 symbolist work based on the theme of war between the proletarians and the capitalists. It was rewritten to make it a piece of Bolshevist propaganda; the action was moved forward to accord with the then-current civil war on the Crimean Front between the Red and White armies. A striking, skeletal visual format, involving silver-gray cubo-futurist geometric scenery, was diminished by a poorly trained company of actors whom Meyerhold had difficulty integrating with his scenic concept. Barely any movement was used in this coldly formalized work. The most unique device was the use of nightly reports on the daily occurrences at the front, mixing actual war news into the drama's structure. Actors dressed as spectators sat in the house to help rouse the audience's emotions when the reports were read. The night the news of the final victory of the Reds was announced, the audience broke into applause and rose to their feet, standing silently as a singer performed a moving revolutionary hymn.

Attacked by critics, particularly Lenin's wife, Meyerhold was forced to revise the text to make it politically more orthodox. Still, audiences enjoyed it and it had a healthy run.

In May, he directed a revised version of *Mystery-Bouffe* suggested by recent political events. The author was very involved in rehearsals and practically codirected the play. This broadly comic poster-style presentation starred Igor Ilinsky, a student of Meyerhold's who for years was his leading actor, especially in satirical grotesque roles. The play's political message was sharpened, but even more important was the open attack—in the new verse prologue—on realistic theatre. Many theatricalist ideas were incorporated in the work, including an apron stage, acrobatics, and circus techniques. The highly stylized costumes were made from old newspaper scraps, and the set by Malevich was an early example of the constructivist style shortly to play a vital role in the regisseur's work.

Theatre RSFSR 1 was closed by the government following this production. Meyerhold's final work at the theatre under this name was Ibsen's *The League of Youth* (1921). When the theatre reopened in 1922, it was known as the Actors' Theatre; its premiere production was the version of *A Doll's House* called *Nora*.

BIOMECHANICS

At Russia's first directing school, the Meyerhold Workshop, organized in 1921, Meyerhold worked on his new theories of revolutionary art, especially the technique he called "biomechanics." Biomechanics was an acting method that had a theoretical foundation linked to such scientific notions as the time-

motion discoveries of Frederick Winslow Taylor and the research into condi-
tioned reflex behavior of William James and Ivan Petrovich Pavlov. Meyerhold,
like the futurists, saw in the machine the representative symbol of modern life,
and attempted to create an acting system as technically precise as the miracles
of technology. The machine represented the answer to man's problems in its
adherence to empirical scientific laws. Biomechanics was an appropriate response
to a materialistic worldview in which the old social conventions of morality, art,
and social relations were abandoned in favor of clear-cut mechanical principles
based on objective, verifiable data. (In later years Meyerhold—while continuing
to support its artistic validity—admitted the spurious scientific basis of biomechanics.)

Movement was to have no superfluous aspects, only those pertinent to the
expression of a given idea. All movement had to be based on rhythm, a center
of gravity, and stability—concepts Meyerhold believed were essential to any
trained worker. His system took great pains in teaching actors to master metrical
patterns and musical timing. In his view, actors were no different from nontheatrical working men and women. He wanted an actor so thoroughly trained
that he could respond immediately, as if by reflex action, to the needs dictated
by his part or by the director. At first, the biomechanical actor was deemed
capable of bearing the entire mise-en-scène within his performance; instead of
wearing an identifying costume and makeup, he could wear no makeup and
simple work clothes like any other honest proletarian, transforming himself into
a theatrically interesting entity through gestures and movements. If the actor
could conquer the physical problems of biomechanics, he could go beyond the
needs of psychological character depiction and "grip" his audience emotionally
through physiological processes. The correct postures and moves would lead
naturally to an emotional state in the actor and, by extension, affect the audience.
These notions are related but not identical to Stanislavsky's "method of physical
actions." Sonia Moore has explained the essential differences:

Meyerhold thought that certain movements of the highly trained body would stir inner
processes within the actor, whereas Stanislavski spoke, not of a movement, but of a
purposeful action, which involves the consciousness of the actor. An action is an un-
breakable organic psychophysical process—that is, what the actor thinks, experiences,
and does physically in the character's circumstances. . . . Biomechanics . . . is based on
physical movement only, and thus divides the actor's physical from his psychological
behavior.[9]

(However, the published remarks of various Meyerhold actors make it obvious
that the director was consistently concerned to see that all behavior on stage was
psychologically motivated. He understood that no system works the same way
for every actor and that each actor should be allowed to approach the inner life
of a role by whatever means was best for him.) Meyerhold did not require his
actors to perform abstract gestures. All movements were rationally based. "Every

movement is a hieroglyph with its own peculiar meaning. The theatre should employ only those movements which are immediately decipherable,''[10] he pointed out.

Earlier in his career Meyerhold had used studio exercises resembling those of biomechanics, especially during the period when he was intensely engaged in exploring the techniques of commedia and Asian theatre. These earlier ideas were also behind his biomechanic schematic treatise, "The Actor's Emploi," in which he broke down dramatic characters into seventeen male and seventeen female types, each with its own specific requirements of voice, appearance, and dramatic function, and supported his divisions with examples drawn from numerous classic and modern plays. By thus reducing all characters to types, he rejected outright the individualization of character psychology in favor of a more schematic approach. Individualization was developed in the director's free interpretation of each role-type. According to his theory, casting against type was one way he could exercise this artistic technique, as some actors are far better in roles for which, on the surface, they seem not well suited. In the struggle to subdue their personal traits, they often emerge far better in such roles than could be imagined. Type casting produces lazy actors and only a challenge can make an actor work to his fullest abilities.

Also significant in the world of Meyerholdian acting was the idea that actors were to use their many skills not to embody their characters as fully rounded individuals with whom they could completely identify, as in the theatre of Stanislavsky, but to consciously comment on the character by remaining clearly distinct from it. The audience would thus see a bipartite construct, the actor and the character played by the actor. In 1931, critic Boris Alpers noted: "The actor enacts, as it were, not the character itself, but his own attitude to the given character—thus does the Meyerhold theatre define the fundamental principle of the actor's craftsmanship.''[11] Bertolt Brecht would soon be calling for precisely the same thing in his theoretical essays.

THE MAGNIFICENT CUCKOLD AND CONSTRUCTIVIST PRODUCTION

A production of Ferdinand Crommelynck's *The Magnificent Cuckold* (also known as *The Magnanimous Cuckold,* 1922), cast with Meyerhold's workshop students, was a classic example of biomechanical acting techniques combined with constructivist design. Partially for reasons of economy, and partially for aesthetic reasons, the curtainless set designed by Lyubov Popova was stripped to bare essentials, even revealing the brick wall at the rear. Meyerhold chose to reveal the austere set to his actors as the lengthy rehearsal period was nearing its end; the actors were surprised to learn that there would be no conventional flats, drops, or wings. A "machine for acting," or construction which combined ramps, slides, platforms on various levels, swinging doors, a curved bench, a practical windmill, and two wheels offered the actors an amusing playground for their performances. In addition to responding to the main characters' emotional moods, as when its windmill wheels revolved at speeds corresponding to someone's feelings, the set could be used to make ironic comments on the action. Locales were not depicted with specificity nor, at first, were characters clearly differentiated in dress. The actors all wore dark blue overalls. Technical staff as well as actors were permitted to go about their offstage duties just as though they were hidden from view by scenery.

Seven months of thorough preparation went into *The Magnificent Cuckold,* making it the most polished of Meyerhold's post-Revolutionary works to date. The acting was a wonderfully exact demonstration of acrobatic techniques, especially as represented by three performers who worked together in perfect rhythmic harmony. Biomechanic techniques of pantomime allowed the actors to comment on, in addition to playing, their characters, making their relationships to the situations more vivid to the audience. The somewhat exaggerated contours of the costumes heightened the mechanical movements. "The body, in movement, is shown to be made up of working parts in much the same sense as the working parts of the stage construction."[12]

All movements were correlated with aspects of the setting; the patterns and attitudes of gesture and pose were linked organically to the structural components of the scenery. When Norris Houghton viewed a revival in the 1930s, he observed how the lover made his entrance to the heroine.

Meyerhold places the lady at the foot of a tin slide, the lover climbs up a ladder to the top of the slide, zooms down it, feet first, knocks the lady off onto the floor, and shouts something that sounds like the Russian for "Whee!"[13]

Constructivism was the scenic counterpart to biomechanics. It was a functionalist method based on utilitarian, scientific principles, incorporating industrial materials in a simple and economical fashion. All nonessential decorative features were avoided, atmospheric and illusionistic conventions were discarded, and the setting was reduced to its undisguised minimum requirements. Although biomechanics was an invention of Meyerhold, constructivism was not. It was one of several currently fashionable trends in modern art which Meyerhold cleverly exploited. In time, its "scientific" foundations were exposed as specious and it was seen, and criticized, as merely another interesting decorative technique.

In 1922 came A. Sukhovo-Kobylin's 1869 satire, *The Death of Tarelkin.* An earlier version had been staged by Meyerhold at the Alexandrinsky in 1917. This was a work which had been repressed for years by the tsarist regime and only received its premiere performance in 1900, in a greatly censored version. Using his student actors again, Meyerhold had them wear striped, loose-fitting uniforms that resembled prison clothing. Varvara Stepanova designed a constructivist set for the wild and farcical antics of the biomechanical players. Departing from his earlier conception of the play as a grotesque Kafkaesque farce, the director now turned it into a satire on the pre-1917 bourgeoisie, a point of view which would color many of his subsequent works.

At this time Meyerhold also began to direct plays for a group called the Theatre of the Revolution, where he supervised the production of two German expressionist plays by Ernst Toller and directed Alexy Faiko's *Lake Lyul* (1923) and Ostrovsky's *A Profitable Post. Lake Lyul,* a satire on the typical NEP businessman, was performed in expressionistic style and employed a semiconstructivist set that allowed for specific locales to be represented. Costumes were individualized and theatrically exaggerated. Action occurred everywhere throughout the three-story setting.

Ostrovsky's play was presented as part of a "Back to Ostrovsky" celebration, commemorating the late playwright's hundredth birthday. Meyerhold's popular production of this anti-tsarist satire was done on a modified constructivist set with a shallow stage, behind which ran a wall high enough to mask the back wall. A staircase, such as was soon to be found in any number of variations in Meyerhold's productions, ran from a single doorway up center in the wall. Lighting progressed from the unlocalized techniques of Meyerhold's previous work to a more selective representational style. Costumes were authentic recreations from the writer's period. The acting was less overtly physical than heretofore and depended largely on clearly individualized impersonations.

In 1923, Meyerhold also directed Sergei Tretyakov's adaptation of Marcel Martinet's *Night,* renamed *Earth Rampant.* It was done in March, two months prior to *A Profitable Post. Earth Rampant* continued in the style Meyerhold had chosen prior to the Ostrovsky work. Agit-prop methods were used for this blatantly political work. Audiences were greeted with a gigantic posterlike spectacle, utilizing techniques of constructivism, biomechanics, and unlocalized lighting. Projections reminded the audience of the play's contemporary relevance. Actors, scattered among the audience, shouted appropriate slogans. The bleakness of an essentially bare stage, revealing the rear brick wall, was relieved by a huge cranelike scenic construction. A fleet of actual army vehicles entered the theatre, moved down the aisles and, via ramps, onto the stage. Other actualistic props were used as well, including a field telephone, field kitchen, harvester, and machine gun. One of Meyerhold's best-known satirical touches in this piece was a scene in which a defeated emperor attended to his physical needs with a chamber pot.

Ostrovsky's *The Forest,* done in January 1924, was considerably edited and rearranged so that its five-act structure was converted to thirty-three brief scenes. A filmlike montage effect of alternating scenic moods and attitudes brought out the director's satirical and ironic interpretation. This technique of dividing established plays up into many episodes of varying lengths became a distinguishing feature of Meyerhold's adaptations; the effect was, in some eyes, like that of a "dramatic revue" in its alternation of fragmentary scenes. Ostrovsky's realistic comic genre study became, in Meyerhold's hands, a biting Bolshevist satire on the landed gentry of the nineteenth century. This outstanding success eventually was given over 1,700 times.

A set design, employing modified constructivist principles, was presented as a bare nonrepresentational background with an apron built out over the orchestra. On the curtainless stage was a long table at center, behind which a sweeping semicircular suspended bridge rose from the floor at stage right to a height of over six feet at the rear. A man-sized bird cage with two live doves in it and a clothesline slung across the stage were the only other important scenic furnishings. At the rear could be seen the brick stage wall and an impromptu-like arrangement of masking curtains and flats. A title for each scene was projected on a screen. The lighting was harsh, nonlocalized, and nonillusionistic, exposing the make-believe elements of the stage world. Props and furniture, however, were realistic and of mixed periods. Costumes were also of mixed periods and suggested a world of grotesques through their often violent contrasts. Exaggeratedly colored wigs, one of flaming red, another of green, another of gold, completed the strange visualization.

The use of props, furniture, and scenic units in *The Forest* exemplified one of the regisseur's most creative techniques during these constructivist-influenced years; they were conceived as neutral elements that came to life only as they were employed by the actors, so that the same object could have multiple functions or represent various locales. The bridge construction, for example, could be a road, a bridge, a hill, or a trysting place for lovers. A set of chairs in the play were used in their normal manner as seats during a wedding scene, gymnastic equipment for a character doing exercises, and, thrown at a crowd of people during the finale, the bricks and beams of a house that has been torn down. In another scene the characters Arkashka and Ulita were seated on a seesaw for a love scene, and Meyerhold used the action of the seesaw for offcolor humor.

D.E. (Give Us Europe!) followed *The Forest*. This was an agit-prop revue based on the work of four writers, the principal source being Ilya Ehrenburg's novel, *The Give Us Europe Trust* (also called *The D.E. Trust*), in which the healthy Soviet proletarians were intended to be favorably contrasted with the decadent capitalists of the West. Unfortunately, the homogenized Soviets in Meyerhold's production seemed far less intriguing than the jazzy Westerners, whose sophistication had considerable appeal. This rapid-paced satire used many actors playing a large variety of roles, relying on quick-change techniques. Igor Ilinsky had one fifteen-minute passage in which he played seven different roles. Speedy transitions were made from scene to scene throughout the seventeen-episode piece by means of a clever setting conceived by Meyerhold. It consisted of erect movable wooden panels on rollers which could be rearranged instantly to create different backgrounds; they often became part of the action as actors ran in and out among them as they were shifted about. As in other recent works, projected titles informed the audience as to locales and specific episode titles, and rhythmic and pantomimic acting overshadowed verbal acting techniques. An American jazz band (Sidney Bechet's Quintet) appeared onstage in one scene and is said to have led to the ensuing Soviet passion for jazz. *D.E.* is considered the last in Meyerhold's sequence of agit-prop productions.

Alexy Faiko's *Bubus the Teacher* was done in January 1925; it presaged a new direction in Meyerhold's work in its turn away from constructivist-influenced settings and its concern with a more overtly aesthetic—although still nonillusionistic—environment. It was much less dependent on the actors to bring it to life than the previous plays. Henceforth, the exposed walls of the stage would be hidden by elements of scenic masking, and the sets would evoke a specific atmosphere for each play. This rather unsuccessful political satire made extensive use of musical accompaniment to provide rhythmic backing to the performance. Seated on a high perch at the rear of the stage, a pianist in tails played forty-six selections, mainly chosen from Chopin and Liszt, to underscore each character and element in the comedy. Meyerhold was extremely fond of accentuating characters by individual rhythmic leitmotifs. The unusually attractive setting consisted of a semicircular curtain of vertical bamboo rods marking off the acting area. Realistic and beautiful, though sparse, furnishings—including a rich circular carpet, chairs, and a practical fountain—adorned the stage. The characters wore highly decorative costumes and makeup.

Most significant of the production's features, and the one which seriously damaged its audience appeal, was the use of "pre-acting." Pre-acting was a method created by Meyerhold to clarify each moment in the play by having each actor present his every transitional attitude toward an event, in the form of a pantomimic reaction preceding his actual physical or verbal response. The technique served merely to retard the action, obscure the text, and bore the audience. Like Brecht (to whom so many of Meyerhold's ideas can be related),[14] he sought to convey through pre-acting the actor's relationship to his character and his character's choices and behavior. He wrote, "The actor-tribune acts not the situation itself but what is concealed behind it and what it has to reveal for a specifically propagandist purpose."[15] Convinced of the ideological basis of drama, he felt each play and character had a definite message to communicate. The theatre's purpose was to change its audience's thinking. The "pre-acting" technique was subsequently modified, and Meyerhold's later work would often be marked by a solemn, even static, pace and by the frequent inclusion of thoughtful, expressive pauses and poses.

Meyerhold's next important production was Nikolai Erdman's *The Warrant* (also known as *The Mandate,* 1925), a new Soviet play starring Erast Garin. It was to be Meyerhold's last Soviet work for two years. He wanted very much to do Tretyakov's *I Want a Child!,* but though he worked on it for years and helped develop a provocative constructivist set, censorship prevented its presentation. *The Warrant,* a literary satire on the bourgeoisie who refused to acknowledge the impact of the Revolution, was turned by Meyerhold into a grotesque and biting tragi-farce at the expense of those it satirized. These characters were universalized by Meyerhold to suggest Russian emigrants as well as those remaining in the country; to convey what the regisseur viewed as their tragic fate—the fact that they are nothing more than hollow persons—he revealed them at the end as once elegant but now crumpled jackets, coats, and gowns. A simple set used no levels other than the flat stage floor, the sunken orchestra pit, and a double revolving platform; barely any scenic decor was displayed aside from the realistic props and furnishings with which Meyerhold liked to dress his "empty" stages. The revolve brought characters on and took them off, frozen in tableaus. Exaggerated costumes, makeup, and acting emphasized the "grotesqueness" of the characters.

THE INSPECTOR-GENERAL

Nikolai Gogol's *The Inspector-General,* Russia's most famous and best-loved satirical comedy, was staged by Meyerhold in 1926. It became his major production and one of the most memorable of the century. It was unique interpretations of the classics such as this that led to the numerous imitations of his style, later branded as "Meyerholditis." Over a half-year of rehearsals followed an extensive period of research and planning. The total reworking of Gogol's script by Meyerhold and Mikhail Korenyev was considered a sacrilegious act in the eyes of many. The new script was a compilation derived from all of Gogol's many drafts, with interpolations from the rest of the author's oeuvre. As usual, the intent was to make the play speak to current concerns. Meyerhold believed a director of his stature had the right to freely adapt a text in keeping with his own vision. His adaptation of Gogol's masterpiece deepened the play's tragicomic tone, brought out the intense bitterness of its attack on the bureaucratic mentality, and greatly heightened its fantastical ingredients.

The production was greeted by severe criticism; Meyerhold was assailed for having a reactionary attitude which inhibited the progress of Soviet theatre art and did not elucidate this classic play. Nevertheless, *The Inspector-General* became a standby in his repertory and was produced frequently for many years.

Gogol's five acts were arranged in fifteen titled episodes. To make the theme more universal, the locale was changed from a small provincial town to a major city, presumably St. Petersburg. Instead of exploiting the full stage space, as was Meyerhold's custom, he restricted most of the action of the localized scenes to constricting areas on small platforms—twelve by sixteen feet, which were rolled into position on tracks. Scene changes were made rapidly as one platform was rolled off and another on. Lighting illuminated only the specified acting areas. These platforms were usually rolled on with a crowd of characters frozen on them in tableau, suggesting miniature nineteenth-century genre paintings. As the lights hit them, the actors would slowly unfreeze.

The acting style was based on silent film techniques—each character being sharply delineated, often through the use of freezes in which everyone held still while the character in focus performed. The actors were told to emulate the economy of Charlie Chaplin and Buster Keaton in creating large effects in cramped spaces. Extreme physical expressiveness was required to make the most of these conditions.

New characters, such as the "Officer-in-Transit," who do not appear in the original, were added to increase the feeling of mystery. The officer acted as Khlestakov's shadow and said nothing, but was always with him as if viewing events with the ironic detachment of the audience.

The traditional characters, especially Khlestakov, were totally unlike their conventional interpretations. Assuming a different "social mask" for each episode, Khlestakov was capable of total physical transformation according to the needs of each situation. For example, in one episode he was a card-playing cheat, in another a government official bent on seducing his superior's wife, in the next a cruelly condescending officer, in another an excessively affected poet from the big city, in yet another a robot-like bribe taker. He had, therefore, many costume and makeup changes.

Most famous of Meyerhold's innovations was episode nine, "Bribes," in which he replaced the bribery scene of the original text with one in which all the officials entered simultaneously through the eleven doors in the beautifully paneled, semicircular screen which formed the set's back wall. As they entered, they proferred their bribes, as if creating an overwhelming indictment of the act of bribery as one inimical to the old regime. Khlestakov sat at center, staring upstage at the paneled screen; the sleeping officer and Ossip, his servant, were at his sides. Nick Worrall describes the scene in sharp detail.

The rear doors became like coffins standing on their ends, and the figure of Khlestakov . . . that of an undertaker. . . . A crack developed in all eleven "lids" simultaneously and eleven disembodied hands, with the same gesture . . . held out little white packages, like conjuror's rabbits. Then, as the bodies attached to the hands slowly emerged through the cracks they began to chant their lines like an eleven part fugue . . . on the theme of bribery.[16]

Khlestakov, robotlike, moved to each and plucked the money from them one by one.

Among the many other dazzling pieces of staging was that arranged for the final moments. Khlestakov's impersonation having been discovered, a riotous scene of noise and movement erupted, culminating in the thirty to forty onstage characters shrieking and wailing as, holding hands, they snaked offstage and through the audience in a macabre Dance of Death. When they were gone and silence fell on the theatre, a white curtain—on which the message of the real inspector's arrival was printed—ascended slowly from the orchestra pit and disappeared above. As the curtain passed, the stage, which had been empty, now revealed an array of life-sized costumed wax mannequins representing every character in the play. The bizarre and awesome effect was "as if Death had come to each, unexpectedly, as he might to victims of a volcano disaster just unchipped from a preserving mould of lava."[17]

Of great importance to the production was Mikhail Gnessin's background music, to which all the acting was precisely set. Each episode had a different musical motif and rhythm, which captured perfectly the Gogolian spirit desired by the director.

WOE TO WIT

Meyerhold continued in the mode of tragicomic social satire with his anti-bourgeois adaptation of Alexandre Griboyedov's nineteenth-century classic, *Woe from Wit,* now retitled *Woe to Wit* (1928). He took textual liberties with this play similar to those he made in *The Inspector-General.* As with the latter play, a barrage of invectives rained down on him from official sources for his artistic and ideological "distortions."

The play's contemporaneity was stressed by turning the leading character, Chatsky, into the equivalent of a modern radical. His intellectual aspects were toned down and his emotional ones underlined. Various aspects of his character were developed in the manner used for Khlestakov. Classical music, selected for its ability to reflect the various strains in Chatsky's character, was played throughout.

Meyerhold's involvement in designing the production was intense, as it had been for most of his recent work. He was essentially the codesigner, if not the sole designer, for all his productions from *The Forest* on. *Woe to Wit* had a constructivist-influenced set consisting of a very high balcony at the rear with a spiral staircase leading up to it from the stage. At either side of the stage, railed balconies ran forward along the side walls, with curved staircases leading down to the stage floor at the ends nearest the apron. Loosely hung draperies only partly masked off the bare stage walls. The modernist metallic look of the set contrasted strongly with the period costumes and furnishings. When the piece was revived in 1935, a somewhat similar floorplan was followed, but more period features were incorporated into the architectural decorations.[18]

MOUNTING PRESSURES

With his theatre plagued by economic problems, and unable to find suitable new Soviet plays, Meyerhold went to France for five months in 1928, returning in December. At the time, it was feared he would emigrate to the West. Stalin's power had increased greatly, especially with his victory over the Trotskyites in 1927. Bureaucratic pressure on the director began to grow. The NEP was abolished in 1928, and the first five-year plan was inaugurated. Artistic experiment was looked on scornfully. Meyerhold also began to lose his actors, one reason being the overbearing attitude of his wife and leading actress, Zinaida Raikh, toward other company members. Raikh was an attractive though not exceptional actress whom Meyerhold had trained with great success. His casting her in parts for which she was not always right also led to company dissatisfaction. Only Igor Ilinsky remained faithful to Meyerhold.

In February 1929 Meyerhold directed a highly controversial work—one which actually pointed the finger of satire at the current government bureaucracy— Mayakovsky's *The Bedbug,* starring Ilinsky. Dimitri Shostakovich provided a striking and original score. Success with the public brought a measure of financial stability, but it also marked Meyerhold's growing unpopularity in Stalinist circles. It soon became almost impossible to produce anything considered contrary to official dogma, political or artistic.

The Bedbug's first half was designed in semirealistic style by a team of cartoonists called the Kukrynsky, and the second half was done in modernist-constructivist fashion by Alexandre Rodchenko. Life in the communist future was mocked in this amusing play, which told of an NEP man frozen in ice and restored to life in 1979. Thus, the set contrasted the life of the present with that of the future through two totally different scenic conceptions. Many of the exceptional directorial ideas stemmed from the author, who acted as codirector. Buffoonery and vaudeville-type antics enlivened the acting style.

Ilya Selvinsky's Soviet propaganda play *The Second Army Commander* followed in late 1929. It represented a departure from Meyerhold's satiric style and was done in a classically austere manner suggestive of Greek tragedy. The formal setting showed a tall, curved wooden back wall across which ran a sweeping semicircular staircase. The realism of costumes and props extended in one scene to the use of a real horse. Choral speaking and singing, with powerful music by Vissarion Shebalin, played a crucial role. Yet, official criticism castigated this and similar plays for "over-emphasizing the tragic or underlining individual conflict."[19]

Meyerhold returned now for his third collaboration with the popular Mayakovsky and staged his *The Bathhouse* in March 1930. As in *The Bedbug,* Soviet bureaucracy was the butt of the joke; Meyerhold was dealing with material too hot to handle, however, and overestimated the lengths to which he could go in poking fun at the new breed of Soviet leaders. Utilizing a performance style recalling the biomechanical devices of earlier years, the play satirized the contrast between the grossness of the contemporary world and the spare and clean-lined society of the future. The abstract setting, which employed the revolving stage, had a backdrop composed of a slatlike construction resembling venetian blinds; each slat had a slogan printed on it. A constructivist platform and step arrangement allowed the actors ample opportunity for precision choreography and circuslike techniques. *The Bathhouse* lasted only about a week. Meyerhold then took his company on a tour of Germany and France. He was in Berlin when he heard of Mayakovsky's suicide.

On his return to Moscow he staged a revised version of *D.E.* (now called *D.S.E.*) and then did a new Soviet play, *The Last Decisive* (1931), a nonliterary propaganda play about the navy, ranging loosely in style from broad satire to posterlike heroics, created at rehearsals in collaboration with the writer Vsevolod Vishnevsky. It was damned by the critics and found little popular support.

More conventional was Yuri Olesha's *List of Assets* (1931), another critical failure. He gave the play, about a famous actress' conflict between political commitment and personal interests, in a rather realistic manner. The point has been disputed, but it seems at least possible that Meyerhold was simply trying to placate the government by finding a happy medium between his desire for artistic freedom and the official requirement that art follow a prescribed dogma.

A *List of Assets* had a set placed diagonally on the stage, providing unusual scenic angles for the action and breaking down the aesthetic confinement of the proscenium arch. *Camille,* a more important production done in 1934, also made effective use of this arrangement.

A Leningrad revival of the famous Alexandrinsky Theatre *Don Juan* staging was offered in 1932, followed by Yuri German's anti-Western heroic tragedy, *Prelude,* in Moscow the same year.

FINAL CREATIVE PERIOD

After *Prelude,* Meyerhold moved into what was to be his final creative period (1933–38), during which he worked mainly on classic plays. In addition to those described below, there were two new stagings of *Masquerade* (1933, 1938), a revision of *Woe to Wit* (1935), several radio works, and two operas, Peter Tschaikovsky's *Queen of Spades* (1935) and Verdi's *Rigoletto,* which he codirected with his old mentor, Stanislavsky, in 1938; it was his final work.

In 1933 he returned to Sukhovo-Kobylin's *Krechinsky's Wedding*, having first mounted it in 1917; now, however, he used highly selective sets and area lighting to suggest the shift in locales. Projected titles were provided for each episode, and the play was converted into an anticapitalist tract. It was notable for being acted with a sense of polish and depth rather new to Meyerhold's work.

This interiorized development in Meyerhold's style found a fruitful outlet in his lovely staging of *Camille,* a production he justified on the basis of Lenin's having wept at this play because he could not bear to see the enslavement of women under nineteenth-century capitalism. *Camille,* more than any other new production of the twenties and thirties, represented the old aesthetics of Meyerhold's St. Petersburg period. There were numerous subtle revisions in the text, though many were unaware of them, a fact that the director attributed to his masterful skill at adaptation. The play was moved forward in time several decades to take advantage of the artistic and social background of the late 1870s. Such a decision emphasizes even further the degree of aestheticism with which the production was imbued. It was played in a style heavy with a mood of decadence and world-weariness, with a decor inspired by French impressionism. Painters Edouard Manet and Pierre-Auguste Renoir were vital influences on the pictorial style. (Norris Houghton, however, found that it "looked like an unfinished high-school production.")[20] Raikh's performance of the leading role drew ideas from the great interpreters of the part, Eleanora Duse and Sarah Bernhardt. Shebalin provided the music, which he often used as "ironic counterpoint" to the action. It was influenced by the atmosphere of Parisian cabarets, the can-can, waltzes, the risqué songs of Mistinguette, and the music of Jacques Offenbach.

Camille's "realism" was so relative only to Meyerhold's other productions. Despite the profusion of realistic props and costumes, Houghton declared that the style was far from realistic: "there could be no doubt," he wrote, "that this was complete theatricality." While waiting for the play to start, the spectator heard a sudden "crash on a huge gong and the lights flashed out—another crash and the stage lights snapped up and the play began."[21]

Another American, Lee Strasberg, then a director with the Group Theatre, thought the director's ability to make felt the presence of death was remarkable. He described how Meyerhold had a masked actor dressed in black and standing against a black background suddenly appear from nothingness. All those in the scene were horribly frightened and Camille screamed.

Then the man takes the mask off, and it is one of the people whom we had seen previously at the party. The shock and the theatricality is so impressive that later on in the scene, when Camille tells Armand that she is afraid of death, so are you—afraid for her because you have just seen it, experienced it.[22]

An evening of Chekhov one-acters, titled *Thirty-three Fainting Fits* by Meyerhold after the number of times characters in the plays swooned, was done in 1935. Meyerhold underlined what he found in the play of an antibourgeois bias, symbolized by the evening's title—a reference to the innate weakness of the bourgeoisie. Shostakovich's music accompanied the play, notably in one scene in which a brass band marked each man's fainting spell and a string quartet each woman's. A scoreboard was set up to denote the number of faints.

Meyerhold was feeling the hot breath of the government more intensely now, but refused to capitulate to demands that he work in a homogenized realistic vein. He was not allowed to show his new productions, *Natasha* (1937) and *One Life* (retitled from *How the Steel Was Tempered,* 1937). A Western theatre artist, designer Stewart Chaney, was fortunate to have witnessed what must have been a preview performance of the latter, perhaps one given for the benefit of Soviet officials. He disputed the oft-heard accusation that Meyerhold's work was unemotional and cerebral, for he found this work, despite its nonillusionistic methods, "the most real and touching picture of Soviet life . . . , it is terribly moving and beautiful." An exceptional moment was the death scene.

Using orchestral music as a necessary accompaniment, Meirhold [sic] has . . . caught the essence of the moment when consciousness leaves the body, as never before conceived in a theatre. He does this by utilizing a droning, humming tone from the orchestra which is monotonous, insistent, feverish. This is broken by a vision of the dying boy, in which he dreams his home is being raided by the Cossacks. In his horror he shrieks above the new chaotic rhythm and melody of the orchestra. This subsides into the droning hum again—then comes another melody—his sister is playing on the piano. It is piercingly sweet. Again the droning noise, and then his head drops—and silence. Surrounded by his comrades, with bowed heads, the broken figure on the bed becomes a pieta.[23]

END OF A CAREER

In January 1938 Meyerhold's company was officially liquidated. He was out of a job, and only Stanislavsky came to his rescue. Meyerhold finished out his active career working with the great actor-director, whose theatrical approach was usually so widely at variance with the younger man's. Two months after Stanislavsky died in August 1938, Meyerhold took over his role as director of the MAT Opera Studio. He was hanging onto his career by a very tenuous grip. Publicly he had been chastised and all his "sins" exposed; all Soviet theatres had been forced to condemn him; and only the ailing Stanislavsky had been able to offer a temporary reprieve. All of Meyerhold's recent artistic compromises had gone for naught with the government.

The final blow was precipitated by a speech Meyerhold delivered at the First National Convention of Theatrical Directors in Moscow, June 1939, where the official purpose was to firmly establish socialist realism as the predominant style of Soviet theatre art. It was generally believed that Meyerhold would renounce his past and affirm a commitment to the approved aesthetics. Instead, he spoke for artistic freedom, attacked socialist realism, and claimed art in the USSR was being slaughtered by the government's demands. Despite the "mistakes" for which he reportedly apologized, he claimed the right as a "master" to experiment, no matter what the result. This speech led to his arrest and imprisonment in a distant concentration camp, where he soon died (he is presumed to have been executed). Shortly afterwards, his wife was found murdered in their apartment.

DIRECTORIAL ACHIEVEMENTS

Meyerhold's contributions were diverse and far-reaching. He was a true theatricalist in his attempts to manipulate the audience's response to his work through an open admission of the theatre's basis in accepted conventions. Himself an accomplished violinist, his use of music to support, accentuate, and comment on the action was integral to every production. He introduced some of the finest modern Russian composers to the theatre and worked closely with them to blend their creations with the actors' movements or to select effective music from the composers of the past.

Few modern directors have done so much to develop a systematized approach to theatrical movement. Biomechanics may have been founded on pseudoscientific principles, but his actors' acrobatic agility and perfect timing provided excitement and delight for many thousands of spectators who had no idea of its theoretical bases.

Meyerhold was part musician, part actor, part director, part choreographer, part playwright or literary adapter, and part designer. In addition to the many novel sets he created or inspired, he also knew how to take the best of contemporary trends in art and make them practical in theatrical terms. His greatest contribution here was in the style of constructivism. His stage became a stripped-down acting machine on which his sets progressed aesthetically from spare, austere arrangements to beautiful decors whose layouts on varying levels and angles showed the source from which they had evolved. Modern scene design still finds inspiration in the sets which Meyerhold helped to develop.

He also made important contributions to the realm of theatre architecture, though the new theatre he planned to build—within the walls of the old Zon Theatre—never was to become his domain. He envisioned a theatre without proscenium, curtain, or footlights, in which the auditorium and stage were in a shared spatial relationship—the audience surrounding the actors on three sides, and viewing the action axonometrically, from above and to the side, in steeply raised tiers of seats. Natural lighting from a glass-domed roof, a pair of elevator-revolves back to back, the absence of any impediments to sight lines, and many other features were planned for this epoch-making theatre. Eventually, the plans were revised and the building converted to the concert hall known as Tschaikovsky Hall, on Mayakovsky Square.

James M. Symons finds Meyerhold an eclectic in terms of the diversity of theatrical devices he used in each production.[24] Actually, despite their diversity, Meyerhold's devices were essentially unified within a fairly consistent aesthetic. Similar techniques recur frequently, though in increasingly unusual permutations and applications. Meyerhold is eclectic in the sense that different periods of his work represent different interests and emphases, but each period is developed fairly consistently within its own parameters. Though something like the same course may be discovered in the work of Reinhardt, the Austrian director during his peak periods shifted artistic gears with such dizzying alacrity—especially in the variety of stage environments he used—that one never knew what to expect from him. Meyerhold's tragedy may reside in his having been unable to create with the same artistic freedom afforded a man like Max Reinhardt. Believing as he did in the need to use the theatre didactically and in the service of the state, he was then confronted by a state that did not want his personal slant on politics, and was unhappily adrift in a world where his creative expressions were forced to survive the rigors of a programmatic concept of the arts. Given these restrictions, he nevertheless produced a body of work that belongs among the greatest imaginative conceptions the world of theatre yet has seen.

AUTOCRATIC DIRECTOR

Vsevolod Meyerhold was the quintessential autocrat-director. He left nothing to chance, requiring that his actors follow his directions explicitly. Nevertheless, he was open to those accidents in rehearsal that often produce artistic revelations, and frequently included such improvisatory discoveries in his productions. His theoretical writing revealed a desire to be accepted as a collaborator in an actor-centered theatre. In a 1907 essay, "First Attempts at a Stylized Theatre," he talked of two types of actor-director relationships. In one the director is the undisputed boss and dictates every move and inflection, rehearsing his actors only in order to realize his personal image of the play. He pointed out that only virtuoso actors without individuality could succeed at this method. The second type of relationship had the actor as the dominant element. This "Theatre of the Straight Line" was the best arrangement, schematically laid out by Meyerhold as a triangle:

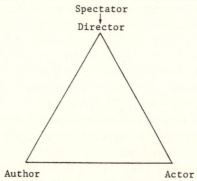

Here the actor had the freedom to reveal his talent as best he could, with the director being merely an expert guide and instructor. The director assimilates the author's ideas and in their new permutation, conveys them to the actor, who in turn develops his interpretation on their basis. The performer-spectator relationship is the crucial one. Many have disputed that Meyerhold actually achieved his ideal actor-director relationship; they claim that Meyerhold's actors were like automatons, fulfilling his desires rather than their own as creative artists. However, various sources close to Meyerhold have argued that, given talented players, Meyerhold could be a most creatively stimulating director. Mikhail Sadovsky, who joined Meyerhold's company in 1934, claims that unimaginative actors, whom Meyerhold, in frustration, was forced to treat like puppets, were responsible for spreading untrue allegations of dictatorial tendencies. Like leading Meyerhold actor Igor Ilinsky, Sadovsky insists that Meyerhold inspired his casts by the vivid nature of his methods, which required him to actively demonstrate what he wanted an actor to do.[25]

Although actors would be shown their business precisely and expected to duplicate it, Meyerhold did not want an exact copy, but a transmutation in terms of the actor's personal qualities. Anything less might anger him. Many commentators have remarked on his brilliant talent at acting something out for his actors. Using no props or costumes, he could make himself seem to hold a prop the correct way or turn into any character merely by gesture and pantomime. Once, when an actor turned down a role, Meyerhold responded by rising wearily and playing the part himself with such comic genius that the actor broke up in laughter and agreed to accept it.

Even in his sixties his boundless energy allowed him to dance and romp in the most lighthearted way as he showed various movements with suppleness and skill. Teaching a group a dance routine he would go through it with them at each repetition, bending, lying down, rising, lying down again, rising, bending once more—never flagging. No matter how energetically he worked, the well-dressed director's clothes never seemed to rumple or lose their elegant fit. He demonstrated tirelessly until he got the appropriate result. At one rehearsal he was seen to go back and forth from house to stage sixty-one times, not sitting down once the entire time, though he was at the time past sixty. Unfortunately, some actors could do no more than offer a blind imitation of his demonstrations; thus, an actor like Ilinsky was cherished for his infinite flexibility in responding sensitively to what the director wanted of him. Ilinsky, realizing that the director preferred not to offer analytical talks on his demonstrations, always sought to discover the psychological truth beneath the physical behavior presented by Meyerhold. The less the actor's ability, the more Meyerhold had to demonstrate explicitly. André Van Gysegham, for example, witnessed Meyerhold having trouble getting a specific effect from two actors in *Camille* through other means, and then leaping on the stage to show

them how each little jerk of the head is connected with the following movement and forms a link in the whole chain of movement which constitutes the mise-en-scène. Gradually he builds up the little scene until the . . . masked figures are the essence of stupidity.[26]

An assistant of Meyerhold's, Alexandre Gladkov, transcribed his impressions of the director while engaged in rehearsals for *Boris Godunov* (ultimately abandoned) in 1936. When the actor Lev Sverdlin confronted an obstacle in delivering a certain speech, Meyerhold began to explain the ideas within it and then to read it aloud. Soon he removed his glasses, put down the book, and accepted an assistant's prompting. Having finished the thirty-four-line speech, he improvised brilliantly in verse, in the manner of the great Russian actor Malmont Dalsky, whom he wished Sverdlin to emulate. Gladkov was ecstatic:

Brilliant! Yes, this is incandescence! But he doesn't stop. He continues to perform, improvising iambs. He knocks a glass off the table and no one dares to pick it up. . . . And it continues. He is already standing on the table. We hadn't even noticed him jumping up there.

Is this Meyerhold? Is this Malmont Dalsky? No, it is a frenzied, drunk, wild Alfanasi Mikhailovich Puskin, a living man of the seventeenth century with his hurt, his pain, with his uncontrollable anger. . . .

This is impossible! After all, he is over sixty. What a flow of temperament! What a fury of passions! What a frenzy! . . . It is almost terrifying. . . .

And suddenly he stops, jumps lightly from the table and turns to Sverdlin: "Is that clear?" Everybody is silent. . . . Only after a long pause does applause ring out. . . . This is what a Meyerhold demonstration was.[27]

Those actors who merely offered a Xerox copy of the business demonstrated received Meyerhold's wrathful reprimand. "Put your foot there and your arm here. Speak all the phrase in one tone! Close your eyes, they express nothing anyway,"[28] he would shout at an actor unable to invest the business with internal life. Despite such an approach with his own company, Meyerhold could alter his technique with other actors. When he directed a never-to-be-shown production of *Boris Godunov* for the Vakhtangov Theatre (1925–26), the actor Boris Zakhava noted that Meyerhold considered himself a representative of Evgeni Vakhtangov and thus worked in a manner resembling that of the other man. "He rarely went on stage. He did very little demonstrating. Sitting on a director's stool in the back of the auditorium he would from there toss up to the performers his ideas and advice."[29]

PREPARATION FOR PRODUCTION

Extensive research and thought went into the preparations for a Meyerhold production. The director often spent several years studying and conceptualizing a play, investigating its historical background, including the economic, artistic, and social conditions of the period. He believed the director must engage in travel and a wide range of reading as part of his preparations, and that he must also visit libraries, museums, and every other source of pertinent information.

Using his research, the director had to develop a key idea or central production concept. This was a mental image that developed gradually and took form over a lengthy period of gestation. Meyerhold kept all his staging ideas locked up in his brain and often committed nothing to paper. He gave up the use of prompt-books early in his career and chose to come to rehearsals with a mental image which he would bring to life through his actors. Putting every detail down on paper would not give him the freedom to create in the process of rehearsals. He needed to discover the capabilities of his actors in determining how his conceptions could be carried out. Nevertheless, there exist production scripts of his which bear evidence of careful notes, just as there are those without a single comment. At any rate, his research and preparation prior to rehearsals was great, and he knew precisely what he wanted when he confronted his actors.

THE REHEARSAL PROCESS

At the first company meeting Meyerhold would discuss his ideas quite amply. Loathe to waste rehearsal time in analytical discussions, he preferred to dispose of all theoretical concerns at the first meeting or two, when he would talk on the nature of the production, the basis of his interpretation, the history of the play in the theatre, the characters, and so forth. In talking to the cast of *The Inspector-General*, for instance, he showed how he would take the idea of the emploi (e.g., traditional role type) and use it creatively. He wanted the actor of Khlestakov to realize the character's place within the tradition of fops and imposters, and since Gogol's work was not the end of a tradition, but a novel approach to one, the role had to be played in an innovative way. It was vital that the actors should familiarize themselves with the author's other works, as this would help them find ideas they could use in performance. Khlestakov, especially, would benefit from such a tactic.

At the first rehearsal of *Thirty-three Fainting Fits*, Meyerhold sat onstage at a table surrounded by the entire company. Filled with dynamic energy, he appeared ''to be almost in a state of spontaneous combustion!''[30] He began his remarks by defining his approach to theatre—to find the author's idea and clothe it in an appropriate form, a *''jeu de théâtre.''* For his *jeu* in this production, he chose the idea of the thirty-three fainting spells undergone by the characters in the three one-acts. He then read the script to the company, noting as he did where the fainting occurred. Next, he had his designer describe and draw on a blackboard the scenic idea. Music also was discussed. With these explanations concluded, the rehearsal was adjourned.

The second rehearsal was usually the company's reading of the script. This process was constantly interrupted by the director as he tried to get the actors to read the lines as he had done. Meyerhold felt his understanding of the characters was essential to the production and insisted that his line readings be followed. When an actor began to read the first speech, Meyerhold would stop and launch into an analysis of each line, ''of the juxtaposition of words and sounds that made up the line, of the meaning of it, of the characterization, of the style of the play as it would be set by that opening speech.'' The director's view predominated, Meyerhold giving everything possible to the actor, from reading and facial expressions, to business and blocking. Houghton heard him say, for example, ''Watch me! This is the expression Chubukov must wear to point his absurdity. My expresion now. . . . Do you see? Now you try it.''[31] Lengthy ''at table'' preparation was distasteful to him because of the declamatory style actors were apt to fall into when reading from the script. Better the actors should be on their feet being fed their lines by the prompter than to be preoccupied following the words with their eyes.

As soon as he could, Meyerhold began his blocking rehearsals. Whenever possible, he would provide props, furnishings, and appropriate lighting to assist the actors in grasping the needs of the blocking. Meyerhold often spent many hours creating the lighting effects so they would be ready for the first blocking rehearsal. As he staged a play, a corps of assistants noted down his every word, including every correction and adjustment he made in the course of rehearsals. The eight to fifteen assistants who performed this chore were divided into three groups—one being in charge of all matters related to the dialogue; another to record all the physical action; and another to deal with the wealth of miscellanea developing during rehearsals. The notes were organized and collated daily to provide what Houghton said was "probably the most elaborate and detailed prompt book"[32] in the world. These books were for the use of Meyerhold's directing students and for his assistants when he himself could not be present at a rehearsal.

Most rehearsals lasted several months, often half a year or more, because Meyerhold loved to refine and vary his ideas. Rehearsals were for him an experimental period during which he tried out all his ideas and finally chose those which he found best. He spent many hours working on tiny bits of business, going over and over them until he was satisfied with their execution.

From the early rehearsal period on, as many as twenty to thirty spectators were allowed to sit in on rehearsals, and Meyerhold would often ask them for their opinions, just as he might the theatre's cleaning man.

WORKING WITH ACTORS

Meyerhold would usually direct by sitting in the house at a special raised table fitted with a high stool that allowed him to dominate the proceedings. Seated near the notebook-filled table were his assistants. A ramp or plank connected to the stage gave him easy access to the actors. As he began to block he would provide instructions for every move and gesture, being as explicit as he could, and almost always demonstrating. Whereas Ilinsky recalled that Meyerhold disliked giving explanations of his staging ideas, others noted that each demonstration was provided with precise comments on character and attitude, suggesting that his methods evolved in terms of his company's needs. Thus, in *Thirty-three Fainting Fits* he told an actor he was to wear an oversized hat because, being an uncouth rustic, he's had to borrow a hat from his father to make a formal call; the father's head being bigger than his, the comic possibilities began to suggest themselves and the hat became an important prop, as when the actor let it slide down and cover his ear when startled by a loud sound. This business led to the realization that the ear would have to be made more visible to point up the later business.

Although Meyerhold used no notes, his ideas seemed to spring forth in a steady stream as if he were a directing machine. A magnificent combination of inspiration and careful preparation gave many the false impression that everything was being made up at the spur of the moment. One director, who worked with him in the thirties, recalled that Meyerhold would never cease working on the play outside of rehearsals, even working through the night. "And he liked very much to flaunt the unexpectedness of what he had made up."[33] Sometimes Meyerhold began to direct at so rapid a pace, talking of scenes not yet being considered, that an actor would be totally confused. The regisseur would then comfort the baffled player and tell him that he need not worry about the future scene until the time for it arrived.

Nevertheless, Meyerhold could sometimes dry up while waiting for an idea;

he is said to have gone for several weeks while staging *Camille* with barely a helpful word for the actors. Yet, just as they began to turn disconsolate, the idea which had been growing in his head would spring forth and be so clever that spontaneous applause would greet it. Houghton witnessed one such sparkling moment in *The Proposal*, one of the plays on the Chekhov bill. An actor had practically exhausted all the variations possible for business with a glass and carafe of water. Struck by a new thought, Meyerhold stopped the rehearsals, told the actor to watch him, and spoke the line:

"If it were not for these terrible agonizing palpitations, Madam, if it were not for the throbbing in my temples————." He paused, looked about him wildly, seized the carafe, held it in his outstretched hand a moment, then lifted it and emptied its entire contents over his head! With his hair and nose streaming water, he finished the line: "I should speak to you very differently!"[34]

As applause broke out, Meyerhold ended the session.

Normally, however, the impression given by Meyerhold's rehearsals was of extreme sloppiness, haste, and chaos. A quality of haphazard improvisation, generated by the director's restless energy, kept everyone on their toes, solemnly focusing on his every word and motion. All seemed in a state of creative growth and flux. To have taken the time to work in an orderly fashion would have suggested an excessive sense of leisure. Instead, things were always on the go.

His inventiveness never seemed to cease. When rehearsing *Camille*, he had a female character wearing a train sing to a group around a piano. As she sang, she had to move with "an accompaniment of running steps." Meyerhold had her repeat the business again and again, "with the train held up, with the train on the floor, with much ogling of the pianist, with a fan, without a fan, loudly, softly—until it would seem that the singer must drop from sheer fatigue."[35]

As he rehearsed, Meyerhold would shout "good, good" to his actors when pleased, or applaud them vigorously. Or he might yell out: "No words! No words!... More unity! More unity!... Legs! Legs! Where are your legs!... Laughter! More laughter!"[36]

Obviously, he could grow cross and even ill-tempered when confronted by stupidity or carelessness. His caustic tongue often made him enemies. He did not accept others' unsolicited suggestions very openly, pursuing his own intentions without rest, driving his actors mercilessly until he reached his goals. If he suspected someone of having betrayed him, he was determinedly unforgiving. Once when a former assistant, whom he had fired and told never to return, showed up at one of his rehearsals thinking Meyerhold would let bygones be bygones, the director refused to go on working until the man was removed from the premises; he even screamed abusively at him before the entire company.

Watching Meyerhold direct was often as exciting as seeing one of his productions. An observer, noting his rehearsal technique for *The Inspector-General*, wrote that the director was giving his actors obstacles—so they could create a strong interest in their attempts to overcome them—when suddenly an idea hit him:

Has anybody got a cloth or scarf? (They bandage the Mayor's head.) There! Walk all around him beating your breast, put mustard plasters on his feet to draw the blood away from his head. . . . Everybody close together. Nobody over there. . . . Enter the Mayor. . . . He groans. You [to the German doctor] are preparing the mixture. . . . When everybody says "What, an inspector!" it must be in unison. Some say "in-spec-tor." There must be a variety of logical intonations.[37]

He moved excitedly among all the actors, giving each a specific piece of business to enact. Comments poured forth from him on stage positions, pace, reactions, intonations, energy levels. As he saw new possibilities in the scene he tossed them in, constantly adjusting, enriching, underlining, and heightening. He knew precisely how to tell an actor what he expected from him. In a rehearsal of Erdman's *The Suicide* (never shown) three men entered to console the heroine on hearing of her husband's suicide. Meyerhold told one: "Begin again please. . . . You understand: your voice must express deliberation, victory, irony. It must be gentle, then gloat, then crackle. Again please."[38]

A girl had to measure the reclining figure of the heroine for a mourning dress. Meyerhold wanted to play the scene for its satirical value.

"Size of back 94 cm," she says. "Won't do!" Meyerhold stops her. He is on his feet again and with one deft movement he lifts the reclining figure so that the lady's back is unmistakeably to the audience. The imaginary tape is spread boldly around her hips. "Size of *back* . . . 94," he emphasizes. "This is satire. Throw the *back* into the public; stop after the word for one significant moment." "But no one ever measures that way," the modiste timidly objects. "Of course not," Meyerhold rejoins. "But in the theatre we must translate everything into theatrical terms. We do not seek to reproduce reality of detail, but to point the irony of a situation."[39]

At rare moments, Meyerhold would suggest that the actor was the one who could provide the answer to a problem. During a rehearsal of *The Inspector-General*, he told the Judge where to pause, giving him a precise reading, but followed with: "I don't know how you should say it. You know best, but don't bother about it now, otherwise the line will lose its spontaneity."[40]

A peculiarly Meyerholdian technique was for him to shout out, as needed, the words "retard" and "reject." The first was used when he wished a scene's pace to be slowed down to make for a more vivid contrast with what preceded or succeeded it. "Reject" was employed as a device to insert a momentary hesitation as represented by a pause or carefully selected physical action to heighten what ensued. He likened this to the drawing of a bowstring before shooting a bow.[41]

Although he found the presence of an author an irritant in the first few years of his career, Meyerhold started to change his policy in the 1920s. Faiko, Erdman, and Mayakovsky, among others, all took part in productions of their plays. Mayakovsky was Meyerhold's favorite, the director admitting, "I simply couldn't begin to produce his plays without him."[42]

Meyerhold and Mayakovsky shared an intimate collaboration owing to their mutual respect for one another. Mayakovsky not only made whatever alterations in his texts the regisseur found necessary, but he even went onstage to work with the actors. Meyerhold held this writer's work in great respect and barely altered it except in minor ways. Working on these plays, he gave great consideration to the poet's linguistic style and worked with him in getting the actors to read the lines appropriately.

At the polishing rehearsals Meyerhold's interruptions, though continuing, grew less and less frequent as the actors ran their scenes. New ideas kept arising, but far less abundantly than they had months earlier. Soon there were no interruptions, and he concentrated on tempo and general shaping. He would run an act over and over, sometimes doing it three times in a row, followed by notes in the intervals.

Lighting rehearsals received a great deal of attention during the run-through stage and were as carefully rehearsed as the acting. Meyerhold usually lit his own shows, even focusing the instruments himself. He kept up a constant stream of advice to the technicians when he returned to watch the effects onstage. According to Robert Leach, "His two favorite states of lighting were an even, overall wash effect, and sharp directional lighting."[43] Meyerhold also preferred, especially in his post-Revolutionary work, to allow the lighting instruments to be exposed, much as did Brecht a bit later. There were few theatre jobs he did not master, from composing music to designing sets: he was a Craigian artist in more ways than one.

CONCLUSION

Seeing him in 1934, Van Gysegham found the tall, well-dressed director

no longer young in years, and his deeply lined features and stooping figure betray the vigour with which he has enjoyed life, but the youth has not gone from his brain—it peers out at you from those keen, steely eyes, and the enormous hooked nose has a strength and defiance about it which reveals the dominance of a character that has forced a whole continent to accept him as a creative artist.[44]

Meyerhold's presence still peers out at us today, in the "innovative" work of Peter Brook, Yuri Lyubimov, Andrei Serban, Liviu Ciulei, and many other theatricalists and conceptualists. His influence on Brecht is apparent, and, by extension, on all those current directors who believe they owe their artistic genesis to the ideas of the German playwright-director. Meyerhold is the first great objective theatricalist of the century, the first to successfully tear off the theatre's mask of illusionism and draw attention to its innate character as a world of accepted conventions. His work would be as fresh today as it was when first produced.

NOTES

1. "Meyerhold Ousted from the Soviet Stage," *New York Times,* 9 January 1938.

2. "Soviet Police Arrest Meyerhold," *New York Times,* 24 June 1939.

3. "Resurrections in Moscow," *New York Times,* 1 August 1956.

4. Had he staged *Hamlet,* Meyerhold might have cast his wife, Zinaida Raikh, as the Prince, or he might have had two Hamlets to represent warring aspects of the character's nature; he expressed an interest in both these notions, among many others concerning the play, and even considered writing a book to be called *Hamlet: The Story of a Director,* in which his plans for the play would be detailed so that some future director might carry them out in his name.

5. The notion of masks remained a vital one in Meyerhold's work. By the late 1920s, Marxist critics were to see in it an unhealthy adherence to the "fixed" character types of the pre-Revolutionary world, and an inability to reflect the dynamic forces of the allegedly more complex persons of the post-Revolutionary USSR.

6. Vsevolod Meyerhold, "The Fairground Booth," in *Meyerhold on Theatre,* ed. and trans. Edward Braun (New York: Hill and Wang, 1969), p. 127.

7. See Paul Schmidt, ed., *Meyerhold at Work* (Austin: University of Texas Press, 1980), pp. 11–15.

8. James M. Symons, *Meyerhold's Theatre of the Grotesque: The Post-Revolutionary Productions, 1920–1932* (Coral Gables, Fla.: University of Miami Press, 1971), p. 41. During the next few years, the theatre changed its name several times. These name changes were bureaucratic, not an indication of a change of building. From 1921 to 1922 it was the Actors' Theatre, and from 1922 to 1923 it was the Theatre of GITIS (an acronym for a name meaning State Institute of Theatrical Art). It was called the Meyerhold Theatre from 1923 to 1926 and was renamed the Meyerhold State Theatre, a name it retained until 1933, even when Meyerhold relocated to the less satisfactory Passage Theatre while he waited for the older building to be remodeled. During these years, the theatre was often closed for one reason or another.

9. Sonia Moore, "Meyerhold: Innovator and Example," *Players* 48 (October-November 1972): 37–38. For an excellent account of biomechanics and the influences upon it, see Mel Gordon, "Biomechanics," *Drama Review* 18 (September 1974): 73–88.

10. Meyerhold, "Biomechanics," in *Meyerhold on Theatre,* ed. Braun, p. 200.

11. Boris Alpers, "The Theatre of the Social Mask" (Moscow-Leningrad, 1931), trans. Mark Schmidt (ms. of unpublished translation sponsored by the Group Theatre, 1934).

12. Nick Worrall, "Meyerhold's Production of *The Magnificent Cuckold,*" *Drama Review* 17 (March 1973): 22.

13. Norris Houghton, *Moscow Rehearsals* (New York: Harcourt, Brace, 1936), p. 34.

14. The close relationship between Meyerhold's and Brecht's ideas is the subject of Katherine Bliss Eaton's *The Theatre of Meyerhold and Brecht* (Westport, Conn.: Greenwood Press, 1985). Eaton argues convincingly that Brecht was strongly influenced by

the Russian regisseur's work; perusal of the Brecht chapter in the present work will reveal many pertinent parallels.

15. Meyerhold, "Pre-Acting," in *Meyerhold on Theatre,* ed. Braun, p. 206.

16. Nick Worrall, "Meyerhold Directs Gogol's *Government Inspector,*" *Theatre Quarterly* 2 (July-September 1972): 91.

17. Ibid., p. 94.

18. For a complete description of this work, see Alma H. Law, "Meyerhold's *Woe to Wit* (1928)," *The Drama Review* 18 (September 1974): 89–107.

19. Marjorie L. Hoover, *Meyerhold: The Art of Conscious Theater* (Amherst: University of Massachusetts Press, 1974), p. 202.

20. Houghton, *Moscow Rehearsals,* p. 32.

21. Ibid.

22. Lee Strasberg, "Russian Notebook (1934)," *Drama Review* 17 (March 1973): 109.

23. Stewart Chaney, "From the Drama Mailbag: Note on Russia," *New York Times,* 23 January 1938.

24. Symons, *Meyerhold's Theatre of the Grotesque,* p. 135.

25. Schmidt, *Meyerhold at Work,* p. 44.

26. André Van Gysegham, *The Theatre in Soviet Russia* (London: Faber and Faber, 1943), p. 34.

27. [Alexander Gladkov], "Meyerhold Rehearses," trans. Alma H. Law, *Performing Arts Journal* 3 (Winter 1979): 82–83.

28. Schmidt, *Meyerhold at Work,* p. 44.

29. Quoted from Boris Zakhava, *Sovremniki,* in Symons, *Meyerhold's Theatre of the Grotesque,* p. 44. See also Schmidt, *Meyerhold at Work,* pp. 91–99, which provides a full account of Zakhava's experience with Meyerhold in the direction of *Boris Godunov.*

30. Houghton, *Moscow Rehearsals,* p. 117.

31. Ibid., p. 126.

32. Ibid., p. 124.

33. Schmidt, *Meyerhold at Work,* p. 167.

34. Houghton, *Moscow Rehearsals,* pp. 131–32.

35. Van Gysegham, *Theatre in Soviet Russia,* p. 33.

36. E. Zozulya, "Vsevolod Meyerhold," *International Theatre* (October 1934): 5.

37. Quoted from *Teatri dramaturgiya,* in Meyerhold, "Meyerhold at Rehearsal," *Meyerhold on Theatre,* ed. Braun, p. 223.

38. Bryllion Fagin, "Meyerhold Rehearses a Scene," *Theatre Arts Monthly* 16 (October 1932): 834.

39. Ibid.

40. Meyerhold, "Meyerhold at Rehearsal," *Meyerhold on Theatre,* ed. Braun, p. 225.

41. For a more detailed description of these terms, see Schmidt, *Meyerhold at Work,* pp. 171–82.

42. Quoted from Meyerhold, "A Word about Mayakovsky," in *Meyerhold on Theatre,* ed. Braun, p. 165.

43. Robert Leach, *Vsevolod Meyerhold* (Cambridge, Eng.: Cambridge University Press, 1989), p. 104.

44. Van Gysegham, *Theatre in Soviet Russia,* p. 31.

CHRONOLOGY

1873   born in Penza, Russia

1896   leaves Moscow University law school to study theatre at Moscow Philharmonic
          Society; marries Olga Mikhailovna Munt

1898   becomes charter member of new MAT

1902   leaves MAT to cofound touring troupe

1902–5   tours Russian provinces; stages about 150 plays and other entertainments

1905   Stanislavsky sets him up in Theatre-Studio; *The Death of Tintagiles; Schluck
          and Jau; Snow; Love's Comedy* (Studio closed by Stanislavsky before any
          public showing)

1906   directs for Vera Komissarjevskaya's St. Petersburg theatre: *Hedda Gabler; In
          the City; Sister Beatrice; The Eternal Story; Nora (A Doll's House); The
          Fairground Booth; Miracle of St. Anthony*

1907   *Love's Tragedy; Love's Comedy; Wedding of Zobyedy; The Life of Man; To
          the Stars; Spring's Awakening; Pelléas and Mélisande; Victory of Death*

1908   tours various Russian cities with troupe comanaged with R. A. Ungerna: *Sister
          Beatrice; The Fairground Booth; Vampire; Electra; Hedda Gabler; Victory
          of Death; The Life of Man; Hostages of Charlemagne; The Master Builder;
          At the Gates of the Kingdom*; assumes directorship of Imperial Theatres,
          Alexandrinsky and Marinsky; latter used primarily for operas, St. Petersburg;
          Alexandrinsky: *At the Gates of the Kingdom*; Mikhailovsky Theatre: *Salomé*
          (cancelled by censors); "The Seashore" (Lukomore): *Petrushka; Fall of the
          House of Usher; Honor and Revenge*

1909   Alexandrinsky: *A Lawsuit*

1910   private apartment: *Paul I*; Tower Theatre (private apartment): *The Jest of
          Tantrise; Adoration of the Cross*; Alexandrinsky: *Don Juan*; as "Dr. Dap-
          ertutto," explores cabaret-like experiments in private venues; House of In-
          terludes: *Columbine's Scarf; The Transformed Prince*

1911   Alexandrinsky: *The Red Café; The Living Corpse*; Assembly Rooms of the
          Nobility: *Harlequin, the Marriage Broker*

1912   private home: *Being in Love*; Tenishevsky Hall: *Three Dawns*; Fellowship of
          Actors, Writers, Artists, and Musicians, Terioky, Finland: *Being in Love* (new
          version); *Harlequin, the Marriage Broker* (new version); *Adoration of the
          Cross* (new version); *Crimes and Crimes; You Never Can Tell*; Alexandrinsky:
          Hostages of Life

1913   Chatelet Theatre, Paris: *Pisanella*; Suvorin Theatre, St. Petersburg: *Seville
          Café*

1914   Alexandrinsky: *Mid-Channel*; Tenishevsky Hall: *The Unknown Woman; The
          Fairground Booth*; Suvorin: *Mademoiselle Fifi*

1915   Alexandrinsky: *Two Brothers; The Green Ring*; *The Constant Prince; Pyg-malion*

1916   Alexandrinsky: *The Storm*; Comedian's Rest: *Columbine's Scarf*; *The Romantics*; edits magazine *Love for Three Oranges*

1917   Alexandrinsky: *Krechinsky's Wedding; Masquerade*; School of Scenic Art (Mikhailovsky): *An Ideal Husband*; *The Case*; *The Death of Tarelkin*; *The Lady from the Sea*; Russian Revolution

1918   Alexandrinsky: *Peter the Baker*; Workers' Theatre: *Nora*; Theatre of Musical Drama (Petrograd): *Mystery-Bouffe*; joins Communist party; head of Theatre Division of the Education Commissariat

1919   nearly executed by White Army; freed by Reds, takes over municipal theatre at Novorossiysk

1920   heads Theatre Division of the People's Commissariat of Enlightenment (resigns 1921); First Soviet Theatre in the Name of Lenin, Novorossiysk: *Nora*; New Theatre RSFSR 1, Moscow: *The Dawns*; theatre undergoes various name changes 1920–23 (see theatres named 1922–23, below)

1921   New Theatre RSFSR 1: *Mystery-Bouffe* (new version); *The League of Youth*; first Russian directing school, the Meyerhold Workshop; begins work on biomechanics; marries second wife, Zinaida Raikh

1922   Actors' Theatre: *Nora* (new version); *The Magnificent Cuckold*; Theatre of GITIS: *The Death of Tarelkin* (new version)

1923–26   his theatre called the Meyerhold Theatre; all subsequent productions at Meyerhold Theatre (MT; Meyerhold State Theatre from 1926), Moscow, except where noted

1923   MT: *Earth Rampant*; Theatre of the Revolution: *A Profitable Post; Lake Lyul*

1924   MT: *The Forest*; *D.E. (Give Us Europe!)*

1925   MT: *Bubus the Teacher; The Warrant*

1926–33   theatre called the Meyerhold State Theatre (MST)

1926   MST: *The Inspector-General*

1928   MST: *The Magnificent Cuckold* (new version); *Woe to Wit*

1929   MST: *The Bedbug; The Second Army Commander*

1930   MST: *The Bathhouse*; tours Germany and France with company; *D.S.E.* (revision of *D.E.*)

1931   MST: *The Last Decisive; A List of Assets*

1932   State Drama Theatre, Leningrad: *Don Juan*; MST: *Prelude*

1933   MST: *Krechinsky's Wedding* (new version); State Drama: *Masquerade*

1934   MST: *Camille*

1935   MST: *Thirty-three Fainting Fits*; *Woe to Wit* (new version)

1937   MST: *Natasha*; *One Life* (neither opened to public)

1938   government liquidates company; Pushkin Theatre, Leningrad: *Masquerade,* last solo production

1939   completes Stanislavsky's production of *Rigoletto*; denounces socialist realism at First National Convention of Theatrical Directors, Moscow; arrested

1940   dies in prison camp

Max Reinhardt

(1873–1943)

Max Reinhardt was not, in the technical sense, an *homme de théâtre*. He was an actor, a producer, and a director. He did not, however, create stage designs, write plays, or publish significant theoretical treatises as did so many others in this book. Within the somewhat more proscribed area of his talents, however, Reinhardt's directorial achievements rival, in their range and overall breadth of expression and imaginativeness, those of almost any other director the century has produced. He was a master with chamber plays, immense spectacles, avant-garde exercises, operas and operettas, and the classics of the contemporary and antique repertory. He explored almost every type of theatre architecture known to his day, from conventional proscenium stages, to arena theatres, to "found" locations. So diverse were his creations and so broad his scope that historians and critics, unable to classify his methods under some comprehensive label, are forced to describe him as an eclectic, perhaps the greatest the theatre has known.

EARLY YEARS

Reinhardt's eclecticism grew out of a tradition with which he had become familiar in his youth. Reinhardt was born Max Goldmann in September 1873 in Baden, Austria, a popular resort town for the Viennese; his early theatre-going experiences included Vienna's renowned Burg Theater, a playhouse supporting one of Europe's finest ensembles playing in a repertory of considerable catholicity. The Austrian and German theatres of the time produced many plays each season, selecting them from the standards of the classical and modern stage. The diversity of a typical theatre's repertory is underscored by the fact that, as a young actor-in-training, Reinhardt himself played forty-nine different roles in the one winter season of 1893–94.

The first ambition of this son of a less than affluent merchant family was to be an actor; for this he entered a Viennese theatre school in 1890. He soon showed outstanding talent and by 1893 was a leading character actor in the Salzburg Stadttheater where, despite his youth, he specialized in the roles of old men. Otto Brahm, the famed critic-director who founded Berlin's Freie Bühne and introduced a program of intense naturalism to the German stage, seeing the student Reinhardt act in 1890, was impressed. In 1894 Reinhardt became an important player at Berlin's Deutsches Theatre, of which Brahm had become the artistic director. A year later, recognized as the brightest light among Brahm's younger players, he was beginning to experiment as a director with other actors in the company.

CABARET

Brahm's proclivity for photographic naturalism soon began to weary Reinhardt, and he developed various ideas for a more theatrical style of presentation. In 1898 Reinhardt and a company of Brahm's players performed works by major modern writers such as Henrik Ibsen, Leo Tolstoy, and Knut Hamsun in Prague, Vienna, and Budapest. Two years later, he made his formal directorial debut with Ibsen's *Love's Comedy* at the Deutsches. Shortly afterwards, in 1901, Reinhardt became leader of a group called "Die Brille" (The Eyeglasses), and, while still employed as an actor by Brahm, began directing its members in musical and dramatic sketches designed for cabaret performance. Their first public show was an evening of parody scenes produced to raise money for a poet-friend so he could enter a sanatorium. Friedrich Schiller's *Don Carlos* was burlesqued in naturalistic, symbolistic, and strolling-player styles. Die Brille was so well received that weekly performances were introduced under the name "Schall und Rauch" (Sound and Smoke) at a cabaret rented and decorated in Greek temple style.

THE KLEINES THEATER

These intimate evenings of satire and burlesque began at midnight and went on all night. They afforded Reinhardt many opportunities for experimenting with theatricalist and musical techniques. So popular did they become that the group moved to a hotel where they built a small theatre. In August 1902 it was named the Kleines Theater (Small Theatre) and soon began a policy of producing straight plays. Among those of their first season were August Strindberg's *There Are Crimes and Crimes*, Oscar Wilde's *Salomé* and *The Importance of Being Earnest*, and Frank Wedekind's *Earth Spirit*. Most were very advanced and daring dramas at the time; among them were plays that allowed Reinhardt to demonstrate theatricalist techniques in the symbolist style that so sharply differed from Brahm's emphatic naturalism. *Salomé,* for one, was so effective, that Richard Strauss was inspired by it to write his famous opera version. In later years, Strauss' *Elektra* was also inspired by a Reinhardt production.

By 1903 Reinhardt was able to sever his ties with Brahm and to emerge as an independent producer-director. He continued to act in productions he staged or produced, including an excellent interpretation of Luka in *The Lower Depths,* a major mounting codirected with Richard Valentin. This *Lower Depths* outdid Brahm at his naturalistic game and accrued over 500 performances within two years of alternating repertory. Reinhardt's interests in acting were fast receding before the force with which his directorial and producing genius was burgeoning.

THE NEUES THEATER

While continuing his Kleines activities, Reinhardt rented the larger Neues Theater (New Theatre) in 1903 and operated it concurrently. The same playhouse eventually became the home of Bertolt Brecht's Berliner Ensemble. Here he was soon responsible for plays by Ludwig Thoma, Ludwig Anzengruber, and Maurice Maeterlinck (*Pelléas and Mélisande*). His Kleines repertory for the 1903 spring season included his direction of Hugo von Hofmannsthal's *Elektra.* This Austrian playwright's neoromantic poetic plays were to figure importantly in Reinhardt's career.

The two-theatre system allowed Reinhardt to produce about twenty plays a year and to provide audiences with the widest range of plays. Reinhardt's success with the large theatre/small theatre concept was enormously influential, and many institutions (including colleges and universities) eventually adopted a similar system. Unlike those contemporaries of his who specialized in a narrow range of theatrical approaches, Reinhardt felt that each play was a separate entity with its own inherent style and that the director's task was to discover and then transmit this style through the production. The play always came first, not the director. As a result, his productions reflected most of the century's significant theatrical modes, from naturalism to romantic and selective realism to symbolism to expressionism, and so on.

A MIDSUMMER NIGHT'S DREAM

The apex of Reinhardt's early career was the 1905 Neues production of *A Midsummer Night's Dream.* In what was then considered a revolutionary staging, Reinhardt and designer Gustav Knina combined the totality of the theatre's resources in scenery, costumes, lights, sound effects, and machinery to provide the most exciting German Shakespeare production of its day. Shakespeare has long been one of Germany's favorite playwrights, although, in Reinhardt's formative years, productions of his plays were in the reverent and heavily pictorial style epitomized in the late nineteenth century by the work of the Meiningen company. Rarely did such productions have the life, color, and vitality with which Reinhardt imbued his first presentation of the Bard. His uncut version used a revolving stage to make the action move swiftly from scene to scene. Discarding the conventional two-dimensional painted scenery of wings, borders, and backdrops, Knina created a three-dimensional forest of thick tree trunks and grassy glades. Although still heavily indebted to an illusionistic viewpoint, the result was a charmingly unconventional blend of naturalism and romanticism.

Reinhardt saw the forest as central to the play. His forest convincingly suggested the supernatural world inhabited by Shakespeare's magical creatures. All aspects of the forest, including a tiny lake, could be viewed as the set slowly revolved. According to Ernst Stern, who became a leading Reinhardt designer, "the elves and fairies ran through the forest, disappearing behind the trees, to emerge behind the little hillocks. These beings in their green veils and leafy crowns seemed . . . to form a part of the forest itself."[1] Stern was disturbed by the director's conventional use of a female for the role of Puck, but he was pleased to note that the fairies were attractive and sensual young females instead of the stodgy-looking ballerinas used so frequently in past productions.

A Midsummer Night's Dream was staged by Reinhardt many more times in his career. He was an inveterate lover of Shakespeare and directed or produced twenty-two of his plays for a total of 2,527 performances. Of these, 427 were devoted to the *Dream*. (His 1913–14 season was known as the Reinhardt Shakespeare Festival; it saw his staging of ten plays from the canon.) In each of his *Dream* revivals he found a new approach, doing it in varying styles, from the classical to the romantic, each time in a new environment. One production would be intimate, another extravagant, one in a private park, another on a university campus, and still another in Florence's Boboli Gardens or Los Angeles' Hollywood Bowl. Best known today, of course, is his 1935 American film version, codirected with William Dieterle.

Reinhardt's Shakespearean stagings blended Elizabethan ideas with modern ones, although he held to no specific method. Some works were as visually simplified as the Elizabethan reconstructions of William Poel, others approached the elaborate pictorialism of Herbert Beerbohm Tree. Reinhardt's Shakespeare went from solid realistic sets built in naturalistic detail on a revolving stage to impressionistic, minimalist versions to outdoor presentations done amid preexisting environments. At times he would abandon the proscenium arch and build a forestage into the house. He rarely cut the texts, and arranged the action to move swiftly with a minimum of waits. In Reinhardt's hands Shakespeare was reborn for the twentieth-century German stage; Shakespearean production blossomed all over Central Europe in the wake of the regisseur's eye-opening revivals. According to J. L. Styan, Reinhardt's frequent Shakespeare presentations, in which he constantly sought to refine his staging methods,

established what many thought to be the characteristic style of Shakespearian performance in the twentieth century—free flowing, highly rhythmic, leaning towards a symbolist use of colour and design, seeking the right visual images for each play's mood and atmosphere, and catching the most telling emphasis in action and characterization.[2]

THE DEUTSCHES THEATER

It was not long before Reinhardt capitalized further on his great success with the *Dream*. In October 1905 he assumed control of the Deutsches Theater, the scene of his early Berlin acting triumphs. For a quarter of a century this was to be the center of his theatrical fiefdom.

The Deutsches was one of Europe's best-equipped theatres. Reinhardt fervently believed in the technical resources of the modern stage and made elaborate use of the Deutsches' sixty-foot-diameter revolving stage, its plaster cyclorama inset with thousands of tiny bulbs to simulate stars, a cloud projection machine, and an elaborate Fortuny lighting system. He continued to expand and refine his acting company, bringing in new and unformed talent and establishing a training school for them. Its advanced curriculum included work in the Dalcroze system of eurythmics. The company, as with most Reinhardt companies before and after, operated as a true ensemble, without stars. Even recognized performers had to play cameo roles in the repertory. Gertrud Eysoldt, Alexander Moissi, Friedrich Kayssler, and Rudolph Schildkraut were among the best of the early actors.

THE KAMMERSPIELE

The Deutsches opened with Reinhardt's staging of Kleist's *Käthchen von Heilbronn*. Within two months four more plays under his direction opened there, including an extremely successful *Merchant of Venice*. His last work at the Neues was Offenbach's operetta, *Orpheus in the Underworld*. This theatre was abandoned in favor of a new house called the Kammerspiele (Chamber Theatre) next door to the Deutsches. This converted dance hall seated 292; had no orchestra pit, balcony, or boxes; and had a low stage allowing the already intimate environment to become even cozier. Exquisitely decorated, the Kammerspiele was intended to provide an outlet for the small-scale plays that Reinhardt found inappropriate for the large Deutsches stage. Small-scale, conversational, literary dramas were staged here with an intimacy between audience and actor that few other theatres then could achieve. Ibsen, Wedekind (including, in 1906, the first production, albeit edited, of the long-banned 1891 *Spring's Awakening*), Gerhart Hauptmann, Hofmannsthal, Maeterlinck, Shakespeare, Molière, Carl Sternheim, Strindberg, Johann Wolfgang von Goethe, August von Kotzebue, August Stramm, and Carlo Goldoni were the chief authors interpreted here by Reinhardt. Since he was busy directing at the Deutsches and elsewhere, however, his productions at this theatre were done sporadically, sometimes three or four a year, sometimes one or none. His last Kammerspiele staging came in 1930.

With two companies operating at the Kammerspiele and Deutsches, Reinhardt was able to offer Berlin, within a single week's span, up to ten plays, both new ones and those already at the end of long runs. Casts were changed often to keep the older plays fresh. A dual theatre system like this required the most disciplined managership. With Reinhardt's brother Edmund in charge of the managerial end, the complex mechanism operated smoothly, allowing the enterprise to reap both artistic and financial rewards. Admittedly, the system often was rough on those who found themselves cast in plays being done simultaneously at the two theatres. Passersby often were greeted by the sight of actors, finished with one performance, dashing from playhouse to playhouse, adjusting their makeup as they went, in order to be on time for an entrance in the other play.

The Kammerspiele's history began in 1906 with Reinhardt's symbolist production of *Ghosts,* in which he also acted. This sensational performance revealed his venturesome visual tastes. He hired Norwegian modernist painter Edvard Munch to do the sets, resulting in

a scene that used outward forms only for the purpose of deepening the central mood of the play by the way it arranged its lines; vertical most of them, horizontals and curves, repeating as it were, the play and clash of ideals in a play and the clash of lines.[3]

Reinhardt's use of advanced painters like Munch demonstrated how deeply in touch he was with the major artistic currents of the day. He employed many artists of the radical new trends just as he chose plays reflecting all the important new literary tendencies. He had a special gift for inspiring the proper scenic decor for each play to make its presentation totally effective.

Moving back and forth between the classics and modern dramas during the next few seasons, Reinhardt divided his time fairly evenly between both theatres. In 1909 he put on *Faust I* (generally considered unstageable before this) in a spectacular production at the Deutsches. Fascinated by this immensely challenging work, he staged it often in later years, and even produced *Faust II,* similarly thought unproducible, as well as Goethe's original version of the play, the *Urfaust,* in its premiere production. In the 1909 *Faust I* he employed the full resources of the revolving stage to show the multiscened drama with three-dimensional realism yet with barely any delay between scenes.

THE REVOLVING STAGE

Reinhardt was the undisputed master of the revolving stage. Together with his designers, notably Stern, he solved numerous problems through its use and successfully overcame its primary problem—the narrow space to which it restricted scenes set on it. The revolve was then a fairly new phenomenon in European theatre, an electrically operated one having been installed at Munich's National Theater in 1896 by Karl Lautenschläger. The revolve was used in darkness and also in light, as in *A Midsummer Night's Dream,* so that movement of the actors as they went from locale to locale could be incorporated. This technique is fundamental to Japan's *kabuki* theatre, where the turning stage was invented by a playwright in the mid-eighteenth century. In its fullest development a multiscenic production could tie all scenes together in a continual flow, regardless of how many interiors and exteriors were needed. In Stern's designs one could often view exteriors through spaces incorporated in interior settings, these exteriors being in part composed of other elements included on the revolve. What served for an interior wall in one scene would often reveal its other side, thus allowing scenic units built in three dimensions to serve for both indoor and outdoor action. The scenes on the revolve could be varied from as little as a dozen feet to the full stage, through the use of curtains within the proscenium arch.

DIRECTORIAL DIVERSITY

It was in 1907 that Reinhardt became an international director when his company toured to Budapest with a repertory of Sholem Asch, Hauptmann, Wilde, Wedekind, and Strindberg. In addition, Reinhardt's services were increasingly requested by other German cities. Of considerable importance in this regard were the three summers (1909, 1910, 1911) during which he operated Munich's controversial Kunstlertheater (Artists' Theatre). Reinhardt's various successes here were in sharp contrast to the successive failures of the theatre's founder, Georg Fuchs, who had helped design its much-discussed "bas-relief" stage (which Reinhardt disparagingly dubbed "the little kiddie coffin"). So favorable was the reception afforded the Austrian director's work in the Bavarian capital that the mayor even offered to rebuild the Kunstlertheater to accommodate Reinhardt's spatially expansive productions. In addition to Munich, the regisseur's work was often to be seen in Budapest, Prague, Frankfurt-am-Main, Vienna, Stockholm, Zurich, Amsterdam, Moscow and other Russian cities, Cologne, the Hague, Copenhagen, and other Scandinavian, German, and Swiss cities, not to mention Paris, London, New York, Hollywood, and elsewhere.

While adding new productions to his credits, Reinhardt also was making a practice of reviving plays he already had staged. In so doing, he usually employed an assistant who worked from carefully prepared promptbooks. Unless the occasion was especially important to him or he had a totally new conception, Reinhardt was often too busy to attend to all the preliminary rehearsals and would only show up in the latter stages when he would help bring the work to performance level. However, critics have observed that this practice frequently led to sloppy productions, especially in the postwar years.

Among the many plays that kept reappearing in his repertory were *A Midsummer Night's Dream, Faust, Hamlet, The Winter's Tale, Twelfth Night, Oedipus Rex, The Miracle, Everyman* (Hofmannsthal's version), *King Lear, Othello, The Merchant of Venice, Much Ado about Nothing, Romeo and Juliet, Minna von Barnhelm, Judith, Spring's Awakening, Clavigo, Love and Intrigue,* and *The Imaginary Invalid.*

SUMURUN

Much of Reinhardt's work involved the use of pantomimic action. His 1908 *Lysistrata,* for example, was a feast of visual delights in which color and movement predominated over the spoken word. It seemed a natural progression, then, when he undertook to stage a wordless drama in 1910; this was the visually enchanting mime-drama with music called *Sumurun*. Soon to be an international success, with performances in London, Paris, and New York, it was first staged, of all places, at the intimate Kammerspiele. Based by Friedrich Freksa on *The Tales of the Arabian Nights,* it was an exquisite presentation, harmoniously blending movement, lighting, scenery, and Victor Hollaender's music. Its complex melodramatic plot was concerned with a love triangle and involved delightfully theatrical characters such as a sheik, adulterous lovers, a hunchback, and members of a harem. An austere white background with only a suggestion of an Arabian motif set off the gorgeous display of colorful costumes.

Reinhardt and designer Ernst Stern added a new device to the store of Western theatrical techniques, a runway through the theatre for important entrances. He did not employ the runway, borrowed from the *kabuki* theatre's *hanamichi,* in many other productions, but its use apparently influenced American musicals and revues.

Reinhardt had begun to feel that the theatre had been losing touch with its audiences and was becoming too remote. With *Sumurun* he tried to reunite the stage and spectators by eliminating overelaborate sets and costumes, seeking instead a simplicity of decor that would capture the spectator's imagination and hypnotize him into yielding to the influence of the production. Asked by a journalist if Reinhardt was indeed a hypnotist, one of his assistants, Richard Ordinski, said,

That is the idea. His scheme is to appeal to the imagination of his audience so strongly, if possible, that they will forget they are in a playhouse and for the time being imagine they are spectators of some happenings in real life.[4]

The interesting thing about Ordinski's remark is that it referred, not to a modern play in the realistic tradition, but to a work conceived as a pure fantasy. Reinhardt realized that stage reality did not depend on external fidelity to life; a sense of reality could be evoked by means which brought out the truth inherent in the work itself, no matter how unrealistic its subject or treatment.

OEDIPUS REX

Sumurun was a first for Reinhardt, and would be followed by other wordless spectacles, a group of plays which forms an important genre in his career. Another first, also produced in 1910, was his staging of Hofmannsthal's version of *Oedipus Rex* in the three-quarters round. The impetus for the production came from an invitation Reinhardt had received from a Bavarian folk-festival organization that sought to create an apolitical coalescence of Munich's politically segmented populace by offering classical plays in a festival atmosphere. As in so much of his other work, Reinhardt attempted in *Oedipus* to manipulate the actor-audience relationship in the direction of greater active audience participation—active, that is, on the emotional and psychological, not the physical or intellectual, level. The first of the spectacular *Oedipus* productions was at the Munich Musikfesthalle in September; it soon played in various Central European cities and came to Berlin's Zirkus Busch (a circus arena about five minutes from the Deutsches Theater) in November. *Oedipus* represented Reinhardt's earliest try at what he called the Theatre of the 5,000—presentations, staged in huge environments, which sought to capture the awesome power of the ancient theatre by using vast crowd scenes, broad heroic acting, and majestic scenic back-grounds. The many seats would allow the masses to attend cheaply. The three-quarters-round arrangement would also allow everyone to be closer to the action than in a proscenium playhouse.

The Munich staging of 1910 was at a large exhibition hall, and the Berlin production (and many of those in other cities) was in a circus arena. In both, the audience surrounded the action on three sides. The entire performance space was used for the acting, and crowds of supernumeraries numbering in the hundreds surged and swelled in carefully rehearsed choreographic patterns. No masks were worn, and the chorus of twenty spoke sometimes in unison, some-times individually, in a free adaptation of the original distribution of their lines. The production was not in a style contemporaries considered suggestive of the fifth century B.C.; instead of stately, measured drama, it was passionate, emo-tional, and in constant movement, swelling at the seams with dramatic power. Scenery resembling a Greek palace was at one end of the space; a horseshoe-shaped thrust stage had been pushed forward into the arena. Actors emerged into the arena from the vomitoria beneath the spectators.

A vivid description by Eva Elise Vom Bauer conveys the excitement of the opening moments. The play began, she tells us, in

Egyptian darkness, out of which rang, clear and loud, a clarion trumpet-call. Then four lithe youths, clad in the altogether, and bearing their torches on high, ran out from the centre entrance opposite the stage, up the vast steps, to kindle the calcium lights, resem-bling ancient altar fires, that stand at either side of the palace. Where and how these youths disappear, one doesn't notice, as the attention is distracted by a rumbling that is neither thunder nor the rolling of nine pins! . . . louder it grows, nearer it comes, and with a jostling gray mass of human beings that pours into the arena through three entrances. Their inarticulate cries and wails grow more intense; pierced here and there by the shrieks of a woman or the groan of a man's voice, they finally concentrate into the insistent demands for "Oedipus."[5]

This famous production played in many cities, including London, where it was placed on a proscenium stage at the Covent Garden Opera House in 1912, and starred Sir John Martin-Harvey and Lillah McCarthy.

THE MIRACLE

Enthused by the reception of *Oedipus*, Reinhardt continued his circus stagings, producing *The Oresteia* and *Everyman* (in Hofmannsthal's adaptation) in 1911,

both at the Zirkus Busch (although the former had premiered at Munich's Musikfesthalle). The same year his most famous production, Karl Vollmoeller's
elaborate mime-spectacle, *The Miracle*, with music by Engelbert Humperdinck,
was produced. Reinhardt was still directing revivals of this enormously successful
pantomime as late as 1932. The first version was done not in Berlin but in
London. This was the type of Reinhardt work which exported best, because the
audience needed no German and could concentrate instead on the expertness of
the staging values. Consequently, Reinhardt's reputation in England and America
was more as a director of spectacles than as one of small-scale dramas, although
German-speaking audiences found his skill at the latter even more impressive
than his work on larger canvases.

An enormous company of 1,800, including actors, dancers, orchestral ensemble, and choir were involved in the vast undertaking of presenting *The Miracle*
at Olympia Hall. Reinhardt had to work with a team of assistants to stage the
mammoth show. Vollmoeller's script, based on Maeterlinck's *Sister Beatrice*,
told the tale of a medieval nun who leaves her convent for a worldly existence,
only to have her place at the convent taken by a statue of the Virgin Mary which
miraculously comes to life. The simple but powerful story, moving from temp-
tation to sin and then to redemption, was told through movement, sound, lighting,
and scenic effects, with a musical and choral accompaniment. Reinhardt's vision
was an outgrowth of his Theatre of the 5,000 idea, although some performances
played to as many as 30,000. Olympia Hall's vast rectangular space was fitted
for a three-sided seating arrangement with a scenic area at the fourth side. Actors
entered and left through large openings beneath the bleachers. Scenery was
moved in and out and up and down by mechanical means. Powerful overhead
spotlights, part of an elaborate electrical setup requiring up to ten miles in cable,
could isolate small areas for intimate effects. This was Reinhardt's first totally
environmental production in the sense that the interior of the hall was converted
into the semblance of a Gothic cathedral.

Even more awesome, perhaps, was the 1924 New York revival, designed with
totally new sets and costumes by Norman Bel Geddes (Stern had done the
originals). Reinhardt was impressed by the aspiring visions of Bel Geddes'
soaring imagination. Bel Geddes shared Reinhardt's growing distaste for the
proscenium arch and sought solutions to the problems of the audience-actor
relationship, which he, too, wished to see established on a deeper than usual
level of communion. In New York the Century Theatre, a large proscenium
house at Columbus Circle (several blocks uptown from the Broadway district),
was used, so Stern's old sets could not be adapted. Bel Geddes' unusual concept
disturbed not one permanent feature of the auditorium or stage but managed to
transform them into an overwhelming cathedral which gave spectators the feeling
they were present at a religious service. The aisles were filled with ritual proces-
sions surrounding the audience with the smells, sounds, colors, and movement
of medieval church life. It took twenty to thirty tons of scenery to effect the
transformation, with sets shifted almost supernaturally by hanging all the movable

scenery from tracks and moving them by electric motors. The extremely complex lighting plan was executed by a single technician seated before a switchboard in the second balcony and controlling the hundreds of instruments, none of which the audience could see.

Only in the opening and closing scenes were realistic costumes used. The intervening dream scenes were highly formalized, everything being united by a motif based on a medieval craft product such as woven hangings, stained glass, enamel, and sculptural elements; inexpensive imitations gave the impression of the real thing.

The critics were hugely impressed by the event and reviews appeared on the front page of the New York papers. They effused about the stained glass windows, the thousands of candles, the religious statues and statuettes, the organ music, the exciting use of crowds in medieval garb, the nuns, crucifixes, Gothic arches, cloisters, incense, thickly carved doorways, towering choir and apse, and pewlike seating, not to mention the monumental grandeur and spiritual euphoria of it all. George Jean Nathan thought it the most beautiful and effective production ever "chronicled in the history of American theatrical art."[6]

Unhappily, Reinhardt's next mime-spectacle collaboration with Vollmoeller, *A Venetian Night,* which opened in London in 1912, was a flop.

NEW THEATRES, NEW STYLES

A new Berlin theatre came under Reinhardt's control in 1915—the Volksbühne, where he soon began directing more classics. His prolific contributions streamed forth from year to year now, with Shakespeare represented the most. In 1918 he began a series of striking productions of the new expressionist plays, beginning with Walter Hasenclaver's *The Son.* Already familiar with the essentials of the style from his work on the proto-expressionism of Wedekind and Strindberg, he staged such plays as Reinhold Sorge's *The Beggar* (1917), Reinhart Goering's *A Sea Battle* (1918), and August Stramm's *Powers* (1921), all done under the auspices of the avant-garde group Das Junge Deutschland (Young Germany). Many others were staged under his aegis as producer.

Yet another Berlin theatre was added to Reinhardt's domain in 1918, the Kleines Schauspielhaus (Small Playhouse), an intimate venue for modern dramas and an occasional classic. His first directing jobs here were Goethe's *Clavigo* and Wedekind's *Spring's Awakening,* both of them standards in his repertory. Before long, however, his attention reverted to his earlier ambitions, and he began to prepare for his most grandiose conception, a permanent theatre for the masses.

THE GROSSES SCHAUSPIELHAUS

Reinhardt returned to the Theatre of the 5,000 concept in typical earthshaking fashion in November 1919 when he opened his newest acquisition, the Grosses

Schauspielhaus (Large Playhouse), with his production of *The Oresteia*. From 1920 to 1922, when he abandoned the place, massive productions of such classics as *Hamlet, Julius Caesar, Lysistrata, The Merchant of Venice, A Midsummer Night's Dream,* and Schiller's *The Robbers* were given, as were elaborate stagings of plays by such modern writers as Romain Rolland, Gerhart Hauptmann, Georg Kaiser, and Ernst Toller.

As early as 1901 Reinhardt had begun to dream of a vast theatre of the masses. His dream never left him; it was made concrete in his original circus presentations, but its most significant expression was the Grosses Schauspielhaus, itself a remodeling of the Zirkus Schumann. Here, in what was then the world's largest playhouse (it seated 3,300), he wished to produce towering dramas dealing with man's most universal concerns. Still seeking to cast a hypnotic spell over the spectators, he created a dynamic symphony of lights, sounds, music, and color. A three-step system of (1) wide proscenium stage, (2) jutting apron, and (3) a sixty-six-foot-long, U-shaped arena was surrounded by tiers of seats over which hung a colossal circular network of scalloped ceiling decorations resembling stalactites.

Few theatres were as fully equipped technically. The proscenium stage had a huge revolve, a vast plaster cyclorama, and advanced cloud projection machinery. A great many powerful lighting instruments made the action visible in the broad expanses of the acting area. Sets and costumes were of appropriate grandeur and simplicity, for all that smacked of the fussiness of everyday detail could have no place in so titanic an environment. As soon as the spectator took his seat, he was drawn into the atmosphere of the ensuing drama, as the curtainless stage setting was immediately visible. Here was no fourth-wall naturalism with its self-contained existence, playing away as though the audience was a secondary concern. Reinhardt's goal was audience involvement, an immediate sensation by the spectator that he was one of "the people" within the world the actors were portraying. His theatricalist realism demanded an electrical interplay between the audience and the performance for the work to be complete. To intensify this relationship, his productions often had actors mingled with the audience so that a sense of shared commitment between the two could be effected.

As it happened, though, architect Hans Poelzig's epoch-making project was generally condemned by critics and public alike for its garish, cavelike appearance, its poor acoustics, its severe lighting problems, and its awkward combination of different and basically incompatible (proscenium and arena) stages.

The Grosses Schauspielhaus productions made use of hundreds of extras for their crowd scenes (practically a prerequisite for a play produced here). Two hundred of them helped create the excitement necessary for the depiction of the French Revolution in Rolland's *Danton* (1920). In the courtroom scene the crowd filled the stage and arena on a set occupying the complete acting area backed by gigantic windows at the rear of the stage proper. Walter Volbach witnessed the effect of the actors mixed in with the audience:

A member of the crowd standing in the arena before the tribunal began to shout; almost at once the entire mob took up the shouting; then, suddenly actors scattered throughout the upper rows joined in the yelling. The effect was indeed provocative and inflammatory for those seated not too close to the yelling people. I could observe that some spectators in the neighborhood of a "revolutionary" felt like joining, others like protesting. During later performances, when this trick was general knowledge, the audience scarcely reacted to it.[7]

Julius Caesar boasted a brilliant performance by Werner Krauss and crowds of extras that may have totalled four hundred. A four-hour performance of the uncut tragedy was moved along swiftly by use of the revolving stage. Reinhardt used all three scenic areas, with realistic sets placed on the proscenium stage to represent streets and the inside of homes. Well trained in their roles, the masses of extras provided an unforgettable picture in the battle and forum scenes, although Volbach remembers the battle as being inferior on the overly large arena.

Volbach, who worked as an assistant to the regisseur at the time, believes *Hamlet* to have been Reinhardt's most impressive production at the giant amphitheatre.[8] A semimodern dress production, with some military costumes strongly reminiscent of the German uniforms of World War I, was played against a Stern set in which tall and simply decorated flats were moved about to suggest many locales. The dialogue of Shakespeare and other poetic playwrights, though, was no match for the lofty reaches of the theatre and doomed such productions from the start. Reinhardt's modern-dress interpretation—one of the century's earliest—was a further attempt to bring the performance into intimate contact with the audience. When the play began in the arena, and the players took their places near the audience railings, spectators tried without success to pick out from the ensuing blend of actors and audience members dressed in evening clothes the famous Alexander Moissi in the role of the Dane.

Reinhardt's hilarious staging of *Lysistrata* was perhaps his most successful 1920 project at the Grosses. His activity there in 1921 was mainly with plays he had staged before; they were typical of those which he entrusted to an aide while he himself only came to do the touch-up work. Several of them revealed the difficulty of staging works in the theatre's awkward space. *The Merchant of Venice,* for example, displayed an insurmountable gap between actors and spectators, while for *A Midsummer Night's Dream* the gap was filled with seats placed on the arena floor, turning the work into a more or less conventional proscenium staging.

Reinhardt's work at the Grosses ended in 1922 following his stagings there of Hauptmann's *The Sunken Bell* and Toller's *The Machine Wreckers.*

SALZBURG FESTIVAL

Reinhardt's international activities led in 1920 to the establishment of a permanent liaison with his native Austria. In 1903 he had begun to think of creating a theatre festival in his beloved Salzburg, where Mozart festivals long had been held. He became involved in serious plans for such a festival in the postwar

years, especially after taking up residence there in 1918 in the palatial surround-
ings of Schloss Leopoldskron, a baronial estate in which he lived like a king.
With a council consisting of himself, Richard Strauss, Franz Schalk, Hugo von
Hofmannsthal, and Alfred Roller, Reinhardt got the festival under way in August
1920 with his production of *Everyman,* which was staged on the steps of the
Salzburg Cathedral with the audience seated in the open square of the Domplatz.
Except for interruptions occasioned by the Nazi invasion of Austria and the
privations of World War II (1938–45), the production has been put on yearly
and may still be seen. Though he had produced *Everyman* in a variety of indoor
locales, beginning with the Zirkus Schumann in 1911, Reinhardt was fascinated
by the idea of doing this religious drama in an outdoor environment which would
serve as a natural setting for the action. The Renaissance architecture of the
cathedral and the surrounding square was supplemented by a set consisting of
little more than a platform erected on the cathedral steps. Reinhardt's dramatic
imagination made the best use of his opportunities. Martin Esslin pictures the
action for us:

After the prolog had been spoken, calling upon the audience to be attentive, the voice
of the Lord resounded mightily from high up inside the cathedral. When the figure of
Death appeared to acknowledge his summons, it was as though one of the statues adorning
the facade had come to life. And when, during a rumbustious banquet on the platform,
Everyman was being summoned, the voices calling him came from all sides, echoing
and reechoing from the towers of the many churches of Salzburg.[9]

Reinhardt's Salzburg activities continued to expand in the ensuing years. In
order to pursue his outside interests, such as Salzburg, he had temporarily given
up active involvement at the Deutsches Theater, but still retained ownership and
occasionally staged a play. He resumed management in 1924. Meanwhile, Salzburg had seen his production in 1922 of Hofmannsthal's version of Pedro Cald-
erón de la Barca's seventeenth-century *auto sacramentale, The Great World
Theatre,* retitled *The Great World Theatre of Salzburg.* This allegorical work,
produced without an intermission, and reminding the audience of the brevity of
life and the promise of the hereafter, was done in the baroque surroundings of
Fisher von Barlach's eighteenth-century Jesuit Kollegienkirch. (The money
raised by the production helped save the old church from destruction.) Alfred
Roller's crimson cloth settings, the mystical choir music of Einar Nilson, and
the direction of Max Reinhardt combined to create a deeply holy atmosphere.
Angels—who appeared and disappeared as if by some supernatural agency—
were placed in the church's highest reaches to sing their lines. Critics were most
impressed by the bone-chilling dance of Death, one of the chief figures in the
piece.

Molière's *The Imaginary Invalid* was given two Salzburg productions in 1923,
one at Schloss Leopoldskron and the other at the Stadttheater. The former was
actually in the nature of a dress rehearsal for an invited group of international

guests in the great hall of Reinhardt's castle. Max Pallenberg, in the lead role, acted as host, welcoming the audience to the candlelit home by greeting them as they entered.

THE REDOUTENSAAL

Yet another unusual theatrical environment had been explored by Reinhardt in 1922. An exquisite Viennese baroque court ballroom dating from the time of Empress Maria Theresa was converted into a playhouse called the Theater in der Redoutensaal. Located in the Hofburg, this charming hall decorated with Gobelin tapestries hanging on the high-ceilinged walls, and with the convolutions of cornices, pilasters, and moldings, with stage and auditorium illuminated by superb crystal chandeliers, had a proscenium-less stage erected at the room's balconied end. A bridgelike double staircase led to the upper-balconied end from the stage. Against this delicate permanent architectural facade were placed simple scenic elements in no way designed to hide the fixed decor. Only the use of footlights and a curtain drawn on wires, used when necessary to mask scene changes, were throwbacks to the theatre of fourth-wall realism. Houselights remained on throughout the performance.

Reinhardt's productions here of *Clavigo,* Pedro Calderon de la Barca's *La Dama Duende*, Goethe's *Stella*, and Etienne Rey's *Beautiful Women* in 1922 were his chief contributions to a theatre of nonillusionistic presentationalism. Unlike his work in theatres and environments where his aim was to convince the audience through representational staging that the scenic world was integral to the world of the play, the Theater in der Redoutensaal admitted openly that the stage was a stage and that the actors, usually accepted as the *embodiment* of the characters, were actors *playing* the characters. Nevertheless, this theatre's acoustics did not satisfy Reinhardt, and in 1924 he took over another theatre in Vienna, the old Theater in der Josefstadt, which he opened with Goldoni's *The Servant of Two Masters,* staged with irrepressible mirth and energy in commedia style. The play became one of his favorites and was often repeated on other stages in other cities. When, later the same year, he opened his next Berlin venture, the Komödie Theater (Comedy Theatre), it was with the same play.

THEATER IN DER JOSEFSTADT

A wealthy backer had allowed Reinhardt to gain control of the 1822 Viennese playhouse, Theater in der Josefstadt, which he thoroughly renovated as a luxurious resort. An 800-lamp chandelier—which flew to the ceiling, lights fading, as the play began—was the decorative centerpiece. (A similar concept is now used in New York's Metropolitan Opera House.) Reinhardt's productions here included classics and contemporaries, and were produced annually from 1924 to 1927, and in 1930, 1931, 1934, and 1937. The final production, Franz Werfel's *In One Night,* ended his European career when, as a Jew, he was forced to flee from the threat of the Nazi terror. One of his unusual stagings here was of Somerset Maugham's *Victoria* in 1926. The play was done expressionistically with cubist furniture; all the movement and dialogue were set to the jazz accompaniment of a piano.

Although commentators often stress his success at this playhouse with light sophisticated comedy and farce, Reinhardt's mountings at the Theater in der Josefstadt also included the heavier material of Schiller, Shakespeare, Pirandello, and Werfel.

DEVELOPMENTS IN SALZBURG

With the economy of Salzburg booming in the wake of its new festival, Reinhardt conceived a gigantic Festival Playhouse complex to be designed by Poelzig, with an 800-seat theatre for Mozart concerts and a larger one for drama. His hope was to re-create the conditions of the great medieval festivals when the theatre was sponsored by the church. The new playhouse was never built, although Reinhardt made ample use of other local spaces, including a one-time-only performance of *Twelfth Night* (1931) on a tiny island in the lake before Schloss Leopoldskron. The audience watched from the mainland. Rain, however, a constant threat in Salzburg, canceled the show in the middle. Of more importance were Salzburg's Riding Schools, once used by the nobility. There were two, an indoor one for winter and an outdoor one for warmer weather. Reinhardt staged plays in both. The outdoor school had its seating built into the surrounding rockface of a mountain. His most famous production here was a new version of *Faust I* (1933–37), with a spectacular set built according to the medieval principle of simultaneous staging; all the play's numerous locales were visible at once. Lighting was employed to isolate each as needed. Esslin declares that the result was

a realization of the Baroque concept of the theatre as an image of the whole world on all its levels: Heaven and Hell and, in between, the earth, with life as an endless process of rising and falling from one sphere to the other.[10]

Adjoining the outdoor school was the indoor one, converted by Reinhardt into the Festival Playhouse in lieu of the grand new theatre of which he had dreamed. He staged plays here, usually past successes of his, from year to year. His last Salzburg season was in 1937, after which the Festival closed down for the duration of the Nazi reign.

LATE TWENTIES, EARLY THIRTIES:
THE PERIPATETIC REINHARDT

Meanwhile, America was welcoming the regisseur, first with his 1924 production of *The Miracle*, and then, in 1927–28, with a season of seven plays using his German ensemble. Throughout the winter months New Yorkers visited the Century Theatre to witness *A Midsummer Night's Dream*, *Everyman*, and Georg Büchner's *Danton's Death*. The more intimate pieces in the repertory were viewed at the Cosmopolitan Theatre; they were Czech playwright Frantisek Langer's *The Ragged Edge* (also known as *The Outskirts*), *The Servant of Two Masters*, Leo Tolstoy's *The Cause of It All*, *The Living Corpse* (also known as *Redemption*), and Schiller's *Love and Intrigue*. In the company were Moissi, Hermann and Hans Thimig, Lili Darvas, Vladimir Sokoloff, and Paul Hartmann.

As the twenties gave way to the thirties, Reinhardt's directorial energies showed no signs of flagging. He continued his hopscotch life of staging plays in Berlin and Vienna, with frequent sidetrips elsewhere. In 1928 a theatrical conservatory, the Max Reinhardt Seminar (still in operation), was founded in Austria. When he had time he taught there.

His last production at the Deutsches was Hofmannsthal's *The Great Theatre of the World* (1933). Soon afterward the Nazi regime forced him to relinquish his German theatres. In 1932 and 1933 he worked in England, Switzerland, Austria, Italy, Romania, and France. Among his notable productions were outdoor versions of *A Midsummer Night's Dream* in Florence's Boboli Gardens and at Oxford for the Oxford University Dramatic Society.

Another memorable outdoor staging was in 1934 when Reinhardt directed *The Merchant of Venice* at Campo San Trovaso, Venice. The same year he was once more in the United States to do an enormously ambitious presentation of the *Dream* at Los Angeles' huge Hollywood Bowl for a crowd of over fourteen thousand. The entire Bowl area was used for this environmental presentation. Mickey Rooney, soon to star in Reinhardt's film version, played Puck. San Francisco, Berkeley, and Chicago were shortly to see approximations of this spectacle.

AMERICA: THE DECLINING YEARS

Reinhardt moved his family to America in 1935, although he continued to visit Vienna for two more years. In America he directed a number of productions until 1943. These included several student productions with young actors he was training at an acting school he established in Hollywood in 1938. His most important staging was the world premiere of Werfel's *The Eternal Road* (with a score by Kurt Weill) in New York in 1937. After a career during which he had produced eye-opening pageants honoring Christian ideals, Reinhardt paid his homage to his Judaic origins with this Brobdingnagian mounting (in English) of Werfel's biblical saga. The work, Broadway's most expensive to date ($750,000), ran for 153 performances but lost its investment despite critical acclaim and sold-out houses. Its huge running costs (it had a cast of 60 principals, 40 dancers, and 120 singers and others), exacerbated by Norman Bel Geddes' uneconomical design concept, were too high to keep the production open.

When weather and legal problems obstructed Reinhardt's plans to stage this giant show in a mammoth tent in Central Park, he had Bel Geddes architecturally make over almost the entire Manhattan Opera House. The first thirteen rows of the auditorium were removed, and the pit deepened by dynamite blasting, to build the "cave of the synagogue" scene. Not only were these valuable seats withdrawn, but also the huge forestage area created such poor sight lines that the entire top balcony had to be closed, losing even more precious income-producing seating.

The proscenium arch was cut open to give it more height, an undertaking which in pictures today reveals both Bel Geddes' vision and also his impractical business sense. His sound track was the Broadway theatre's first use of effects recorded on tape. Extraordinarily successful effects of thunder, wind, and rain, as well as music, were thus achieved. The colossal set incorporated imaginative mechanical devices, with hills that opened and closed, and temples that rose on elevators (until the latter were scrapped because of technical difficulties).

Thornton Wilder's *The Merchant of Yonkers,* written at Reinhardt's suggestion that the author adapt an old Nestroy farce, was staged late in 1938. Harry Horner blames Broadway producer Herman Shumlin for interfering so seriously with the director's concept of the work as a folk play with a commedia-like spirit of fun, that the compromises Reinhardt made led to the show's demise.[11] As is well known, it was resurrected and revised years later to become *The Matchmaker* and, ultimately, the great hit musical, *Hello, Dolly!*

Other productions of these declining years included an outdoor modern dress *Faust I* (1938) and Somerset Maugham's *Too Many Husbands* (1940) in Los Angeles, a rather successful Broadway adaptation of *Die Fledermaus* called *Rosalinda* (1942), and, finally, in New York, Irwin Shaw's *Sons and Soldiers* (1943), with Geraldine Fitzgerald and Gregory Peck. Reinhardt died in New York, after suffering a stroke. Once king of the European stage, he parted from the world stripped of his theatres, his money, and, judging from the reactions to his final ventures, respect for his creative genius.

CRAIG'S PAUL

Max Reinhardt was thought by many to be the embodiment of the prophetic dreams of Gordon Craig, who viciously attacked Reinhardt in his periodical, *The Mask,* for stealing his ideas. George Jean Nathan called Reinhardt "Gordon Craig's Paul."[12] Yet, as Craig pointed out, Reinhardt's ideas were not really identical to his. For one, Reinhardt did not believe in the notion of the master director, the one supreme power responsible for total artistic control of every facet of production. Instead, he was a collaborative artist, working in intimate relationship with a team of artists—writers, composers, designers—and accepting from each his best ideas, which he would blend through the filter of his own artistic genius. If Reinhardt believed any artist to be the focus of a production, it was the actor. The director's art was seen as secondary to the actor's art and, consequently, he gave his actors great creative freedom. As a director he guided the collaborative process by "his creative imagination, his judgment in selection, his sense of proportions and his ability in co-ordination."[13]

Craig probably realized that his ideas and those of Reinhardt were not as close as he later claimed; otherwise, he might have followed through when Reinhardt invited him in 1905 to stage *Macbeth, The Taming of the Shrew,* and Shaw's *Caesar and Cleopatra,* and in 1908 to design *King Lear, The Oresteia,* and *Oedipus.*

Some of Reinhardt's ideas do resemble Craig's, though. For example, he conceived of an ideal combination author-director-actor, a man like Shakespeare or Molière, although he himself had only the latter talents. He felt that too many writers wrote more for the reader than for the spectator and that, if they shared the practical experience of the director and actors, their plays would be more stageworthy. He would have liked a play to be so written that the director's intervention became unnecessary, the staging possibilities being implicit in the lines and situations.

More noticeably, Reinhardt's scenic achievements often resembled Craig's innovations in design. His use of mood, color, lighting, the highly selective disposition of forms, and the lack of realistic detail in many settings suggest the impressionistic influence of Craig. Yet Craig was only one of a myriad of forces and pressures acting upon Reinhardt's seismographic artistic temperament. He was receptive to all the current ideas and movements in the arts and reflected their influences in his numerous productions. He worked with each new concept in a suitable production and rarely stayed with one long enough to be identified with it. Reinhardt's main purpose was to serve the text; he rarely threw upon the stage effects geared toward demonstrating his own cleverness or that of any other in the ensemble. Anything less would be a distortion. He sought whatever ways he could to bring the play and the audience together in a shared experience.

THE SEARCH FOR THEATRICAL ENVIRONMENTS

Reinhardt went from style to style in search of that most fitting to each play. He saw a play in total terms, considering it not only in terms of acting, theme, decor, and music, but also in terms of what architectural arrangements were best suited to it. He made a habit of acquiring different theatres, so that plays could be staged as best befit their needs. From gemlike playhouses to stupendous circus arenas, from conventional stages to imperial ballrooms, from cathedral squares to church interiors, and from forest parks to Venetian plazas, Reinhardt placed his productions in the most appropriate environments.

Once ensconced in the proper surroundings, he immediately began to wring every theatrical possibility from them. We have seen how the towers of Salzburg played so crucial a role in the sound effects of *Everyman.* In preparing the same play, he noted there were hundreds of pigeons roosting under the cathedral eaves. Thus, he conspired to have a big trunk lid slammed down at one moment, startling the birds into flight so they would swoop around the square in a circle, creating a thrilling effect. In his outdoor Oxford University Dramatic Society *Dream,* the play opened with the men and women of the court hiding behind trees. When they abruptly stepped forward where they could be seen, the vista took on sudden, unexpected life.

Reinhardt tried to make each production a Wagnerian work of total theatre art—a *gesamtkunstwerk.* He drew upon any theatrical idea, old or new, to reach his goals, and emphasized no one element at the expense of any other. All elements were in perfect harmony in the presentation. He studied theatre history, looking for inspiration from the Greeks, Japanese, Chinese, Italians, Elizabethans, and others. But he was no mere copier or theatrical archaeologist. Each new principle he encountered was transformed by his showmanship, artistic taste, and imagination until it became as original and fresh as if it first had come from him.

In his early days he was classed among a group of theatrical innovators recognized essentially for their attempts to cast off the pall of nineteenth-century tradition. This group, seceding from the dry, literary, discussion-oriented problem and thesis dramas of the time—some even called them Secessionists—moved toward a more theatricalist employment of the theatre. They saw the theatre as an art important for its own sake and not for its use as the mouthpiece of a program or idea. Manner came before matter to these aestheticians and they turned the theatre into the temple, not of propaganda, but of beauty and delight. The leader of the movement was Reinhardt, the stage director to whom cold academicism in art was tiresome and dull, who rarely pontificated, but who never stopped laboring to make the theatre theatrical.

Reinhardt's theatricalism did not estrange his audience, except on rare occasions, but looked instead to create an atmosphere in which nothing mattered but the play and the mood it evoked. In most of his productions, he tried to create a feeling of complete illusionism, using simple but expressive backgrounds and realistic acting. Whatever techniques he could devise to envelop the audience in the drama's atmosphere were put to work. Alexander Bakshy discriminates two principal methods in Reinhardt's work, the passive and the active. In one, the spectator becomes the observer of the action as if he were an onlooking participant in the dramatic world; in the other, he is practically an engaged participant in the action. The former is akin to a bystander at a real street accident. Though the world onstage is an imaginary one, the spectator's involvement is so developed as to project him into that fictive world as if it were real. Bakshy describes this distinction from the "illusion of reality of the play enacted" as an "illusion of 'reality of onlooking.' " But when Reinhardt extended the conventional proscenium stage to include the auditorium as part of the scenic unity (as in *The Miracle* or the outdoor productions), the audience member—surrounded by a decor like that onstage and by actors seated in the auditorium—became an imaginary participant in the action. A measure of objectivity remains when the actors and scenery are perceived by the audience as part of a separate world within the same structure, but when the theatre (the amphitheatre) becomes crowded with mob scenes, the separation becomes less clear:

The continuity of the amphitheatre is then extended from end to end of the theatrical building, and the audience, drawn into the whirl of action in the Arena, is lifted, so to speak, to the state of potential actors, which brings the performance almost to the verge of action.[14]

CROWD SCENES

In the economically straitened circumstances of much contemporary theatre, it is rare to experience crowd scenes of any sort, much less to consider the handling of crowds as a sign of directorial expertise. However, crowd scenes were once a common feature of large-scale productions, and—in the wake of the Meiningen company's accomplishments in this domain—directors were generally prized for the brilliance with which their mobs were managed. Because of the scope of many of his productions, Reinhardt was constantly testing his crowd-handling skills; as may be imagined, he was considered a master at this difficult art. Reading descriptions of Reinhardt's crowd scenes, it is not difficult to envision the compelling effect they must have had. He marshalled hundreds of extras, all thoroughly drilled by a team of assistants, and directed them to speak their lines with careful rhythmic emphases and to move with predetermined gait and gestures. Every crowd sound, such as shouting or clapping, had its part in a clear rhythmic structure and was never improvised. The sounds were built on a three- or four-part basis, rising, getting louder, dying down, rising louder again, only to die, and once again reach a crescendo. This created a striking effect of unity.

Reinhardt was a master at the use of lighting to bring out all the dramatic excitement of a crowd scene and to make his mobs seem larger than they actually were. Heinz Herald described the dynamic effect of the lights as seen in *Danton's Death*:

The impression of tremendous plenitude and variety of life, the impression of passionate movement, was obtained by lighting up only one small part of the stage at a time whilst the rest remained in gloom. Only individuals or small groups were picked out in spotlight whilst the masses always remained in semi-darkness, or even in complete darkness. But they were always there and they could be heard murmuring, speaking, shouting. Out of the darkness an upraised arm would catch the light, and in this way thousands seemed to be where hundreds were in fact.[15]

Another Reinhardt practice, seen in other directors known for their effective crowd direction, was the employment of dialogue written especially for members of the mob. Styan provides a sample from the promptbook of the 1905 *Merchant of Venice* courtroom scene. (Cf. Tyrone Guthrie's crowd dialogue in the companion volume, *From Belasco to Brook*.)

DUKE: (strongly). No, Shylock, no! you may not have that.
BASSANIO: (emptying a bag of coins on the table, left). Here is the money, you Jew;
    take three times the sum.
GRATIANO: Unfeeling Jew, shame! We won't stand for this.
SALARINO: On your life, let justice be done!
SOLANIO: A wolf rules your doglike spirit.
FIRST JUDGE: Not even the metal of the executioner's axe has half the edge of your
    bitter resentment.
SECOND JUDGE: Shylock, listen to us!
THIRD JUDGE: Let charity be your guide, Shylock![16]

For all their power and imagination, however, some found the Reinhardt crowd scenes to be even less effective than his handling of intimate scenes. He needed very few actors to gain his greatest effects of theatrical truth.

ENSEMBLE COMPANIES

Reinhardt's acting companies, composed of the finest actors he could obtain, were expertly trained and were as flexible as any such ensemble could be. Numerous cast changes in the long-running or often-repeated plays allowed the actors many opportunities in challenging roles, and replacements for important parts were rarely any problem. A company of actors, all of whom could have been stars with other groups, subordinated themselves to the no-star principle so strongly stressed by Reinhardt. Company harmony was thus maintained, and many actors stayed with Reinhardt for the better part of their careers. Actors considered it a mark of great prestige to be called a "Reinhardtschauspieler" ("Reinhardt actor"). He paid his actors well, except for the early postwar period when his company was forced by inflationary pressures to disband and the actors boosted their incomes by acting in films. During the summers at Salzburg, however, he drew them together again, even in this period of adversity.

An important criticism of his use of these great talents is that Reinhardt did not achieve a truly heightened acting style with them. All plays were acted realistically, with a sense of truth and freshness, but this realism was not always appropriate to the demands of the play. Realism in nonrealistic plays was accepted for lack of a more organic style. Only occasionally did he manage to enhance a production by an original theatricalist approach to acting. His actors sometimes jarred with the scenic style, which was normally executed in a suggestive, not minutely literal, mode.

SCENIC STYLE

Reinhardt and his designers examined a wide range of visual methods in the mise-en-scène, but these essentially conformed to a pattern of selective or stylized realism, or, as one form of it was called, impressionism. He worked essentially with three-dimensional scenic elements, employing interesting scenic levels for the actors and breaking up the stage picture in the manner of Adolphe Appia's designs. Suggestion replaced representation, though to today's eyes the sets often seem excessively realistic in their solidity. Still, their simplicity at the time was revelatory, especially in the unity of effect with which lights, colors, and costumes blended on the stage.

Pictorial conceptions continued in Reinhardt's work off and on throughout his career, especially when the revolving stage was used to depict a multiscenic play's many locales; however, he was more likely than not to create the impression of a place by the careful selection of a detail rather than a fuller re-creation. Thus, part of a bush was enough to evoke a garden, an architectural detail could summon up a street, and a church could be imagined by the proper placement of a pair of columns.

Though highly simplified, the scenic elements rarely were abstract. Real glass in doors, solid-seeming walls, and floors simulating grass or earth were common. In *The Robbers,* irrespective of the stylized creation of a forest with a few carefully placed trees—their leaves hidden above the proscenium—the tree trunks were so realistic even their bark and moss could be discerned.

MUSIC AND SOUND

Music and sound effects were essential to Reinhardt's ideals. Only through their effective incorporation could his dream of a *gesamtkunstwerk* be achieved. Reinhardt's productions were built on musical and rhythmical foundations, and even when no audible music could be heard, an inner music could be felt through the controlled rhythm of the actor's movements.

He knew instinctively which music was most appropriate for each production. Many plays were done with new music, especially commissioned by Reinhardt. Humperdinck and Einar Nilson were among his favorite living musical collaborators, although important work also was done by many others. When necessary, established music was performed. Molière, for example, profited from old French tunes; Welsh music was chosen for *Henry IV*; Chopin for Strindberg's *The Pelican*; Mozart for *The Servant of Two Masters*; Mendelssohn for *A Midsummer Night's Dream*; Schumann for *Faust II*, and so on.

Reinhardt's exciting mood-stimulating sound effects often came from musical instruments, particularly in his great circus productions. Trumpets, bells, and gongs were used with extreme expressiveness for the openings of *Oedipus, The Oresteia, Everyman*, and *The Miracle*, for instance. In other productions, like *Macbeth,* the mood of a bloody night was suggested by an organ's rumbling tones and the intermittent screams of an owl. At other times, organ tones with few vibrations mingled with the low roll of a kettledrum could create the feel of thunder, seemingly emerging from a mass of extras on the stage.

The human voice was but another instrument which played its carefully orchestrated part in the aural ensemble. Of particular importance were the vocal effects of large choruses in which each word was scored and blended with every other. Parts of a sentence were cut from each group, so that as the groups joined in at preset times—one after the other—the line as spoken would have a cumulative effect, culminating in a powerfully united crescendo backed by the orchestral instruments.

Reinhardt thus attained the goal for which so many modern theatricalists have searched in vain, a brilliant fusion of all the collaborative contributions to a work of theatre art. As Hovhannes Piliakin asserts, "Reinhardt must be considered the first creative genius with an absolute grip of *all* the elements constituting the composite art of the stage. All evidence goes to demonstrate that he alone was the first practical priest of Total Theatre."[17]

PREPARATION FOR PRODUCTION

When Max Reinhardt commenced preparations for a new work, he plunged deeply into the script for several weeks, reading nothing that did not pertain to the play. He often made his preparations during a period of vacation. The play required his complete concentration, usually forcing him to cut himself off totally from all his other affairs so that its characters and situations became second nature to him.

This total immersion procedure led to the writing of a huge promptbook, or *regiebuch*, in which every important detail of a planned production was carefully noted. Each page was covered with neatly written notes on desired vocal tones and inflections, timing, gestures, lighting requirements, mood movement, blocking, properties, key words, costumes, business, music, sound effects, characterization, scenery, scene shifts, and every other technical and artistic consideration.

Numerous sketches of settings and accessories filled the available spaces, as did diagrams of all the blocking. These books were continually revised as Reinhardt worked on a play over the years; different colored writing often differentiated the work from one period to another. So profuse were these jottings that they often occupied more space than the text of the play. When he was directing a translation, he would collate several different translations for reference. It sometimes took six to twelve months for a promptbook being prepared for one of the more elaborate productions to reach completion. Morton Eustis wrote that the *Eternal Road* script

fills two large volumes of double column typewriter pages, written and typed on both sides of the page. In one of the columns on each page are pasted a few lines of the English script; sometimes there may be only two lines of text, sometimes ten or fifteen. The rest of the page is filled with Reinhardt's notes written in German, in precise characters not much larger than the printed text.[18]

WORKING WITH THE DESIGNER

Part of the *regiebuch* was taken up with scenic sketches and ideas. Usually Reinhardt used these only as a springboard for his collaboration with a designer, but on several occasions Reinhardt apparently kept strictly to his preconceived scenic concept. In most cases he took a surprisingly liberal approach to the designer's contribution. He would discuss his own ideas and listen to those of the designer. Taking Reinhardt's verbal and visual hints, the designer would go off and create sketches and models for the director's approval. With some designers, like Ernst Stern, he placed total confidence in their ability to do what they thought best, with only minimal suggestions from him. Other major designers with whom he worked included Karl Walser, Emil Orlik, Ludwig von Hofmann, Gustav Knina, and Alfred Roller.

The designer would study the play intently and show the best of his sketches and models to Reinhardt, modifying where the director advised. Models were especially important for sets employing the revolve, because of the technical problems involved. Norman Bel Geddes tells a story of the freedom afforded by the regisseur. After making more than a thousand drawings for *The Miracle*, Bel Geddes brought them to Schloss Leopoldskron where, in one long evening, Reinhardt examined each one before giving his approval.

Heinz Herald found that Reinhardt's collaborative work with the designer followed four patterns, according to the individual involved.

Sometimes, Reinhardt hands only the play to the painter and expects him first to give his own ideas in regard to the scenery. Then again, he explains with a rough draft of his plan. A third time, the painter faces a project completely outlined, with the form of every chair designed by Reinhardt himself. Sometimes, manager and painter get together and lay out their plans in common.[19]

Reinhardt's theatres were well equipped with their own scene and costume shops; this allowed his productions to be executed precisely as he desired. He preferred the same person to do sets, lights, and costumes in order to preserve the visual unity. Often, the design process was not completed until the designer became familiar with the progress of rehearsals, so he could make necessary adjustments as required by the staging.

CASTING

Casting practices were similar to those of many ensemble companies. The no-star system required everyone to act in small roles, no matter what the actor's position; however, Reinhardt always asked the more important actors for their approval before announcing them in a lesser role. This was a courtesy on his part and no actors are known to have refused him.

He sometimes liked to discuss a role with several possible actors and then cast on the basis of such talks. It was more important to him that an actor have the proper personality for a role than the correct physical appearance. This led him to take chances in casting certain actors from whom other directors might have shied away. He often took young, relatively inexperienced actors and gave them important roles as a way of training them. Reinhardt saw a special quality, for example, in Alexander Moissi, and for years ignored the critics' attacks on this actor as he gradually developed him into a performer of great renown. Moissi also represented the kind of actor who became so dependent on Reinhardt's powers that he could not successfully function in other contexts.

At times the actors Reinhardt had available dictated how a play would be staged. The actors' strengths and talents helped him decide on the degree of realism or stylization a production would have. Actors gifted with graceful and highly expressive bodies and voices might provoke a romantic and decorative treatment while those more psychologically acute and small-scaled in manner might lead to a concrete and realistic approach.

Reinhardt opposed typecasting and did not engage a company in the traditional "lines of business," but believed instead in the actor's innate versatility. Reinhardt expected his actors to be what he called "universal character actors," able to play any role believably. His actors were not all this flexible, but few were those restricted to a single type of character.

WORKING WITH ACTORS

Reinhardt was a director for whom actors loved to work; the list of major artists who trained and played under him reveals how highly he was considered by contemporary players, most of whom worked for him more for the artistic experience than for financial reward. He had the gift for making people work well together, in the true spirit of harmonious ensemble; the warmth and genius of his personality kept great actors with him through large portions of their careers, even when more lucrative offers were available to them elsewhere.

At rehearsals he was a model of courtesy and patience, observing everything without missing a beat, and asserting himself through a presence of quiet self-assuredness. Scarcely anything could ruffle him as he sat with his cigar, concentrating his deep blue eyes on the actors. Temper tantrums were a rarity, despite the boiling pressures under which he labored. A rare eruption came when, no longer his own master, he had to submit to the annoying interference of producer Herman Shumlin during rehearsals of *The Merchant of Yonkers*. Shumlin, at the rear of the theatre, had disagreed with something the director had told an actor and sent an assistant to so inform Reinhardt. Having been rudely interrupted and corrected as well, something he had never before encountered, Reinhardt blew his stack and screamed for the assistant to get away from him; he had to sit down for several minutes to regain his composure.

Reinhardt was a master at working with actors; he knew intimately the workings of their mechanisms. He almost always spoke to them in a respectful whisper, drawing them aside and saying just those one or two pertinent things that could spark fires in their imaginations. He knew just how to come to grips with the fundamental problem of a scene and how to get from his actors the proper responses. His comments rarely missed the mark and actors could remember his helpful comments years after they were spoken. Gregory Peck has recounted his experience with Reinhardt in *Sons and Soldiers*, Reinhardt's last production, staged when the director was "past the peak of his powers." Peck says that Reinhardt sat in the house and either communicated with the actors through his assistant, actress Lili Darvas, or came up onstage where he could whisper with the actor apart from the rest of the cast. "He never directed actors so that anybody who happened to be standing around could hear it, especially if he had something critical to say." Peck, then at the start of his career, was having trouble with a difficult scene requiring him to laugh and cry at the same time. His self-consciousness was preventing him from relaxing and getting the proper effect. Reinhardt came up onstage and spoke privately with the young actor.

I know what you're going through, young man, [he said], but you must throw your self-consciousness to one side and just play, just pretend. We don't mind if you don't do it well the first few times, but you won't do it well at all unless you stop taking yourself too seriously. It's playacting. . . . After all, we in the theater are privileged. We can go on playacting and pretending all our lives. Most people have to stop doing it when they're grown up, but we don't have to stop. It's just play, it's play, that's all it is.[20]

Peck reports that this "key" opened the door to his playing the scene with truth.

At other times, Reinhardt would achieve results by a single gesture that would instantly enlighten a player. Acting in *Love and Intrigue*, Lili Darvas was having trouble with a scene in which her character was

playing the piano while waiting for her lover. He just showed me one gesture—how she impatiently puts her two hands down on the keyboard. That gesture gave me the whole character, and the whole scene; its rhythm . . . built naturally from then on.[21]

Reinhardt worked differently with each actor, drawing from him the best he had to offer, inspiring him with confidence. Some actors he let go their own way, only mildly adjusting their effects; with others, he discussed their problems in detail, although he hated talky sessions; and with yet others, he showed how he wanted something done. He actually was fonder of demonstrating than of describing. Being a gifted actor, this method rarely failed him. But his demonstrations were done so as not to invite an empty mirroring. He did them in terms of the particular actor for whom they were meant. He would watch the actors carefully when they were not onstage and observe their mannerisms and personality traits. These would be remembered and incorporated in the demonstration so the actor would see how he personally could enact what Reinhardt was showing him.

Eustis observed Reinhardt at a rehearsal when he had to get an actor to laugh a certain way. Hearing the actor's version, Reinhardt interrupted with his own method, simultaneously showing how he wanted the actor to move. The actor repeated the laugh as Reinhardt listened. Then the director went onstage to further help the actor. "He laughs with him, exaggerating the tone, overemphasizing the gesture, seeming almost to force the actor by sheer hypnotic power to achieve the desired pitch and intensity of inflection and movement."[22]

Reinhardt was always ready to listen to an intelligent suggestion from an actor. He was famed for his ability to listen to someone as though he were the most important person in the world, and thus he gave people the sense that they counted for something in his eyes. His attitude was like this even at auditions. Actors knew they would always be given a fair opportunity to voice their concerns and display their own interpretations. If he disagreed, he would do so gently; he preferred finding a suitable compromise rather than molding an actor too precisely to a prearranged image. Therefore, his *regiebuch* preparations were often changed considerably in the course of rehearsals.

Watching him at rehearsals gave observers a delight. He would laugh uproariously at comic scenes and weep unashamedly at sad ones, infecting actors by this important feedback method. He would play the clown, the lover, or the soldier, according to the role being rehearsed. He moved from extremes of passivity to activity, depending on the needs of the moment. He could converse with an aide and be aware of everything going on onstage. An assistant would sit by him, taking down all his remarks as the actors worked. Merely watching him direct provided for some a complete theatrical experience.

This look at his rehearsal techniques shows how wide a spectrum he traversed from autocratic to laissez-faire. He insisted he was never a dictator, regardless of the claim by some that he was. Talented actors rarely found him sculpting their performances in detail, although he was likely to be very specific with less able players. When he was forced to dictate a performance, he could coax a good one even from mediocre material.

Early rehearsals normally found him to be more authoritative and demanding than later ones. At these first sessions he manipulated his players considerably, seeking specifics in vocalization and physicalization, at least from those in whom he did not place great faith. It was during this stage that he was most apt to demonstrate what he wanted, giving line readings and inspiring actors with his mimic abilities. He would be constantly on the go, moving from actor to actor and group to group, leaving nothing to chance, including pace and tempo. He would keep referring to the *regiebuch* to check on his preplanned ideas, using it mainly as a guide and allowing his aides to use it when he could not be present at rehearsal.

At later rehearsals the actors took over and dominated, as Reinhardt sat quietly and watched from the house. He would give notes at the end of a scene, often letting his assistant read them out as he enacted them, touching on line interpretations, gestures, business, and blocking.

ASSISTANTS

As the above has made clear, Reinhardt could never have functioned as efficiently or as prolifically as he did without the help of capable assistants at rehearsals. He even allowed such individuals to direct the minor characters while he concentrated on the principals. The assistants would drill the company in what Reinhardt had staged, and he would check and adjust the results. When a piece from his standard repertory was to be revived, he often entrusted its mounting to an aide; during Reinhardt's Berlin days, this person was more likely than not to be Berthold Held.

Reinhardt was in the habit of showing up for rehearsals in mid-afternoon, usually about 2:00 P.M., and letting his assistant carry the rehearsal for the first couple of hours before that. He would drift in as the rehearsal was in progress and watch silently before taking command. His presence was so strong that the actors would soon be aware he was there and whisper to each other, "The Master is here." With the actors warmed up by his assistant, he would take charge, coming like a breath of fresh air to the session.

Assistants, of course, figured significantly in the rehearsal of crowd scenes. Large crowds were broken into units, each in charge of an assistant who would take his group to an isolated corner and work there on the staging and vocalization planned by the director. The latter would blend the results with his inimitable skill so that the seams were hidden. Interestingly, some American actors found these rehearsals far less well organized than those to which they were used. Actress Grace Lynn wrote that they were "chaotic, inordinately slow, almost naively conducted, with a tremendously useless waste of time."[23] She did admit, however, that the results were far superior to those achieved by Reinhardt's American counterparts.

According to Lynn, each crowd member was given a number and required to write down his every cue and movement. In *Elektra*, for instance, number two had a script with these notes:

"So foul to look upon," (take slight step forward)

"Perish forever more," (entire chorus says "aye" and moves forward)

"Orestes comes at last," (general movement of surprise and murmuring)

"Light of day," (all cry "oh"—No. 2 louder than the rest)

"Hands and feet were cut off shamelessly," (recoil)[24]

FINAL POLISHING

Rehearsals usually lasted four or five weeks although extensions were granted when the play needed more work. Reinhardt rarely allowed a play to open until he was satisfied with it. He continued working on the production right up to the opening-night curtain, adjusting, cutting, and tightening as he saw fit. These last days wove a hypnotic spell over all involved as Reinhardt's energies were concentrated ever more sharply on the final stages. He would rehearse, when possible, into the early hours of the morning at this point, and no one left, even those who could have. It was not unusual for a dress rehearsal to begin at ten in the morning and conclude sixteen hours later. A sort of ecstasy hung over the rehearsal space as the piece was brought to perfection by the great Austrian regisseur. Even after a work had opened, he would continue to return to it in order to add new touches.

CONCLUSION

It was artists such as Max Reinhardt who made the regisseur's role this century's major contribution to the art of theatre. He was a brilliant collaborator, a man able to draw upon the talents of artists in every facet of production and put to work the best ideas current in the worlds of art, theatre, and music. Above all, he was an actor's director, one of whom stage and film director Otto Preminger, who worked for Reinhardt in the thirties, could say, "Reinhardt knew more about actors and about the nature of acting talent, than anybody in the history of the theatre."[25]

Reinhardt was almost single-handedly responsible for making Berlin a theatre capital on the level of Paris or London. He was enormously prolific; some years saw him do as many as twenty productions, and in 1916–17 he was credited with an astonishing forty-eight. Styan estimates his total output at over 500 new productions.[26] These represented every contemporary and classical style and showed his sensitivity both to the most advanced (and controversial) dramas as well as to the greatest classics; his vivid revivals of the latter, especially Shakespeare and the German and Greek masters, were largely responsible for reestablishing these works as essential parts of the modern repertory. Naturalism, symbolism, impressionism, expressionism, selective realism, and other current theatrical approaches were all appropriated by this theatrical wizard (he was fondly known by his coworkers as "the great magician") and received many of their quintessential realizations in his hands. The modern repertory system of a number of plays performed in alternation rather than seriatim owes him an undying debt as well. He was at one and the same time a genius at monumental crowd scenes and at those requiring the utmost intimacy and delicacy of effect; of pantomimic spectacle and of demanding verse drama. He clarified the possibilities of contemporary scene design and stage technology: he made the revolving stage a distinctive feature of twentieth-century technique, showed how effective cycloramas and sky domes could be, employed all the latest developments in lighting, and was the first major director to realize in practical terms many of the aesthetic theories being propounded by such visionaries as Appia and Craig. He also succeeded in creating works that effectively combined all the arts of theatre, including music, in the *gesamtkunstwerk* manner earlier promulgated by Richard Wagner.

Reinhardt explored the unique characteristics of all sorts of theatrical environments, from the most intimate to the most spectacular, from indoors to out, in spaces designed for theatre and in those built for nontheatrical purposes, as well as in those created by nature. There was barely an area of theatrical concern which he did not somehow affect. It was for these reasons that critic Herbert Ihering called him "the most colourful theatre talent of all time,"[27] and that Styan described him as "arguably the most versatile director the theatre has seen."[28]

NOTES

1. Walter René Fuerst and Samuel J. Hume, *Twentieth-Century Stage Decoration* (New York: Dover, 1967), p. 16.

2. J. L. Styan, *Max Reinhardt* (Cambridge, Eng.: Cambridge University Press, 1982), p. 52.

3. F. E. Washburn-Freund, "Max Reinhardt's Evolution," *International Studies*, January 1924, p. 348.

4. Quoted in Colgate Barker, "Reinhardt," *New York Review*, 2 January 1912, n.p.

5. Eva Elise Vom Bauer, "Max Reinhardt and His Famous Players," *Theatre Magazine* 11 (August 1911): 56.

6. Quoted from the *Journal American* in Norman Bel Geddes, *Miracle in the Evening: An Autobiography*, ed. William Kelley (Garden City, N.Y.: Doubleday, 1960), p. 301.

7. Walter R. Volbach, "Memoirs of Max Reinhardt's Theatres, 1920–1922," *Theatre Survey* 13 (Fall 1972): 18–19.

8. Volbach, "Memoirs," p. 23.

9. Martin Esslin, "Max Reinhardt, High Priest of Theatricality," *Drama Review* 21 (June 1977): 14.

10. Ibid., p. 20.

11. Harry Horner, "Epilogue: Notes on Max Reinhardt's Last Years" (unpublished ms., Research Collection, Lincoln Center Library for the Performing Arts, New York City).

12. George Jean Nathan, *The Magic Mirror*, ed. Thomas Quinn Curtis (New York: Alfred A. Knopf, 1960), p. 77.

13. Rudolph Kommer, "The Magician of Leopoldskron," in *Max Reinhardt and His Theatre*, ed. Oliver M. Sayler (New York and London: Benjamin Blom, 1968), p. 11.

14. Alexander Bakshy, quoted from "Living Space and the Theatre," in ibid., p. 338.

15. Quoted by Ernst Stern, *My Life, My Stage*, tr. Edward Fitzgerald (London: Victor Gollancz, 1951), p. 162.

16. Styan, *Max Reinhardt*, p. 63.

17. Hovhannes I. Piliakin, "Max Reinhardt and Total Theatre," *Drama*, no. 91 (Winter 1968), p. 50.

18. Morton Eustis, "The Director Takes Command, II," *Theatre Arts Monthly* 20 (March 1936): 212.

19. Heinz Herald, "Reinhardt at Rehearsal," in *Max Reinhardt and His Theatre*, ed. Sayler, pp. 118–19.

20. Quoted in Fred Fehl, William Stott, and Jane Stott, *On Broadway* (Austin: University of Texas Press, 1978), p. 57.

21. Lily Darvas, "An Interview," in *Max Reinhardt 1873–1973: A Centennial Festschrift*, ed. George E. Wellwarth and Alfred G. Brooks, (Binghamton, N.Y.: Max Reinhardt Archives, 1973), p. 20.

22. Eustis, "The Director Takes Command," p. 212.

23. Grace Lynn, "Patience Is Reinhardt's First Rule," *Boston Evening Transcript*, 3 March 1928.

24. Ibid.

25. Otto Preminger, "An Interview," in *Max Reinhardt 1873–1973*, ed. Wellwarth and Brooks, p. 111.

26. See the complete list of productions in Styan, *Max Reinhardt*, pp. 128–56. A slightly abbreviated listing is given in the brief chronology below.

27. Quoted by Michael Patterson in *The Revolution in German Theatre, 1900–1933* (London and Boston; Routledge and Kegan Paul, 1981), p. 34.

28. Styan, *Max Reinhardt*, p. 3.

CHRONOLOGY

The listings within each year are not strictly chronological, being organized around the theatres at which Reinhardt directed. Because Reinhardt is credited with an enormous number of productions, and because many of these credits represent repeat presentations of the same play at different theatres within a short span of years, emphasis in this chronology is on his first stagings; most subsequently revived productions are noted with an asterisk on the occasion of their premiere showing. However, the titles of several revivals of note—particularly those of *A Midsummer Night's Dream*—are provided. See J. L. Styan, *Max Reinhardt* (Cambridge, Eng.: Cambridge University Press, 1982), for a fuller listing.

1873   born in Baden, Austria

1892–94   works as an actor in Austria

1894   joins Deutsches Theater company, Berlin, under Otto Brahm

1900   Deutsches: *Love's Comedy**; Somossy Theatre, Budapest: *La Gioconda*

1901   founds cabaret theatre, Die Brille, Berlin; soon renamed Schall und Rauch; directs one-acts

1902   Schall und Rauch: *The Stronger**; *The Bond*; *Boubouroche**; Deutsches Volkstheater, Prague, and Somossy: cabaret sketches; Schall und Rauch moves, renamed Kleines Theater; Kleines: *His Highness**; *Intoxication*; *There Are Crimes and Crimes*; *Ackerman**; *Salomé**; *The Importance of Being Earnest**; *Earth Spirit**

1903   leaves Deutsches to direct the Kleines and the Neues Theaters; *The Lower Depths**; *The County Railway*; *Those Who Sign with a Cross*; *Pelléas and Mélisande*; *Double Suicide**; *A Woman of No Importance*; *Salomé*; *The Tenor**; *The Crows*; *Elektra*; *The Logic of the Heart**; *King Nicholas, or Such Is Life*; *The Fruits of Enlightenment*; *The Stream**; *Among Themselves*; Magyar Szinhas, Budapest: *Youth*; *Idyll of the Family**; *Colleagues**; *His Highness*; *Intermezzo*, and various recent works; recent works also at Deutsches Landestheater, Prague

1904   Neues: *Minna von Barnhelm**; *The Man of Destiny*; *Sister Beatrice*; *Medea*; *Candida*; *A King's Right*; *Flirtation*; *Love and Intrigue**; *He Wants to Play a Joke*; *The Pretenders*; *The Merry Wives of Windsor*; *The Dawn*; *The Count of Charolais**, and various recent works; Kleines: *Mother Highroad**; *The Pastor's Rieke**; *Martyrs*; *Miss Julie**; *The Green Cockatoo*; *Gallant Cassian*; *The Quiet Rooms*; *The Newly Married Couple*; *A Farewell Supper*; *Love's Dream*; Vigszinhaz, Budapest: various recent works

1905   Neues: *A Midsummer Night's Dream**; *Meta Konegen*; *Lovers*; Kleines: *Angela**; *Leaving the Regiment*; *The Bear*; *Sanna**; *Father Riekemann*; *Rosmersholm*; takes over Deutsches; Deutsches: *Käthchen von Heilbronn*; *The Merchant of Venice**, and one revival

1906   Deutsches: *A Florentine Tragedy*; *The Well of the Saints*; *The Commissioner**; *Oedipus and the Sphinx*; *Tartuffe*; *The Accomplices*; *The Winter's Tale**; *The Love King*; *The Merry-Go-Round*; Neues: *Caesar and Cleopatra*; *Orpheus in the Underworld*, and one revival; opens Kammerspiele; Kammerspiele: *Ghosts**; *Spring's Awakening**; *Man and Superman*; Neues Deutsches Theater, Prague, two revivals, including *A Midsummer Night's Dream*

1907   Deutsches: *Brothers and Sisters*; *Romeo and Juliet**; *The Inspector-General**; *The God of Vengeance**; *Robert and Bertram*; *The Prince of Homburg*; *Twelfth Night**; *The Doctor on His Honor*, and one revival (*A Midsummer Night's Dream*); Kammerspiele: *The Feast of Reconciliation**; *Hedda Gabler**; *Aglavaine and Selysette*; *Gyges and His Ring**; *Light o' Love**; *Esther*; *The Servant of Two Masters**; *The Marquis of Keith**; *Catherine, Countess of Armagnac and Her Two Lovers*, and one revival; Vigszinhaz: *The Importance of Being Earnest*; *The Dance of Death**, and various recent works

1908   Deutsches: *The Robbers**; *The Partner**; *Ulrich, Prince of Waldeck*; *The Waves of the Ocean and of Love*; *Medea*; *King Lear**; *Love and Intrigue*; *Fiesco, or the Genoese Conspiracy*; *Revolution in Krahwinkel**; Kammerspiele: *Wedding*; *Lysistrata**; *Death and the Fool*; *Nju**; *Social Aristocrats*; *Terakoya*; *Kimiko*; *Clavigo**; *The Wedding*; *The Doctor's Dilemma**; *No One Knows*; *The Count of Gleichen**; Vigszinhaz: *Links** and various revivals and recent works, including *A Midsummer Night's Dream*

1909   Deutsches: *The Teacher**; *Faust I**; *Don Carlos*; *The Taming of the Shrew**, and one recent work; Kammerspiele: *Wolkenkuckucksheim*; *The Man Who Found No Sympathy*; *The Refuge*; *Major Barbara*; *The Home*; Vigszinhaz; *Hamlet** and various recent works; also recent works at Breslau; Künstlertheater, Munich (including *A Midsummer Night's Dream*); and Frankfurt-am-Main

1910   Deutsches: *Good King Dagobert*; *Christina's Homecoming**; *Judith*; *The Bride of Messina*; *Samson and Delilah*; *Amphitryon*; *The Romantics*; *Master and Servant*; *Othello**; *The Jolly Vagabonds*, and several recent works; Kammerspiele: *The Natural Father*; *Help! A Child Has Fallen from Heaven*; *Sumurun**; *Gawan*; *The Last*; *The Cloister*; *The Forced Marriage**; *The Com-

*edy of Errors**; *The Wounded Bird**; *An Angel*; Musikfesthalle, Munich: *Oedipus Rex**; various recent works at Vigszinhaz; at Burgtheater, Vienna (including *A Midsummer Night's Dream*); at Brussels; at Künstlertheater, Munich (including *A Midsummer Night's Dream*); and at Zirkus Renz, Vienna, and Zirkus Schumann, Berlin (*Oedipus Rex* at the latter two); marries actress Else Heims

1911   Deutsches: *The Treasure*; *Wieland*; *Faust II*; *The Fat Caesar*; *Penthesilea*; *The Small Box*; *Turandot*; *Officers,* and one recent work; Kammerspiele: *Lancelot; The Giant; The Queen; Lanval; Souls Exchanged; Nathan the Wise*; Royal Opera House, Dresden: *Der Rosenkavalier*; Vigszinhaz: *Knickers*; *The Viceroy*; Zirkus Busch, Berlin: *Oresteia**; Zirkus Busch, Berlin; Künstlertheater, Munich: *La Belle Helene*; Zirkus Schumann, Berlin: *Everyman**; Olympia, London: *The Miracle**; London, Riga, St. Petersburg, Stockholm, Prague, Berlin, Budapest, Zurich, Amsterdam, the Hague: *Oedipus Rex*; Leipzig, Munich, and several Berlin theatres: *Oresteia*; also directed at Theater-in-der-Josefstadt, Vienna, for first time, and took *Sumurun* to London

1912   continues to tour with *Oedipus Rex* to major European cities, including Moscow and London; Deutsches: *The Wrath of Achilles*; *Much Ado about Nothing**; *Georges Dandin*; *Hidalla*; *Music*; *Oaha*; *Don Juan*; *Henry IV (I and II)**; *The Blue Bird**, and several recent works; Kammerspiele: *A Happy Marriage*; *I'm Fed Up with Margot*; *Pierrot's Last Adventure*; *Enemy and Brother*; *My Friend Teddy*; *Maria Magdalene*; Royal Opera House, Stuttgart: *The Would-Be-Gentleman**; *Ariadne auf Naxos*; Palace Theatre, London: *A Venetian Night**; Casino Theatre, New York, and Théâtre du Vaudeville, Paris: *Sumurun**; various European cities: *Everyman**; *The Miracle**; Vigszinhaz and Austellungs Halle, Munich: various recent works

1913   Kammerspiele: *Fiorenza*; *Beautiful Women**; *Citizen Schippel*; *The Conquest of Berg-op-Zoom*; *The League of the Weak*; *His Imperial Highness*; *Francisca*; *The Green Coat**; *The Prodigal Son*; *Emilia Galotti*; *Androcles and the Lion*; *The Storm*; *La Parisienne,* and several revivals; Deutsches: *Astrid*; *The Living Corpse*; *Torquato Tasso*; *A Midsummer Night's Dream,* and various revivals (especially of Shakespeare); Centenary Hall, Breslau: *The Centenary Festival 1813*; *The Miracle** continues to appear in various cities; *Sumurun* returns to Paris; other revivals seen in Dresden, Prague, Budapest

1914   Kammerspiele: *The Snob**; *In the Grip of Life*; *The Yellow Jacket*; *The Pelican**; *Freedom*; *The Stone of Wisdom*; *The German Provincials**; Deutsches: *The Prince of Homburg*; *Queue and Sword*; *1914*; *Wallenstein's Camp*; *The Piccolomini*; *The Death of Wallenstein*; *Genevieve,* and various revivals (especially Shakespeare); *The Miracle* continues to appear in various cities; recent works shown in Hamburg, Frankfurt-am-Main, Vienna, Bremen, Budapest, etc.

1915   assumes directorship of Berlin's Volksbühne; Deutsches: *Raimund*; *Schluck and Jau*; *The Fair at Plundersweiler*; *Colleague Crampton*; *The Egg of Nuremburg*; *Maria Stuart**; *The Star of Bethlehem*; Kammerspiele: *The Charm-*

ing Fellow; *The Demon in Woman*; *The Father*; *The Love Potion*; Volksbühne: *The Tempest*; *Traumulus,* and various revivals; Royal Opera, Stockholm: *Macbeth*; *The Beaver Coat**, and various revivals, including *A Midsummer Night's Dream*; several revivals, Christiana, Norway

1916   Deutsches: *The Bores*; *Rose Bernd**; *Soldiers*; *The Suffering Woman*; *Danton's Death**; *The Marriage of Figaro,* and various recent works; Kammerspiele: *The Imaginary Invalid**; *The Shepherdesses*; *The Rapid Painter*; *The New York Idea*; *The Ghost Sonata**; *Poverty and Love,* and one revival; Volksbühne: *Drayman Henschel**; *The People of Mottenburg*; *Master Olof*; *The Rats,* and various revivals; Grosses Schauspielhaus, Berlin, various revivals, as well as at Rotterdam, the Hague, Amsterdam, and Budapest

1917   Swiss and Swedish tour, as well as Bucharest: various revivals and recent works, including *A Midsummer Night's Dream*; Kammerspiele: *The Concert*; *Carnival*; *Madam d'Ora*; *The Children of Joy*; *A Doll's House*; Volksbühne: *Woe to the Liar*; *The Gnawing Conscience*; *A People in Trouble*; *Elga*; *The Mob*; *The Deer*; *Blood Sacrifice,* and one revival; Deutsches: *John Gabriel Borkman*; *Tobias Buntschuh*; *The Miser*; *Winter Ballad*; *The Beggar,* and various revivals

1918   Kammerspiele: *The Coral; The Black Glove; A Sea Battle; The Son*; *The Visitor from Elysium*; *Cain*; *The First One*; *One Family*; Volksbühne: *Hermann's Battle*; *Hannele*; *The Right One,* and one revival; Deutsches: *The Power of Darkness* and three revivals; takes over Berlin's Kleines Schauspielhaus; Kleines Schauspielhaus: *Clavigo*; *Labor*; *Phaedra*; *Pandora's Box,* and one other revival; purchases Schloss Leopoldskron, Salzburg

1919   Kammerspiele: *The Fall of the Apostle Paul*; *The Farce of Life*; *On the Way*; *The Star*; *The Children's Friend*; *Ivanov*; *Advent*; Deutsches: *From Morn to Midnight*; *As You Like It*; *Henry of Aue*; *The Wuppers*; *Job*; *The Burning Briar*; *Cymbeline*; *Jacob's Dream*; *And Pippa Dances*; Grosses Schauspielhaus: *Oresteia**

1920   Kammerspiele: *Semael's Mission*; *The Monster*; *Gabriel Schilling's Flight*; *Stella**; *After the Fire*; *The First Distiller**; *The Gamblers*; Grosses Schauspielhaus: *Judith and Holofernes*; *Danton*; *Helios*; *Antigone*; *Julius Caesar*; *Europa,* and two revivals; Deutsches: *The Fairy Lady**; *Heaven and Hell*; *Lonely Lives*; *Urfaust**; *Chauffeur Martin*; Dagmar Theatre, Copenhagen: *The Big Scene** and various recent works and revivals; various recent works and revivals at Goteborg, Christiana, Stockholm, Aarhus; Salzburg Festival founded with showing of *Everyman* on steps of Salzburg Cathedral (shown annually through 1938 and resumed after World War II)

1921   Grosses Schauspielhaus: *Florian Geyer*; *Florindo*; *The Hobby*; *Gotz von Berlichingen,* and various recent works and revivals, including *A Midsummer Night's Dream*; Kammerspiele: *The Adventurer and the Singer*; *Beyond*; *The King of the Dark Chamber*; *Powers*; *Misalliance*; Deutsches: *The Maid of Orleans*; *Woyzeck,* and one recent work and one revival; a revival, Copenhagen; Dramatiska Teater, Stockholm: *A Dream Play**

1922   Grosses Schauspielhaus: *The Sunken Bell*; *The Machine Wreckers*; Kolle-
        gienkirche, Salzburg: *Beautiful Women; The Great World Theatre of Salzburg*;
        Redoutensaal, Vienna: *Clavigo*; *Beautiful Women*; *The Failures,* and several
        recent works

1923   Schloss Leopoldskron and Stadttheater, Salzburg: *The Imaginary Invalid*

1924   Century Theatre, New York: *The Miracle*; USA tour: *The Miracle*; acquires
        Theater in der Josefstadt, Vienna; Theater in der Josefstadt: *The Servant of
        Two Masters*; *The Difficult Man* and various recent works; acquires Komödie
        Theater, Berlin; Komödie Theater: *Servant of Two Masters*; *Six Characters
        in Search of an Author,* and a recent work; resumes directorship of Deutsches;
        Deutsches: *St. Joan*

1925   Theater in der Josefstadt: *Loyalties**; *Juarez and Maximilian*; *Riviera**, and
        a pair of revivals, including *A Midsummer Night's Dream*; a recent work
        apiece at Kammerspiele, Vienna, Komödie, and Kammerspiele, Berlin; Salz-
        burg Festspielhaus: *The Salzburg Great Theatre of the World**; *The Play of
        the Apostles**; *The Miracle*; Deutsches: *The Chalk Circle*; Theater am Kur-
        furstendamm, Berlin: *Rain*

1926   Deutsches: *The Ragged Edge** and a recent work; Komödie: *Victoria**; Neues
        Deutsches Theater, Prague: *Broadway*; Magyar Szinhaz, Budapest: *Natalie*
        and a recent work; recent work in three Swiss cities and Salzburg; Theater in
        der Josefstadt: *The Prisoners**; *Dorothea Angermann,* and a recent work; San
        Francisco: *The Miracle*; *Everyman*

1927   Los Angeles: *Everyman*; *The Miracle*; recent work in Switzerland; Theater in
        der Josefstadt: *The Good Comrade* and a recent work; several European pro-
        ductions of *The Miracle*; Festspielhaus: *A Midsummer Night's Dream* and
        another revival; Century Theatre, New York (through 1/28): *A Midsummer
        Night's Dream*; *Everyman*; *Danton's Death*; *The Ragged Edge*; *The Servant
        of Two Masters*; *The Cause of It All*; *Love and Intrigue*; *The Living Corpse
        (Redemption)*

1928   Vigszinhaz: *Desirée*; *Robert and Marianne**; Deutsches: *Artists*; Festspiel-
        haus: *The Perchten Play*; *Iphegenia in Tauris**, and a revival; takes over the
        Berliner Theater; Berliner: *Romeo and Juliet*; Theater in der Josefstadt: a
        revival; Schauspielhaus, Zurich: *It's in the Air*; Basel and Zurich, two recent
        works; founds Max Reinhardt seminar, Vienna

1929   Deutsches: *Die Fledermaus**; *The Apple Cart**, and a recent work; a recent
        work apiece in Vienna, Munich, and at Komödie

1930   Theater in der Josefstadt, Theatre Royal, Copenhagen, and Kammerspiele: a
        recent work apiece; Deutsches: *Phaea*; *Elizabeth of England,* and several
        recent works, including *A Midsummer Night's Dream*; Komödie: *The Creature*
        and a pair of recent works; Festspielhaus: several recent works

1931   Theater am Kurfurstendamm: *The Weaker Sex**; Deutsches: *The Captain from
        Copenick*; Stockholm, several Swiss cities, Budapest, Riga, Salzburg, Co-
        penhagen, Vienna, Manchester (England): recent works and revivals; Grosses
        Schauspielhaus: *Tales of Hoffman*

1932   Deutsches: *Before Sunset* and several recent works and revivals; London, Riga, Zurich, Vienna, Salzburg: recent works and revivals; Theater in der Josefstadt: *Mademoiselle*

1933   final work at Deutsches: *The Great Theatre of the World*; Outdoor Riding School, Salzburg: *Faust I* (annually through 1938); Boboli Gardens, Florence, and Oxford, England: outdoor stagings of *A Midsummer Night's Dream*; Magyar Szinhaz, Budapest: *Farewell Supper*; *Is Geraldine an Angel?*, and a revival; Theater in der Josefstadt and Théâtre Pigalle, Paris: several revivals; Nazis compel him to give up his German theatres

1934   Dutch cities, Grosses Schauspielhaus, Milan, Rome, San Remo, Vienna, Prague, Zurich, Basel, Salzburg: various revivals; Theater in der Josefstadt: *The Human Voice*; Campo San Trovaso, Venice: outdoor staging of *The Merchant of Venice* (also 1935); U.S. West Coast and midwest: outdoor stagings of *A Midsummer Night's Dream*

1935   Fovorosi Operettszinhaz, Budapest: *The Princess up the Ladder*; Vigszinhaz: *His New Will*; film of *A Midsummer Night's Dream*; second marriage, Helene Thimig

1937   Manhattan Opera House, New York: *The Eternal Road*; Theater in der Josefstadt: *In One Night*; leaves for exile in USA

1938   opens acting school in Hollywood; Los Angeles: *Sister Beatrice*; Los Angeles and San Francisco: *Faust I*; Colonial Theatre, Boston, and Guild Theatre, New York: *The Merchant of Yonkers*

1939   Los Angeles and San Francisco: various revivals, including *A Midsummer Night's Dream*

1940   Los Angeles and San Francisco: various revivals; Los Angeles: *Fortunato*; *Faust I*; *Too Many Husbands (Victoria)*

1941   opens Max Reinhardt Theatre, Los Angeles; a revival apiece in Los Angeles and New York; Max Reinhardt: ''Shakespeare's Women, Clowns and Songs''; *Girls in Uniform*; *Squaring the Circle*

1942   Forty-fourth Street Theatre, New York: *Die Fledermaus (Rosalinda)*

1943   two additional presentations of *Die Fledermaus*, New York; Morosco Theatre, New York: *Sons and Soldiers*; suffers stroke on Fire Island, New York, and dies

Jacques Copeau

(1879–1949)

Jacques Copeau's appearance on the theatrical scene as a director in the Paris of 1913 could not have been more propitious. A stultifying respect for tradition hampered the Comédie Française from providing the theatre with creative leadership, while the commercial theatres of the Boulevard were mired in the shallow theatrics of a debilitating star system. In this latter arena the playwright's work was little more than a vehicle for the actor's vanity. Commerce crowed loudly from the stages while art had trouble getting past the ticket taker. André Antoine, who had astonished the theatre world in the 1880s with his naturalistic presentations at the Théâtre Libre, was now passé, and few were those who sought to raise again the banner of art in the cause of theatrical production.

New ideas, however, originating in England, Germany, Russia, and Switzerland, were in the air, and one French theatre artist, Jacques Rouché, tried, though unsuccessfully, to make them work for Paris audiences at his Théâtre des Arts, founded in 1906. In a way, Rouché was continuing in the path of Paul Fort and Aurélien-Marie Lugné-Poë, whose symbolist productions of the 1890s first revealed to France the possibilities of antinaturalist theatre art. Despite his own uninspired theatre work, Rouché provided a source of great stimulation to Copeau through his book on the new ideas, *L'Art Théâtral Moderne*.

In 1913, finding the situation stifling, Jacques Copeau, already a respected critic and playwright, created his own art theatre, the Théâtre du Vieux Colombier; within a year he became the leading French exponent of the modern stage, though he had barely any previous professional theatre experience. While professing reverence for such aging masters as André Antoine, Copeau was closely in touch with the newest theatrical developments. He hungrily absorbed the dynamic concepts of Europe's leading theorists and practitioners, especially Gordon Craig, Adolphe Appia, Max Reinhardt, Georg Fuchs, Emile Jaques-Dalcroze, Harley Granville-Barker, and, somewhat later, Konstantin Stanislavsky and Vsevolod Meyerhold. As a result, his audiences soon saw France's finest acting, directing, and decor in the service of a superb repertory made up of outstanding dramas, classical and modern, French and foreign.

EARLY YEARS

Copeau, born in Paris in February 1879, came from a completely nontheatrical background, although his grandfather was an avid playgoer and claqueur at the Comédie Française. His parents were well-to-do bourgeois, his father being in charge of an iron factory. His teenage years saw him involved in a number of amateur theatricals, first as a reader and then, at fifteen, as a director when he staged Racine's *Athalie* with his sisters. He wrote his first play at seventeen and saw it produced at his high school. Playwriting seemed a possible goal during his years at the Sorbonne, though his formal studies came to an end in 1901 when his father died and he had to leave school to help out at home. About this time he traveled to Denmark to marry Agnes Thomsen, a Danish woman seven years his senior, whom, as a high school boy, he had tutored in math. Until 1903, he lived in Copenhagen, teaching French, occasionally visiting Paris, and contributing perceptive theatre critiques to French periodicals that took the bourgeois theatre to task. He then took over the management of his father's iron foundry in northeastern France and saw the business go bankrupt within two years. He turned his attention to literary and theatrical criticism, gaining an outstanding reputation, and becoming a founder of the *Nouvelle Revue Française* (1909). His angry attacks on the venality of the contemporary stage made his name familiar as one of those seeking theatre reform. He received his baptism as a director in 1911 when, at the Théâtre des Arts, he and Arsène Durec successfully codirected *The Brothers Karamazov,* a play on which Copeau had collaborated with Jean Croué. When the play was revived the following season, Copeau alone was in charge of the staging. This experience taught him that, more than a playwright, the theatre was in need of a visionary directorial artist; he resolved to found his own theatre and put his many idealistic and revolutionary ideas into action.

LE THÉÂTRE DU VIEUX COLOMBIER

Copeau rented an old, rundown, out-of-the-way playhouse, the Athénée Saint-Germain, built in 1805, and changed its name to the Théâtre du Vieux Colombier (Theatre of the Old Dove-Cot) after its location at 21 Rue du Vieux Colombier in the sixth arrondissement. Soon readers of the *Nouvelle Revue Française* were apprised of his plans via a manifesto published there under the title "An Essay of Dramatic Renovation."[1] In it, Copeau stated that his new theatre was being created in a spirit of "indignation" against the frivolity and prostitution of present-day theatre art. He wrote, "We wish to restore [the theatre] to its lustre and grandeur."[2] Several years later he informed New York audiences that his company's aims, when they settled at the Garrick Theatre for a two-year residency, were

modesty, sincerity in arduous research, continuous novelty, absolute refusal of compromise towards commercialism or *cabotinage*; fighting in the name of true tradition against the academic, against aesthetic virtuosity, and every affectation of the mind, and this in the name of sensibility, culture, and taste.[3]

From the start, Copeau was aware that clever economies would have to be practiced for his repertory to proceed. His economies extended not only to his methods of organizing and engaging a company, but to the cunning arrangements by which sets and costumes could so be deployed as to serve a wide variety of plays with a minimum of waste. Yet his goal was also to produce theatre that everyone could afford by providing a subscription plan so significantly reducing ticket prices that the Vieux Colombier would be "the cheapest theatre in Paris."[4] Copeau continually shied away from accepting government subsidies because he believed they would somehow mar the independence of his work. Only toward the end of his theatre's existence did he agree to receive the backing required to keep the place open for a temporary period. He had always wanted to prove that, with excellent staging, he could make the theatre pay its own way, despite its unusual repertory.

Nevertheless, Copeau's artistic ideals were constantly in danger of being sabotaged by economic necessity. He chose to perform in a small, intimate theatre seating only 500 (later reduced to 360), though presenting a repertory program that would not bow to the long-run practices of the Boulevard.

In his manifesto, Copeau stated that the new theatre's repertory would be classically oriented. The great old plays were to be held up to view as object lessons for new playwrights, actors, and directors. He emphasized, however, that these works would never be performed in faddish versions.

THE FIRST SEASONS

An enormous response greeted Copeau's initial call for subscriptions. All Paris looked forward with excitement to the new theatre's revolutionary program. After a summer of preparations in the open air of the countryside at Limon, the Vieux Colombier company opened on October 22, 1913, with Thomas Heywood's Elizabethan drama, *A Woman Killed with Kindness,* followed by Molière's *Love's the Best Doctor (L'Amour Médecin)*, both minor masterpieces rarely produced. Other plays of the extremely successful first season were by Alfred de Musset, Georges Courteline, Henri Ghéon, Paul Claudel, and Shakespeare. Molière was represented by three plays, although the biggest hit of the season was Copeau's own *Brothers Karamazov.* These plays were staged in hopes of developing a new theatre audience which would appreciate such works and not attend only revivals of more standard fare. In the new troupe were young actors eventually recognized as leaders of the French stage, among them Louis Jouvet, Charles Dullin, and Suzanne Bing, who became Copeau's mistress and bore him an illegitimate child.

Flushed with success, the Vieux Colombier company toured England by the invitation of the French Institute of London in the spring of 1914. They performed Musset's *Barberine,* Jules Renard's *Household Bread (Le Pain de Ménage)* and Molière's *The Jealousy of Barbouillé (La Jalousie du Barbouillé).* Warm responses were generally their reward. They were especially liked for their ensemble spirit and the excellence of their diction. When they returned to Paris, they scored heavily with *Twelfth Night,* a production which established them as one of Paris' strongest groups. *Twelfth Night* had never been produced successfully in France, and Copeau's staging came as a revelation to most.[5]

Audiences now had to struggle to get a seat at the Vieux Colombier, and the number of subscriptions mounted dramatically for the 1914–15 season. The new program was being mapped out as the company toured to Alsace in June 1914. But soon the guns of August shattered all of Copeau's immediate dreams. With the outbreak of war and the consequent mobilization of all suitable men, the company was forced to break up. Actors such as Jouvet and Dullin were sent into combat and other war-related activities; Copeau was assigned to caring for the wounded. The playhouse was used as shelter for displaced persons and soldiers on leave.

THE WAR YEARS INTERRUPT

From 1915 to 1917 Copeau was unable to reorganize his company. Instead, he occupied himself creatively by translating *The Winter's Tale* and studying *Macbeth* for a future production. He also had to take time out to recuperate from tuberculosis in 1915. Correspondence with his scattered actors was maintained; in it he continued to develop his ideas for the Vieux Colombier of the future. His plans for training actors at a new school also flourished during this directorial hiatus. In 1915, as part of his planning, he visited Gordon Craig in Florence, where the latter ran a theatre school (recently closed because of the war), and stayed over a month, becoming intimately acquainted with the controversial Englishman's ideas on actor training (which were minimal) and stage and lighting design. On his return trip to Paris Copeau stopped in Geneva and visited with Emile Jaques-Dalcroze, through whom he met Adolphe Appia, with whose ideas on lighting and design Copeau had already familiarized himself. Appia's thinking on the primacy of the actor in the mise-en-scène, of the rhythmic foundation of stage activity, and of the crucial role played by light seriously tempered Copeau's views on theatre art. From Dalcroze, himself a powerful influence on Appia, Copeau imbibed important ideas concerning this composer's development of "eurythmics," a method of stimulating creative rhythmic movement. Eurythmics was to become a significant factor in the training program Copeau would institute in association with his theatre.

Copeau's new school began with twelve teenage students and was run by him and Suzanne Bing. He desired a faithful source from which to replenish his regular company, a group of artists trained in a unified way with a distinctively personal group style and sufficiently polished to gain the respect and admiration of audiences. Training activities took up much of his time from 1915 to 1917.

In 1931 Copeau looked back at the disruptions caused in his work by the war and asserted that despite the company's later successes, invisible cracks had already begun to appear in the substructure, cracks which would eventually widen into irreparable fissures and bring the enterprise crumbling to the ground. He had sought to lead the theatre on a course of slow and natural development which would culminate in a successful operation, in both economic and technical spheres. The first season had taught him many lessons, he asserted, for the truth of what the stage and acting are had been revealed to him. He comprehended how the playwright, confronted by and imbued with the conventions of the stage, is inspired by them, striving to be in harmony with them in order to best employ the means at his disposal. He learned, too, that the actor had to be trained to think deeply, the playwright to write with the principles of the stage in mind, and the play to conform to the principles of theatrical architecture in order for theatre art to achieve the sense of unity he dreamed of for it. He knew now that ''it is from these areas that . . . the call for an essential renovation of the dramatic form had to begin.''[6]

THE NEW YORK SEASONS

In 1917 Georges Clemenceau, French minister of fine arts, requested that Copeau go to New York with his company as part of a plan to woo the United States as an ally in the war. When the minister of war refused to free mobilized actors for this mission, Copeau went alone as a sort of cultural ambassador, lecturing in many cities on aspects of modern French culture as well as on his own theatrical ideas. Supported by the financing of the American Otto Kahn, he was able to bring his company over in the fall. Turning down more commercially viable theatres, Copeau chose the less convenient Garrick Theatre on West Thirty-fifth Street between Fifth and Sixth Avenues, renaming it the Vieux Colombier of New York. Once again, theatrical production occupied Copeau's talents. At first the company did without Dullin, whose demobilization was blocked. Most of the others were reassembled and were bolstered by a group of fourteen newcomers.

They opened late in November 1917 with a version of Molière's *The Impromptu of Versailles* that they called *The Impromptu at the Vieux Colombier (L'Impromptu du Vieux Colombier)*, a curtain-raiser outlining the company's goals and introducing the company's actors. Then followed Molière's *The Tricks of Scapin (Les Fourberies de Scapin),* with Copeau in the title role.

Strong critical and public response to the acting, decor, and direction was followed by many problems. *Twelfth Night* and *The Brothers Karamazov* were hits, and another success arrived when Dullin finally joined them in March 1919 as the lead in Molière's *The Miser (L'Avare)*. But other pieces in the repertory fared less well, and public pressures on Copeau insisted that he revise the repertory to stage more commercially acceptable plays.

During the between-season period from April to October 1918, the company rehearsed twenty-three new plays and five familiar ones, including many by playwrights previously condemned by Copeau during his active years as a critic. It was a humiliating experience for this apostle of the new theatre to have to direct dramas, especially those in the "well-made" tradition, for which he had not the slightest respect. He opened the 1918–19 season with Henry Bernstein's *The Secret (Le Secret)* and soon presented works by other popular dramatists, including Erckmann-Chatrian, Edmond Rostand, Alfred Capus, Maurice Donnay, Eugène Brieux, Émile Augier, and Paul Hervieu. Ironically, his greatest new success was Molière's *The Misanthrope (Le Misanthrope)*.

The new repertory failed to turn the tide. Audiences dwindled and critical attention, though largely favorable, tended to look elsewhere to attract viewers. Even the new idea of abandoning rotating repertory for a program of one-week runs, with play following play, failed to save the situation. Making things even worse was a breakdown in the company's ensemble spirit, a problem exacerbated by the conditions of their life in New York; Copeau tried to resolve it by several unsuccessful measures, including ensconcing them during the 1918 summer at Kahn's Morristown, New Jersey, home in hopes of simulating the Limon summer of 1913.

Copeau later renounced the experience.

It was a senseless project. Think about it: in the middle of war, to transplant, without any previous acclimatization, into the milieu most unfavorable to its growth, and even to its cohesion—not a tried organization, but a dream hardly hatched, whose value is completely spiritual—to set up shop in New York. . . . a regular French theatre, which will play every evening, without a star, without material luxuries, without bluff, without any other recommendation except its quality! . . . There was enough there to crush us in the egg.[7]

The company had survived this incredible experience at the risk of their mental and physical health. Close to fifty plays had been produced in the two seasons. "The first season moved along at a tolerable pace. The second was inhuman. Twenty-five productions in twenty-five weeks. Two rehearsals a day. Two matinees a week. A premiere every Monday."[8]

The failure in New York had given Copeau his first true taste of what exploitation feels like to the serious artist. It was like a cancer to him, a tumor which eventually grew to such proportions in his postwar productions that he closed his theatre to find solace from its pain.

THE NEW VIEUX COLOMBIER

Copeau's company returned to Paris where, in 1919, he and Jouvet redesigned their playhouse in the classic form now so well known. Though he would have liked to begin from new beginnings, leaving practical production work in order to devote himself with a band of acolytes to working out a new theatre approach unpressured by the public, Copeau succumbed, he says, to "insane ambition!" How much better it would have been, he felt, "to shelter vital experience from a premature exploitation." As he later pointed out:

So, I had the same experience in Paris as I had in New York, more spectacular, but not much more fertile. I undertook it, with less strength than before, on soil that my dream had long since left. I sustained it for five years, without real hope.[9]

The Winter's Tale was the first production of the revived company; it opened in February 1920 using a strikingly simple and austere setting. Then came *The Coach of the Holy Sacrament (Le Carrosse du Saint Sacrement)* by Prosper Mérimée, *The Steamship Tenacity (Le Paquebot Tenacité)* by Charles Vildrac, Georges Duhamel's *Work of the Athletes (L'Oeuvre des Athlètes), The Tricks of Scapin,* Jules Romains' *Old Cromedeyre (Cromedeyre-le-Vieil),* and a program of three one-acts by Francis Vielé-Griffin, Émile Mazaud, and Jean de la Fontaine and Charles Champmeslé. Settings were consistently simple and pared-down; some sharply critical cavils were leveled at these new methods. On the whole, the season leaned more heavily on new works than classics.

The 1920–21 season saw such new presentations as Molière's *The Doctor in Spite of Himself (Le Médecin Malgré Lui),* Henri Ghéon's *The Poor beneath the Stairs (Le Pauvre sous L'Escalier),* Jean Schlumberger's *The Death of Sparta (La Morte de Sparte),* a single performance of Anton Chekhov's *Uncle Vanya,* and François Porché's *The Dauphin (Le Dauphin)*; the rest of the season was taken up with revivals of earlier shows. During this season the Ecole du Vieux Colombier resumed operations under Jules Romains' guidance.

The double bill of Anatole France's *Come What May (Au Petit Bonheur)* and Louis Fallens' *The Fraud (La Fraude),* presented as the opening program of the 1921–22 season, was a serious failure, the theatre's greatest. Several other productions, however, especially popular revivals, kept the Vieux Colombier filled most of the time. Among other new plays were René Benjamin's *The Joys of Chance (Les Plaisirs du Hazard)* and André Gide's *Saul.*

During the next season, 1922–23, a second company was formed to tour the provinces and to occasionally alternate with the regular troupe in Paris. A largely classical repertory was shown on the Vieux Colombier stage, with fifteen classics dominating the twenty-five productions. Opening the season was Pierre Caron de Beaumarchais' *The Marriage of Figaro (Le Mariage de Figaro).* Among the premieres of the season were Vildrac's *Michel Auclair* and Émile Mazaud's *Dardamelle* (both relative failures). Léon Regis and François de Veynes's comedy, *Bastos the Bold (Bastos le Hardi)*, however, a play written expressly for the Vieux Colombier stage and actors, was a success. Unfortunately, it remained the only new play fostered by Copeau's theatre.

THE COMPANY NEARS ITS END

The acting company had been weakened seriously when Charles Dullin left it during the period in New York. Now Copeau and Jouvet, quarreling constantly over management of the theatre and the repertory system, were forced to part company, the latter leaving to become, like Dullin, one of the greatest forces in contemporary French theatricals. Copeau refused to allow commercial considerations to dictate artistic policy, despite the urging of Jouvet and many others. Still, he never was content artistically, feeling that his activities in the theatre were all the outgrowth of forces over which he had no control.

Copeau wanted time to create the art he envisioned, and the practical realities of running a theatre afforded him none of the leisure to which he aspired. The grind of constant production was beginning to tell on his sensitive nature, for he felt completely drained and worn-out by the inexorable demands of staging play after play. He said in his "Remembrances of the Vieux Colombier":

For five years, I consumed my strength in the discontent of feeling in me goals that I had not the time nor the means to accomplish, that I was not even able to express clearly because, in our art, nothing valid is expressed except by its implementation and its completion.[10]

Copeau's final Vieux Colombier season was 1923–24, which began successfully with Pierre Bost's comic *The Imbecile (L'Imbécile)* and Carlo Goldoni's *La Locandiera*. Revivals and a new one-act by Benjamin were followed by a disappointing production of Copeau's own *The Birthplace (La Maison Natale),* then another new work by Benjamin, *Everyone Must Know His Place (Il Faut que Chacun Soit à sa Place)*, and more revivals.

COPEAU'S REASONS FOR RESIGNING

The great French director felt his spirit spoiled by the exploitative mechanisms of the practical theatre. He had, in only a few years, made the Vieux Colombier renowned throughout the world, yet this acclaim meant nothing to him. He would have been happier to work totally isolated in a cellar, perfecting his artistic visions, creating polished theatre gems that he would never have to leave his "hole" to see. Contentment with what he had conceived would have been sufficient.

Although he recognized the popular, nonelitist nature of theatre art, Copeau felt his existence would have been justified more firmly if he had been allowed to pursue his research and experimentation free from the problems of the marketplace. He insisted he could have saved his theatre from financial debacle, as money to support it would have been easy enough to obtain.[11] But what would he really have gained? Without the leisure to learn from the theatre's everyday experience with its audiences, Copeau could not derive meaning from his work. Only in the laboratory conditions of a school with eager young pupils could he truly explore the theatre's fundamental problems and work toward their solution.[12] It was primarily these factors in 1924 that led him to close the Vieux Colombier and set off for the countryside with a devoted group of students to establish a community of theatre artists who would work in harmony to create an organic theatre concept.

One other major event sharply influenced him; the autobiographical play he had been working on since 1901, *The Birthplace,* was very poorly received when it opened in December 1923. Douglas Paterson suggests also that poor health was taking its toll on Copeau and that his sense of history told him to quit while he was in the flush of victory.[13] Religious crises were also burdening Copeau, who, under the guidance of playwright Paul Claudel, converted to Roman Catholicism not long after the closing of the Vieux Colombier. Whatever his reasons, Copeau's decision was not well received by his colleagues, who felt that he was allowing his personal preoccupations to bring to an end a theatre which had been established as one of the finest of its time.

ACTOR TRAINING

Education of the actor, a principal feature of Copeau's career, ultimately overshadowed his work as a director, which it never did for Stanislavsky or Meyerhold, who also found it a necessary component of their work, and to whom Copeau pointed in explaining his own inclinations. Voice, movement, culture, music, animal mimicry, improvisation, language, and oral reading were among the subjects studied by his students in Paris, with the general public invited to participate in certain selected classes.

The actors in the company did not participate in the school, because Copeau felt their professional habits would taint the freshness of the young students, but he found that he could use the school as a laboratory for working out various problems that arose in the process of working with the veteran players. It was, in fact, partly because of his growing frustration with the professional actors' methods that the next significant phase of his career was born.

MOVE TO THE COUNTRY

In September 1924, Copeau, his family, several actors, and a large complement of students moved to the Château de Morteuil, a large, shabby, electricity-less farmhouse in the Burgundy countryside, not far from the towns of Beaune and Chagny, Sâone-et-Loire. Among the company were his nephew Michel Saint-Denis, Léon Chancerel, four actors from the Vieux Colombier, including Suzanne Bing, and student actors Marie-Hélène Copeau (Copeau's daughter, who would become a well-known theatre artist), Jean Dasté (who married Copeau's daughter and became an important actor-director), and Étienne Decroux (eventually a leader in the art of French mime). Many of the artists were accompanied by their families. Copeau sought to weld this large group of disparate personalities into a cohesive community of dedicated artists, living, working, and studying together in harmony, and behaving according to strict moral standards and discipline in the belief that their theatre work would thus be greatly strengthened. Amid debilitating fall weather conditions which made life at the chateau uncomfortable and unhealthy, the group worked on two one-acters written by Copeau, *The Tax (L'Impôt,* an adaptation of a work by Pierre L'Estoile) and *The Object (L'Objet,* written on the basis of company improvisations, and making extensive use of masks), hoping that the income from the planned performances of these would offset their precarious financial situation. As Copeau noted, "To feed them all, it was going to be necessary to tie myself to a new exploitation, without money and without a repertory."[14] Luck was not with them, for the February performances in Lille were a major disappointment, and the troupe had to be disbanded after only five months.

A courageous core of actors remained faithful to the director; among them were Bing, Chancerel (soon to be replaced by Copeau's son, Pascal), Saint-Denis, and three others—six in all. The local people dubbed the hardy band "les Copiaus." They offered their first program in May 1925, a miscellaneous assortment of short musical and comic pieces highlighted by Copeau's new one-acter, *The Widower (Le Veuf).* Introducing the program was a prologue spoken by Jean Bourguignon (John Burgundy), a character based on the local peasantry who would soon become identified with the Copiaus. The piece flopped, but a new Copeau work, a one-act version of Goldoni's *La Locandiera* called *Mirandolina,* replaced it with success, and was followed in late summer by Copeau's new *Harlequin the Magician (Arlequin Magicien)* and Molière's *The Doctor in Spite of Himself.* Saint-Denis' *The Vacation (Les Vacances)* was added to the repertory a week later. In October came Copeau's *The Blackcurrants (Les Cassis),* a festive work celebrating agriculture that owed more to mime and music than to conventional dramaturgy; it was accompanied by Molière's *The School for Husbands (L'École des Maris).* Another harvest-oriented work followed in November, *The Festival of the Vine and the Vinegrowers (Fête de la Vigne et des Vignerons).* The company was becoming an exceedingly popular attraction among the local populace, who visited it when it played at local fairgrounds and similar public gatherings.

Late in 1925 the Copiaus took up occupancy at the nearby village of Pernand-Verglesses, Côte d'Or. Here the company resumed training according to Copeau's methods, working on mask, mime, and gymnastic skills, and focusing more than ever on the primacy of physical action in performance.

Copeau's tastes had turned more and more to farce and commedia-inspired techniques and away from the literary drama. He was increasingly drawn to the use of a simple rectangular platform stage (*tréteaux*) with stairs attached on each side; this was similar to the unadorned platform he had first set up on the stage of the Garrick for his opening-night presentation of *The Tricks of Scapin* in New York in 1917. The Copiaus' productions would generally begin with the company setting up this trestle stage in front of the audiences as a kind of preparatory ceremony.

In 1926 the Copiaus offered two new works, the more important being *The Illusion (L'Illusion)*, adapted by Copeau from works by Pierre Corneille and Fernando de Rojas. Copeau's final work for the group was *The Woman of Ancona (L'Anconitaine)* in 1927, based on a sixteenth-century play by Ruzzante. Before its dissolution in 1929, the group added two more commedia-inspired works to its repertory, one each in 1928 and 1929, but Copeau, who had gradually grown estranged from his company, was not formally connected with either.

OTHER OPPORTUNITIES

Copeau went to New York in 1928 to direct a Theatre Guild production of *The Brothers Karamazov* starring Edward G. Robinson, Alfred Lunt, Lynn Fontanne, Morris Carnovsky, and Dudley Digges. Working with this mixed group from various backgrounds, he concentrated on their tempos. He attempted ''to get the speech and action speeded up to something like the French pitch; to substitute the quick rush of melodrama for the solemn pace and slow of a solemn tragic muse.''[15] The Americans found him to be a man of great ''energy and persistence'' yet always amiable and patient.

Although the possibility of his heading the troubled Comédie Française was suggested to Copeau in 1929, no real offer was made. Because he wanted to drastically reform the old theatre's bureaucratic structure, he was passed over when the playhouse management decided that he would seriously damage the Comédie's traditions.

Michel Saint-Denis took over the directorial leadership of Copeau's remaining disciples in 1929 and earned enduring fame for this new group, the Compagnie des Quinze, which stayed together until 1934.

FINAL YEARS

Copeau's final years as a director were not prolific, but did lead to several unusual productions, especially in the realm of outdoor religious extravaganzas. The first of these was the fifteenth-century pageant, *The Mystery of Saint Uliva (Sainte Uliva)*, staged with a cast of 150 at the Santa Croce monastery in Florence in 1933. Such productions satisfied an early urge on Copeau's part to produce popular theatre for the masses. His outdoor festival productions of farces in Burgundy had been excellent preparation for these new endeavors. *Saint Uliva* employed a variety of acting areas and a great deal of music, in particular choruses that went from simple spoken passages to fully composed songs. Scenic means (designed by André Barsacq) were highly simplified, so that a setting could be swiftly conjured up, as in Shakespearean stagings, by the appearance of a king accompanied by a pair of standard-bearers. The audience was disposed about three sides of the large, rectangular, outdoor playing site, the marble architecture of which provided a perfect medieval environment. In the midst of this setting Barsacq placed a symmetrical pattern of bridgeways and platforms, with key scenes set on the central platform, and secondary ones on the surrounding areas.

Copeau continued his quest for a theatrical form that would encourage religious communion when he presented Rino Alessi's *Savonarola* in 1935 in Florence's Piazza della Signoria, the actual site of Savonarola's execution at the stake in 1498. Barsacq again contributed the design. Four thousand spectators viewed a gorgeous spectacle employing over one thousand performers (including a speaking chorus, singing chorus, and orchestra) dispersed over a variety of stage areas.

Not all Copeau's outdoor spectacles of this period were of a religious nature, however, the single secular example being a 1938 presentation of Shakespeare's *As You Like It* (renamed *Rosalinda*) in Florence's Boboli Gardens, where Max Reinhardt had recently staged a lusciously sylvan version of *A Midsummer Night's Dream*. Disappointment was expressed at the fact that Copeau did not utilize the gorgeous greenery as effectively as had Reinhardt, choosing a relatively mundane corner of the gardens for his setting; this consisted of an arrangement of scenic pieces dispersed in simultaneous fashion like that of a medieval play, thereby allowing all the locales to be visible at once. He had used a similar, but far simpler, arrangement for his hit production of the same play at Paris's L'Atelier in 1934. Despite being too reminiscent of an indoor approach to the decor, the play benefitted from Copeau's special talents, and one foreign critic wrote:

His keen insight into the poetic values of the play, his sensitive artistry, his ripe theatrical experience served to form a spectacle of opulent fantasy, of almost constant lyric elan, of fluid continuity of rhythm, of direct plastic clarity. . . . The Gallic esthete excelled in fastidious groupings and movements, in happy interpretive finds, in infinite shadings of delicate half-tones . . . in short, a minute elaboration of countless decorative details, achieved with a preciosity of stylization at times bordering on affectation.[16]

During the mid-1930s Copeau honored Paris with three productions at the Comédie Française as well as a number of productions elsewhere in Paris and in Florence. The Comédie stagings were of Molière's *The Misanthrope* (1936), Racine's *Bajazet*, Mauriac's *Asmodie (Asmodée*, 1937), and Roger Martin du Gard's *The Testament of Father Leleu (Le Testament de Père Leleu*, 1938). Both the Molière and the Martin du Gard plays also had been directed by Copeau at the Vieux Colombier. After a period from late 1938 to mid-1940 during which he lived in Burgundy but abstained from directing, Copeau accepted the temporary headship of the Comédie Française. Here he revived several old successes from his Vieux Colombier days—including *The Steamship Tenacity, Twelfth*

Night, and *The Coach of the Holy Sacrament*—and supported the work of young theatre geniuses like Jean-Louis Barrault. In March 1941 Copeau resigned his post, presumably because he had no alternative after refusing a command from the German High Command—now in control of Paris—to end his son's activities as a resistance fighter. (It also has been suggested that Copeau was dismissed for the patriotic act of producing *Le Cid* on November 11, the anniversary of the World War I armistice.) Copeau's final important directorial work was of his adaptation of another medieval play, *Pierre le Changeur, Merchant,* which he transformed into *The Miracle of the Golden Bread (Le Miracle du Pain Doré).* With Barsacq again collaborating on the decor, and Copeau's daughter designing the costumes, he produced it in 1943 in the rectangular courtyard of the Hospices de Beaune, which had commissioned the work to celebrate its 500th anniversary. The architectural features of the old courtyard, including a well which was used to represent hell, and the surrounding deambulatories, in which stood the speaking chorus, singing choir, and orchestra, provided an ideal setting for this saintly work, which made effective use of medieval church music. The play brought spiritual solace not only to those who came to see it but to Copeau himself. Following its production, he retired from active theatre work and lived quietly in the country—occasionally doing battle with an atherosclerotic condition which had plagued him as early as 1924—until his death in 1949.

REPERTORY

Copeau's directing activity at the Vieux Colombier will always be the achievement for which he is best remembered, though it represents so brief a period of his career. Here he sought to produce a rotating repertory of three plays a week, a plan which led to the production of eighty-five plays in seven seasons, including the seasons spent in New York, about twelve per year, most of them staged by Copeau. In the repertory were classics, French and foreign, as well as the best modern plays he could find, including those of the past thirty years and those previously unproduced. Copeau's taste in plays was broad, and his theatre did works from the Elizabethan, medieval, neoclassic, symbolist, romantic, and realistic traditions. For a play to interest him it had to stress character over situation, the latter emanating from the former. If the situations were predominant and the characters there merely to further the action, the play was ostensibly a melodrama or a farce, forms in which he had little interest. A play had to have exciting production possibilities, though; excessive reliance on linguistic qualities weakened the theatrical impact of a drama. To Copeau, Molière and Shakespeare were the epitome of the dramatist who knows his medium because he writes for the stage and not the study. He believed the classical repertory should be based on the works of these artists, for they were unparalleled in their ability to fuse theatrical with literary and philosophical concerns.

In spite of his declarations, the new plays Copeau tended to favor were generally more literary than theatrical, a fact that David Whitton believes was responsible for the negligible number of significant plays Copeau's company added to the modern repertory. As Whitton notes, more than half of the new plays staged by Copeau were the work of novelists, most of them writers he knew from his association with the *Nouvelle Revue Française*. In fact, Copeau overlooked several major contributions from true dramatists, among them Luigi Pirandello's *Six Characters in Search of an Author*, which Georges Pitoëff had the perspicacity to stage in a memorable 1923 mounting. The most successful of the new plays offered by the Vieux Colombier were *The Steamship Tenacity, Old Cromedeyre,* and *The Testament of Father Leleu*. As Whitton observes, it was essentially Copeau's success with the classics that formed the basis of his reputation.[17]

THE IDEALIST

Because of his nearly fanatical idealism, Copeau has been called everything from a theatrical Jansenist to a Benedictine to a Calvinist. Ralph Roeder wrote in *Theatre Arts Monthly* in 1921 that "Copeau has brought into the theatre the temperament of a Luther, the ardor of the reformer, the austerity of the scholar, and the probity of the apostle."[18]

Considering himself an antielitist, Copeau wished to attract a popular audience on his own terms. Though this was not really possible given the conditions of a very small theatre playing in a rotating repertory, he continued to aim his presentations at all classes, no matter what their background, attempting to appeal on all levels, emotional and intellectual, producing theatre at the lowest possible cost to the playgoer. Stirred by the spirit of reform, he tried to change the habits of theatregoers. He therefore banned tips to ushers, begged audiences that they be punctual, showed much concern over noise in the auditorium during the performance, forbade spectators leaving while the play was in progress, and prohibited people entering once the curtain had risen.

SCENIC IDEAS

Students of theatre history are probably most familiar with Copeau's contributions to scenic art and theatre architecture. He saw the director in much the same light as did Craig, as a master artist responsible for all facets of the production; he noted in an important essay that a director should be capable of planning the arrangements of a stage, selecting appropriate furniture and props, and even devising the lighting and composing the music. If incapable of such responsibilities he should be able to guide and supervise those who do these things for him. Although Copeau was not himself equipped to actually design all elements of a play, he was capable of articulating his ideas to those who were. When he first took over the Vieux Colombier, the theatre had a conventional proscenium stage and was dressed in an ornate gilt decor. Strongly swayed by the ideas of Adolphe Appia in the direction of a clean-lined and functional stage minus a proscenium, so that stage and auditorium could be fused in a single architectural unit, Copeau had the place thoroughly refashioned. The typical proscenium theatre he found to be "a cluttered-up and mechanized theater, . . . a closed-in space in which mind and matter constantly wage war on each other."[19]

Like Appia, Copeau believed that it was not the business of stage decor to present a realistically specific locale, but to provide a scenic embodiment of the play's emotional forces in which the actor's dynamic three-dimensionality could flourish. Three-dimensional spatial forms, related to the inner rhythms of the play, must be created in order to establish an integral relationship between the play and its scenic expression. He sought an architectural stage which would be analogous to those for which the Greeks and Elizabethans wrote, one capable of infinite flexibility, with as few mechanical encrustations as possible to allow for freedom of movement by the mind. His manifesto contained this passage:

Good or bad, rudimentary or perfected, artful or realistic, we deny the importance of all *machinery*. . . . For we have the profound conviction that it is disastrous for dramatic art to become involved in a large number of extraneous complications. . . . We do not believe that in order to "represent the whole man in his life" there is need of a theatre "where the sets can rise from below and the scene changes can be instantaneous." . . . On the contrary! The use of the stage and its simplest crafts will act on us as a discipline, by forcing us to concentrate all truth in the feelings and actions of our characters. Let the other illusions disappear, and, for the new work, leave us a bare stage![20]

On this bare stage the actor was clearly the focal point; locale and atmosphere could be communicated through a minimum of means.

The stage used in the 1913–14 season was only a partial solution to the problems posed by Copeau's quest; it covered over the ornate decorations on the old proscenium arch, set an arch-shaped doorway into each black-painted proscenium wall, and placed a false proscenium several feet upstage of the original. The old boxes set along the straight side walls were hidden as well. Compared to the theatre's previous appearance, everything was greatly simplified and stripped down, but the changes were by no means as radical as those yet to come. For one thing, there was no forestage to speak of, although the abbreviated area downstage of the false proscenium suggested one.[21] There were also no permanent steps and platforms, nor was there a balcony unit.

Copeau's architectural ideas continued to evolve during the 1914–19 period, especially after his study of Craigian spatial concepts. His company having been forced to cease operations following the eruption of World War I, Copeau, as we have seen, reorganized it and played in New York from 1917 to 1919. He had the stage of the Garrick Theatre remodeled in accord with his new notions (refined through contact with Appia and Craig). Only 550 seats were used in the auditorium (typically sacrificing a potentially profitable seating capacity of 900 to the needs of his aesthetics), and the stage was a step closer to achieving a permanent architectural arrangement than his 1913 version.[22] The Garrick setting was composed of a very simple but adaptable system of interchangeable elements, including bridge and step units, that could be put together in varying arrangements with the addition of appropriate decorative elements. As in the 1913 version, a simplified proscenium was used, but a short thrust was added (necessitating the removal of several rows of seats), as were proscenium doors at either side leading on a slant to the thrust. Surrounding the basic setting upstage and at either side was a continuous wall pierced by six doorways arranged symmetrically; those at either downstage end were two low arches, those immediately upstage of them were tall, narrow arches, and those in the upstage wall itself were oblongs. Above them all across the wall were seven windows, their panes clearly marked. Since most of the scenic pieces were removable, the *dispositif fixe* was not so much in evidence here.

It was the 1919 Paris stage, designed by Copeau and the great actor-designer-director Louis Jouvet, that established the Vieux Colombier as one of the century's most important playhouses. The 1919 renovations added the permanent feature of a thrust stage, which cut 140 seats out of the house but succeeded in creating an intimate union between actors and spectators. Separating the thrust from the main stage was an act curtain, while a second curtain could be used to divide the upstage area from center stage. Upstage was a large architectural unit consisting of a central archway, a balcony area above it, and steps leading down to the main stage from either side of the balcony. An entrance to the balcony was provided in the upstage right wall, while two other entrances led onto the main stage from the stage right wall below. The thrust area was divided in two, with three steps leading to the lower segment. A system of traps was installed in the lower thrust. The proscenium had vanished. The concrete stage floor allowed only scenic units which did not require screwing down to be set on it, thus making the shifting easier. A major disadvantage was the lack of entrances from stage left. Footlights were absent, with front, overhead, and side lighting replacing them.[23]

Study of the productions staged at the Vieux Colombier reveals an extraordinary variety of designs adapted to this seemingly rigid disposition. Copeau had indeed devised a flexible stage architecture suitable to a wide range of plays. By the ingenious use of curtains, wall plugs, and masking flats, the stage became suitable for dramas from the classic to the modern. Designs were mainly in the sphere of selective realism, with locale depicted by a few carefully chosen scenic elements and props, as well as by an imaginative arrangement of spatial masses. Copeau was not always true to his ideal of simplicity in decor, though, for some of his presentations were quite elaborate in execution; occasionally, masking elements were so heavily used that the stage might easily have been taken to be more conventional in form than it was. Still, austerity was a Copeau byword and most of his work was considerably sparer than that of his contemporaries. By stressing extreme simplicity in the scenery, he displayed a series of beautifully arranged sequences stressing color and rhythm through the movements and groupings of the actors as dictated by the needs of the action. Color played a crucial role in the Copeau mise-en-scène, and the director was fortunate in having the talented Jouvet to design his sets, costumes, and lights in accord with Copeau's own aesthetic tastes. Numerous scenic changes were wrought on the permanent background, but these were never allowed to dominate the spectacle or to distract from the performers. The simpler the background, Copeau felt, the more clearly would the nuances of the performances be conveyed. A "naked stage" would permit the drama's unique theatrical personality to unfold without interference from distracting visual effects.

After discussing in detail a variety of decors for Copeau productions, Paterson reveals how effectively the background could be used.

In *Love's the Best Doctor* and to a degree in *Love's Surprise* [*La Surprise de l'Amour*] it merely serves as a background, not as a functional set of stairs, levels, and so forth. Sharply contrasted to this total visibility of the dispositif are the designs for *The Caprice* [*Un Caprice*] and *The Poor,* in which the architecture is totally concealed. *Death of Sparta*'s set uses bare stairs and platforms as essential acting areas, but uses them with stark obviousness, while remaining shows, like *Coach* [*of the Holy Sacrament*], *Saul,* and *It Is Necessary* [*Il Faut que Chacun Soit à sa Place*] integrate the architecture to varying degrees into more stylized settings. As a background, a formal unit, or a part of a stylized set, or as totally concealed, the dispositif fixe became in Copeau's hands the most versatile element in his permanent stage.[24]

THREE REPRESENTATIVE PRODUCTIONS

Paterson has also closely described three of Copeau's finest and most representative productions, Molière's *The Tricks of Scapin,* Copeau's own version of *The Brothers Karamazov,* and *Twelfth Night.*[25] For the first a practically empty stage was used, devoid of decorative accessories. A two-and-a-half-foot-high platform stage was set up on the regular stage floor.[26] Steps led down to the stage floor at the front, rear, and at either side. Between the two front step units a bench was set. Aside from a plug designed to look like grille work and set into the archway up center, the basic architectural arrangements of the stage made up the scenic background. The entire stage space was made use of by the actors who displayed a great show of commedia-style athletic energy and slapstick skill as they leapt to and from the central acting area. Actors were visible onstage until needed by the dramatic action, when they would leap onto the platform from the stage proper. With Copeau in the leading role as the physically and intellectually nimble Scapin and Jouvet as the dim-witted, lethargic Geronte, the production was a masterpiece of slapstick farce.

A far more detailed scenic background was designed for *The Brothers Karamazov,* which was one of the most naturalistic of Copeau's productions. The few theatricalist touches made a decided impact in the idiosyncratic setting designed by Copeau and Jouvet. Copeau played the role of Ivan to great acclaim, and Jouvet starred in the demanding role of old Karamazov. Striking use was made of a long, meandering stairway beginning at stage left and continuing up and across the balcony area to the stage right wall. This play which had been revived in 1914—three years after its premiere at the Théâtre des Arts—rejoined the repertory during the 1918 season in New York, was staged again in Paris in 1921, and was directed by Copeau in English translation for New York's Theatre Guild in 1928.

Copeau was a satisfying blend of the theatricalistic and the actualistic who presented each closely studied character vocally and physically in terms metaphorically expressive of the role and the world of the play. He invented a completely integrated world of eccentric character traits for the drama. The pattern of postures, nervous mannerisms, and behavioral attitudes worked harmoniously to express the inner life of the great Russian novel.

In *Twelfth Night,* first staged in 1914 and repeated in every subsequent season except those of 1919–20 and 1923–24, an utterly simple but elegantly adorned setting was used; the architectural arrangements were disguised by panels and other scenic pieces. Copeau succeeded in making Shakespeare popular in Paris, where productions of the Bard's plays usually went unappreciated. He made the then radical gesture of producing an almost uncut script and placed the emphasis not on the conventional ingredients of romantic comedy but on the hilarious farce of the subplot characters, Belch, Aguecheek, Feste, and the rest. Copeau, acting the role of Malvolio (also played by François Gournac), de-emphasized the character's serious side and showed him as a farcically nervous little man beset with tics. The play flowed unhampered from one scene to the next, as the same set was employed without changes throughout.

THE COPEAU ACTOR

Copeau's work with actors revealed the same messianic drive that led to his achievements in theatre architecture. His actors were members of a troupe, highly disciplined, with a single purpose—to provide excellent performances through dedication to the concept of true ensemble playing. Copeau saw his company as a band of artist-priests,

unselfish enthusiasts, whose ambition is to serve the art to which they dedicate themselves. To free the actor from quackery—to create around him an atmosphere more suited to his development as a man and as an artist; to cultivate him, to inspire conscience in him, to initiate him into the morality of his art; it is to that we stubbornly bend our efforts.[27]

He wished to take away from the actor the degrading quality he called *cabotinage,* the vulgarization of the theatre through the actor's pandering to the vainest elements of his profession. Immorality of personal behavior, gossipmongering, shallowness of character, and artificiality were deplored as inhuman traits. (It is interesting to note how contrary was Meyerhold's feeling toward the *cabotin.*) To Copeau the actor's profession was a noble calling which had been demeaned; he wished to restore the actor's sense of dignity and moral rectitude.

In order to create this new artistic mentality, Copeau was convinced the actor needed to be removed as often as possible from the decadent city atmosphere and placed in a natural, healthful environment. Accordingly, he selected nine actors for his first company through public auditions and, as noted earlier, took them away to his country home at Limon to prepare all summer for their opening in the fall of 1913. Aware that a close-knit ensemble had to be developed out of a group of strangers, mostly inexperienced, he devised a rigorous training schedule.

Daily rehearsals of the repertory took five hours, with constant alternation of the pieces being worked on to keep the actors interested. Two hours a day were given to sight-reading practice and close study of selected plays with Copeau providing unusually precise explanations of the texts. After dinner came an hour of exercise, sports, and *commedia dell'arte* improvisations. In addition, the ideas of leading theatre figures of the day were studied and discussed. Following their return to Paris at the beginning of September, they devoted another month and a half to training and rehearsal with costumes and sets.

As mentioned, the star system was despised by Copeau, who placed his trust in the ensemble approach. He aimed to serve the play faithfully and strove to eliminate anything which detracted from the author's purpose. His principles stressed full respect for the text, "in its truth, in its exact style, and through the action, the staging and the play of the actors, to release the spirit of the poet from the text of the play."[28] Only a rigorously drilled ensemble, working in total harmony, could satisfy this goal. He trained his actors to develop great pliability and range, to simplify their effects, to trim away all excesses and mannerisms, and to be completely honest.

Copeau considered the actor to be the most important figure in the theatre. After him came the playwright and then the director. He himself became an actor at the same time as he began directing, making his professional debut at the age of thirty-five. His talents as a performer were highly praised, especially in the title role of *The Tricks of Scapin*. His entire approach to theatre was actor-centered, for to Copeau the actor bore the theatre's theatricality within him.

PRODUCTION STYLE

He created an uncluttered performance style, pure, cerebral, dancelike, rhythmical, and poetic, eliminating excessive business and byplay, and filling the stage with expressive moments, even when little of an overtly physical nature was occurring. Self-exploitative acting was strictly forbidden as it smacked of the sideshow acting for which Copeau felt great contempt. His actors had to be in total control of their movements and vocal techniques. The *commedia dell'arte* style attracted his attention, and he used commedia methods extensively, especially improvisation, in his actor training. His ideal actor combined the skills of a dancer, a speaker, a singer, an acrobat, and an improviser.

Kenneth Macgowan and Robert Edmond Jones characterized the Copeau style as "presentational," a style fostered by the theatre's permanent architectural arrangements. "The illusion of Realism and representation is extremely difficult to attain." Though the actors occasionally went to great lengths in creating physical characterizations through makeup and costume, "in the main, [they] keep their own appearance throughout." Like the great personality stars (Bernhardt, Grasso, Booth, Salvini, etc.), they strove for "impersonation in emotion rather than in physique." Mood and attitude were their main methods of differentiating one role from another. A typical performance at the Vieux Colombier was

something intellectually settled upon as an expression of an emotion, and then conveyed to the audience almost as if read and explained. In the school of Copeau, who was once journalist and critic, there is ever something of the expounder. It is a reading, an explanation, in their terms of a theatrical performance. It is, to a degree, presentational, because in every reading, in every explanation, there must be an awareness of the existence of the audience.[29]

COMMEDIA DELL'ARTE

Commedia dell'arte, its character types, its masks, and improvisational style played an increasingly more important role in Copeau's training and productions, both at the Vieux Colombier and afterwards. Albert Katz states that Copeau was particularly fond of improvisation as a way of achieving "the inner resource of characterization which did not rely merely upon the words of the text, and the kind of selfless interdependent acting which resulted in a smooth, integrated ensemble."[30] Copeau was gifted with a comic genius and was especially successful at directing and acting in the comedies of Molière. He found Molière (himself strongly influenced by commedia) and the old Italian comedies of improvisation ideal tools for developing actor versatility in all genres. He grew fond of using improvisation as a production method, moving away from a literal presentation of a play to a greater dependence on the actor's inspirations. So enamored was he of commedia techniques that he attempted to devise a modern equivalent with contemporary types, each played by an actor specializing in only that role. His belief was that such a company of improvisational specialists would eventually develop a new comic genre.

I foresee ten modern personae—synthetic, expandable, representing prevalent traits, quirks, passions, foibles, moral, social and individual. The ten personae of an autonomous theater encompassing all genres from pantomime to drama would be entrusted to ten actors. Each would make his persona his property. It would become himself, he would nourish it with himself.[31]

Planning a commedia ensemble during the World War I hiatus, he wrote to Jouvet describing three of the characters he envisioned:

The *Intellectual* (doctor, philosopher, professor, etc.), the *Agent* (or representative) (deputy, minister, electoral agent, grocery merchant, etc.), the *Adolescent* (the child in his family, the schoolboy, the suitor, the artist, the soldier, in short the "idealist," Pierrot's grandson, with a powder-white face, etc.).[32]

Copeau, of course, never completed his plans for this company, although his love for commedia extended to his hiring the extremely popular circus clowns, the Fratellini brothers, to work with his troupe on clowning techniques. Moreover, a good deal of work was done in Burgundy by the Copiaus in the direction of creating Copeau's commedia company, and several of the actors, notably Jean Dasté and Michel Saint-Denis, made extensive progress toward the creation of individualized commedia characters. A number of the plays produced by this troupe—such as *Harlequin the Magician, The Woman of Ancona,* and *The Illusion*—were closely associated with the commedia. At the Vieux Colombier commedia-influenced plays by Molière and others, such as Carlo Gozzi and Pierre de Marivaux, came to command so large a part of the repertory that the critics took issue with Copeau over their choice.

STAGE MOVEMENT AND INNER TRUTH

Stage movement was a great strength for the Copeau actor. Copeau's stage direction was usually quite choreographic, and he took many pains in arranging moves and positions, giving the actors highly detailed instructions on where and how to move. Obviously, the simple settings required visual excitement such as Copeau's expressive treatment of stage movement afforded. Even in the most realistic of his productions Copeau gave "unusual significance" to gestures and moves. An almost balletic style was evident, for example, in his Molière productions, but without the phony posing and attitudes such a style usually leads to in the work of the less gifted. Copeau's stage pictures were always excellently composed; they made full use of the various levels. Never were the groupings self-conscious, as they flowed naturally from the situations.

Concerned with overt theatricality in his actor-training program and in the physical style of his productions, Copeau never veered from his goal of discovering the internal truth of the characters and situations. Theatre always was a human endeavor to him and not merely a formal artistic exercise. He believed in the theatre's humanizing function as a place where a community could gather and share in the common joys and sorrows of man as reflected in dramatic performance. Seeing Copeau's work as "a fusion of theatricalism and realism," critic John Gassner found him cultivating "the histrionic sensibility of the actor as thoroughly as possible, teaching him to *act out* and underscore or punctuate characterization. But he also expected the actor to enact his role with virtually the same 'inner realism' that Stanislavsky cultivated."[33]

THE DIRECTOR'S FUNCTIONS

To Jacques Copeau the ideal director was the individual who wrote the play being staged, as in the great theatres of the past. Only a playwright-director, like Molière, could best create the harmony of style fundamental to a theatrical production. Aware that the capable playwright-director was a rare phenomenon, he was ever cautious that his work as a director did not distort a playwright's intentions. Directors were too easily convinced that their work was independent of the author's contribution and that they had free creative rein in dealing with it. Viewing the director's functions as essentially interpretive rather than creative, he cautioned against the director's distorting the playwright's contribution in order to ride his own creative hobbyhorse. He saw the director's task as one of confronting the drama, seeking to understand it, and staging it as faithfully as he could.

PREPARATION FOR PRODUCTION

When the director first reads a script, Copeau wrote,[34] the play begins to form living images in his mind, with specific actors in the roles, their gestures, the lights, colors, and emotions coming to imaginary life. Deeper study clarifies these images, and the play's "sensual rhythm" and its "breathing" begin to evidence themselves. The drama's locale is soon specified, as are the physical arrangements and the requirements of furniture and props. These images are necessary before the director can work out the play's life in terms of action.

A great deal of effort goes into the preplanning of all moves and business, as well as such elements of timing as tempo and pauses. Characters are thoroughly analyzed, their positions are preconceived, and the lighting is designed. Each step taken by the director is based on his aiming for a stylistic unity within an overriding idea. This idea, however, is not intrusive or disruptive of harmony in the setting or performance. Copeau thus was a strong believer in the director's thoroughly working out a scheme prior to the commencement of rehearsals, in order to save time and energy. His extensive experiments with improvisation as a rehearsal method did not alter his conviction that a detailed rehearsal plan was a necessity. The discoveries made through improvisations could be adapted to the plan and could enhance rather than weaken the already solid foundation.

Copeau enjoyed working with scenic models in prearranging his staging. A reporter for the *Theatre Magazine* observed him in 1917 sitting before a model of the Garrick Theatre stage, working out all his scenic methods, lighting cues, and blocking, noting each actor's moves and gestures in a ledger.[35]

ECLECTICISM

Eclecticism was the keynote of his direction. Like his contemporary Max Reinhardt, Copeau saw each play as a unique product of dramatic art, with its own inherent requirements. He did not seek to fit his work into any singular school of production but found within each play the seeds of its own style. Reinhardt and Copeau were mavericks in this regard—most of their directorial contemporaries were associated with a single fundamental approach, be it naturalistic, symbolistic, or expressionistic. Probably the most specific stylistic path Copeau followed was in the staging of the classical repertory. In studying an old play, he sought to find within it a heartbeat which could be amplified to be heard by a modern audience. Characters and situations were viewed from the standpoint of contemporary psychology in order to make their reality quite vivid. Nevertheless, he viewed with horror the notion of directing the classics in a gimmicky or faddish way merely because a director claimed thereby to be making the work more accessible.

EARLY REHEARSALS

Copeau began his rehearsals by reading the entire script to the company, hoping to make the actors aware of its intellectual and rhythmic nature. Widely recognized as a brilliant reader,[36] Copeau flourished at these sessions. He was not unique among French directors in reading the play aloud, however, as this method was used widely in France and elsewhere. After the reading Copeau had the cast read the play back to him. Discussion and analysis were crucial parts of such rehearsals. He continued with reading rehearsals as long as he found them useful and the actors did not grow bored, since they helped to unify the cast in one interpretation. Another practical consideration was that the reading rehearsals gave Copeau the opportunity to make personnel changes when he saw that someone had been miscast.

On occasion Copeau's first rehearsals would vary from the approach just described. At these times he would employ improvisations prior to giving his actors their scripts, having them work out basic characterizations and relationships in situations analogous to those in the play. Then, given the actual text, the actors could clarify the focus of their roles while retaining a good deal of the spontaneity evoked during their improvisation. Copeau found that his actors invented many useful details through these exercises, and he capably incorporated them into his directorial scheme.

Following the roundtable readings or improvisational rehearsals, Copeau began to block, telling his actors their moves and helping to justify them. This period allowed him considerable directorial flexibility; the lack of a completed setting permitted changes and adjustments from the prearranged plan, both in the blocking and decor. He hoped to get the blocking out of the way quickly, feeling that the actors would be more confident and at ease knowing their movements so they could bend their efforts to a true interpretation of the drama. He liked to have the actors off their books and relaxed in their blocking so they could concentrate on delving deeply into their parts, although he did recognize the danger of their being so comfortable that their concentration would weaken. The director must make sure the actor does not lose a grip on his character and begin to make tactical interpretive errors. The director must continually inspire confidence in the actor and keep him on the road to truth.

WORKING WITH ACTORS

Copeau disliked the dictatorial manner of directing[37] and tried to avoid forcing his actors to give him what he wanted, refraining religiously from demonstrating moves and readings for them. A director must get his actors to respond through the use of "tact, authority, and persuasion," utilizing his "sympathetic understanding" which he can best employ through his thorough knowledge of each actor's abilities and personal character. A happy medium between "too much freedom" and "blind coercion"[38] must be found.

Copeau worked in close proximity to his actors in rehearsal, moving about onstage with them. As he said, "Intimacy is necessary to them, a rod in the ear, physical contact, personal revelations, a pleasantry, an illuminating gesture, a little foul language, and much criticism."[39] Roger Martin du Gard, a close associate of Copeau's, has left this account of the director at work on the opening production at the Vieux Colombier:

Under the remains of a scaffold which was being hastily dismantled, in the dust from plastering, amid the tapping hammers, his torso moulded in a spinach-green sweater, his jawline buried beneath a fluffy scotch wool scarf, topped off with a soft hat with a wide brim . . . Copeau went at it like a demon. Extraordinarily agile, he leaped carelessly from the auditorium on to the stage, and from the stage into the auditorium. I could distinguish a feverish mask under the shade of the hat. He was re-arranging the blocking of the last act of the play, with the exactitude of a ballet-master, often stepping right to the back of the theatre to assess the total effect, he re-worked ten times over the slow assembling of the actors round the four-poster bed where the heroine is dying.[40]

Although he recognized the value of a lengthy rehearsal period, Copeau felt each play and company had different rehearsal needs. The seasoned actor who knows how to explore his role, layer after layer, will get much out of a long rehearsal period while the less experienced will stop dead at a certain stage and be unable to continue making discoveries. He preferred, as did Stanislavsky, to work in the peace and quiet of the country when possible, because with the reduction of disturbing outside factors he could mold his ensemble more cohesively.

CONCLUSION

Copeau succeeded in providing theatrical productions alive with auditory and visual beauty, tied together by a masterful sense of pace, alternating from slow and sometimes immobile moments in certain plays to bursts of speed and energy in others, depending on the desired effect. His work ranged from the sadly sentimental to the airily intellectual, from the wildly farcical to the charmingly comic. Best known for his work in the intimate environs of the Vieux Colombier, he also made remarkable incursions into the field of spectacular pageant drama, and advanced the means by which religious themes could be successfully presented on the stage.

No other modern theatre artist has had as much of an impact on French theatre as had Jacques Copeau. Louis Jouvet, Charles Dullin, Léon Chancerel, Michel Saint-Denis, and other directors continued to uphold his ideals. Many others, including Gaston Baty and Georges Pitoëff, were swayed by his high standards and commitment to theatre art and might never have accomplished what they did without his example to guide them. Copeau's methods and achievements continue to be revered by French theatre people today. Among his many accomplishments, he pioneered in the field of the noncommercial art theatre devoted to true repertory ideals, broke down the public's insistence on star performances in favor of ensemble artistry, and revolutionized French theatrical training methods; through the work of his nephew, Michel Saint-Denis, he has had a serious influence on theatre training elsewhere, notably in England and America. His *dispositif fixe* has become a familiar form throughout the world of theatre and still provides inspiration for directors and designers who seek simplicity and elegance in a permanent scenic arrangement. Like so many others in this book, Copeau's ideas speak to us today with a freshness that has not been diminished by the years. He was truly an *homme de théâtre*.

NOTES

1. See Jacques Copeau, "An Essay of Dramatic Renovation: The Théâtre du Vieux Colombier," trans. Richard Hiatt, *Educational Theatre Journal* 19 (December 1967).

2. Ibid., p. 449.

3. Program, "The Théâtre du Vieux Colombier," scrapbook, Lincoln Center Library for the Performing Arts, New York.

4. Copeau, "An Essay," p. 450.

5. Actually, *Twelfth Night* was the most often revived classic in the Vieux Colombier's history (176 performances), while the plays with the greatest number of total performances were Charles Vildrac's *The Steamship Tenacity* (205) and Prosper Mérimée's *The Coach of the Holy Sacrament* (179).

6. Jacques Copeau, "Remembrances of the Vieux Colombier," trans. Nanette Sue Flakes, *Educational Theatre Journal* 22 (March 1970).

7. Ibid., p. 5.

8. Ibid., p. 6.

9. Ibid.

10. Ibid., p. 7.

11. Ibid., p. 12.

12. After the theatre's school reopened in 1921, Copeau allowed it to become a major preoccupation, drawing much of his attention away from the actual production process.

13. Douglas Lister Paterson, "Jacques Copeau's Theatrical Image" (Ph.D. diss., Cornell University, 1972), pp. 62–63.

14. Copeau, "Remembrances," p. 14.

15. H. I. Brock, "A Guest Director Comes to Us," *New York Times*, 2 January 1928.

16. R. H., "*As You Like It*," *New York Times*, 31 July 1938.

17. David Whitton, *Stage Directors in Modern France* (Manchester: Manchester University Press, 1987), pp. 65–66.

18. Ralph Roeder, "Copeau, 1921," *Theatre Arts Monthly* 5 (October 1921): 280.

19. Jacques Copeau, "Dramatic Economy," trans. Joseph M. Bernstein, in *Directors on Directing*, ed. Toby Cole and Helen Krich Chinoy (Indianapolis: Bobbs-Merrill, 1963), p. 223.

20. Copeau, "An Essay," p. 454.

21. John Rudlin declares that a small forestage was added, but the architectural illustration he provides reveals only the brief space below the false proscenium. This illustration should be compared with the photo of the original Vieux Colombier also reproduced in Rudlin. *Jacques Copeau* (Cambridge, Eng.: Cambridge University Press, 1986), pp. 53–54.

22. The stage was the product of a collaboration among architect Antonin Raymond, actor Louis Jouvet, and Copeau; Jouvet also served as an important scene designer for the company. At one point, an idea of Copeau's for employing a system of lightweight, interchangeable cubes to establish locales was seriously examined, but was ultimately rejected as impracticable. See ibid., pp. 55–59.

23. The principal illumination came from four octagonally shaped lighting instruments hung in full view of the audience from the suspended bases of ceiling buttresses that spanned the area over the audience's heads.

24. Paterson, "Jacques Copeau's Theatrical Image," pp. 169–70.

25. Douglas Paterson describes *The Tricks of Scapin* and *Twelfth Night* in "Two Productions by Copeau: *The Tricks of Scapin* and *Twelfth Night*," *The Drama Review* 28 (Spring 1984). Rudlin offers descriptions of *The Steamship Tenacity* and *The Tricks of Scapin* in *Jacques Copeau*, pp. 64–81.

26. This platform was based on the simple, unadorned *tréteaux* of the old-time street players, including the *commedia dell'arte*, and, as mentioned earlier, would form an important part of Copeau's later work in the festival presentations during his Burgundy years.

27. Copeau, "An Essay," p. 454.

28. Program, "The Théâtre du Vieux Colombier."

29. Kenneth Macgowan and Robert Edmond Jones, *Continental Stagecraft* (New York: Benjamin Blom, 1964), p. 104.

30. Albert M. Katz, "The Genesis of the Vieux Colombier: The Aesthetic Background of Jacques Copeau," *Educational Theatre Journal* 19 (December 1967): 445.

31. Quoted from André Gide's *Journal 1889–1939*, in Frederick Brown, *The Theatre and Revolution: The Culture of the French Stage* (New York: Viking, 1980), p. 231.

32. Quoted from Jacques Kurtz, *Jacques Copeau: Biographie d'un Théâtre*, in ibid., p. 446.

33. John Gassner, *Directions in Modern Theatre and Drama* (New York: Holt, Rinehart and Winston, 1967), p. 187.

34. Copeau, "Dramatic Economy," p. 216.

35. "Jacques Copeau and His Theatre," *Theatre Magazine* 26 (December 1917), p. 342.

36. Copeau was often in demand to give public readings, and a significant part of his time was devoted to such activities, which also served to provide a necessary income. His insistence on sight-reading as part of his actors' training stemmed from his own reading skills.

37. However, Brown suggests in *The Theatre and Revolution* that, in practice, Copeau was indeed dictatorial, attempting to mold every actor's speech and behavior to his precise specifications, much as Craig would have liked to do with the übermarionettes about which the latter theorized. See, for example, pp. 248ff.

38. Copeau, "Dramatic Economy," p. 218.

39. Quoted from Marcel Raymon, *Le Jeu Retrouvé,* in Paterson, "Copeau's Theatrical Image," p. 118.

40. Quoted from *Souvenirs Autobiographiques et Littéraires* in Rudlin, *Jacques Copeau,* p. 14.

CHRONOLOGY

Titles of plays that remained in the Vieux Colombier repertory to be revived later—some quite frequently—are given an asterisk on their first appearance; revivals of these plays are not mentioned except when given with other companies. For a more complete listing refer to John Rudlin, *Jacques Copeau* (Cambridge, Eng.: Cambridge University Press, 1986). All productions in Paris, except where noted.

1879	born in Paris
1896–98	studies at Sorbonne
1902	resides in Denmark and marries Agnes Thomsen
1903	his critical articles begin to appear in Paris
1905–09	works at Modern Art Gallery, Paris, and writes criticism for literary magazines
1909	helps found *La Nouvelle Revue Française*
1911	Théâtre des Arts: *The Brothers Karamazov (Les Frères Karamazov*; codirected with Jean Croué)
1913	founds Théâtre du Vieux Colombier; *A Woman Killed with Kindness; Love's the Best Doctor (L'Amour Médecin); The Louverne Sons (Les Fils Louverne); Barberine; The Miser (L'Avare)*; Household Bread (Le Pain de Ménage)*; Afraid to Fight (La Peur des Coups); The Play of Robin and Marion (Jeu de Robin et de Marion); Farce of the Mad Bungler (La Farce du Savetier Enragé)*
1914	*The Jealousy of Barbouillé (La Jalousie du Barbouillé)*; The Exchange (L'É-change); The Testament of Father Leleu (Le Testament du Père Leleu)*; The Shuttle (La Navette)*; The Brothers Karamazov*; The Water of Life (L'Eau de Vie); Twelfth Night*; company tours England; tours to Alsace; outbreak of World War I forces company to disband
1915–17	runs actor-training school with Suzanne Bing

1915   visits Gordon Craig in Florence and Jaques-Dalcroze in Geneva

1917   Garrick Theatre, New York: *Impromptu at the Vieux Colombier (L'Impromptu du Vieux Colombier); The Tricks of Scapin (Les Fourberies de Scapin)*; The Coach of the Holy Sacrament (La Carrosse du Saint Sacrement)**

1918   *The New Idol (La Nouvelle Idole); The Surprise of Love (La Surprise de l'Amour)*; The Traverse (La Traverse); Carrot Head (Poil de Carotte); The Evil Shepherds (Les Mauvais Bergers); The Little Marquise (La Petite Marquise); Peace at Our House (La Paix Chez Soi); Françoise's Luck (La Chance de Françoise); The Secret (Le Secret); The Marriage of Figaro (Le Mariage de Figaro)*; Blanchette; Georgette Lemeunier; Cranquebille; The Veil of Good Fortune (Le Voile de Bonheur); Claude's Wife (La Femme de Claude); The Doctor in Spite of Himself (Le Médecin Malgré Lui)*; Gringoire; Rosmersholm; The Son-in-law of Mr. Poirier (Le Gendre de M. Poirier); The Caprices of Marianne (Les Caprices de Marianne); The Burden of Liberty (Le Fardeau de la Liberté); The Romantics (Les Romanesques); Boubourouche; The Enigma (L'Énigme)*

1919   *Chatterton; The Liar (Le Menteur)*; Fritz the Friend (L'Ami Fritz); Pelléas and Melisande (Pelléas et Mélisande); Washington; The Magic Winecup (La Coupe Enchantée)*; The Vein (La Veine); The Misanthrope (Le Misanthrope)**; company returns to Paris and Vieux Colombier; *The Winter's Tale*

1920   *The Steamship Tenacity (Le Paquebot Tenacité)*; Work of the Athletes (L'Oeuvre des Athlètes); Old Cromedeyre (Cromedeyre-le-Vieil); Phocas the Gardener (Phocas le Jardinier)*; The Foolish Journey (La Folle Journée)**

1921   *The Poor beneath the Stairs (Le Pauvre sous L'Escalier)*; The Death of Sparta (La Morte de Sparte); Uncle Vanya; The Dauphin (Le Dauphin); Love's the Best Doctor (L'Amour Médecin); A Caprice (Un Caprice)*; Come What May (Au Petit Bonheur); The Fraud (La Fraude)*

1922   *Love, Book of Gold (L'Amour, Livre d'Or); Happy Death (La Mort Joyeuse); The Joys of Chance (Les Plaisirs du Hazard)*; Saul; Sophie Arnould; The One-eyed Magpie (La Pie Borgne)*; The Beauty of Hagueneau (La Belle de Hagueneau); Master Pierre Pathelin (Maître Pierre Pathelin); Michel Auclair*

1923   *Princess Turandot; Improvised Prologue (Prologue Improvisé); Dardamelle; Bastos the Bold (Bastos le Hardi)*; The Imbecile (L'Imbécile); La Locandiera; The Birthplace (La Maison Natale)*

1924   *Everyone Must Know His Place (Il Faut que Chacun Soit à sa Place)*; Vieux Colombier's final season; Copeau moves with family and followers to Château de Morteuil in Burgundy countryside to continue training

1925   new troupe, the Copiaus, formed to play at rural festivals: *The Tax (L'Impôt); The Object (L'Objet); The Widower (Le Veuf); The Namecalling of Gilles (Les Sottises de Gilles); Girls to Marry (Les Jeunes Filles à Marier); Mirandolina*

The Doctor in Spite of Himself; Harlequin the Magician (Arlequin Magicien); The Vacation (Les Vacances); The Blackcurrants (Les Cassis); The School for Husbands (L'École des Maris); The Festival of the Vine and the Vinegrowers (Fête de la Vigne and des Vignerons); The Magic Winecup; company moves to Pernand-Verglesses

1926   *The One-eyed Magpie; The Illusion (L'Illusion)*

1927   *The Woman of Ancona (L'Anconitaine)*

1928   company tours to England; Guild Theatre, New York: *The Brothers Karamazov*

1929   rejected for leadership of Comédie Française; the Copiaus renamed the Compagnie des Quinze under direction of Michel Saint-Denis

1932   Théâtre des Nouveautés: *Jeanne*

1933   Santa Croce monastery, Florence: *The Mystery of Saint Uliva*

1934   L'Atelier: *Rosalinde (As You Like It)*

1935   Piazza della Signoria, Florence: *Savonarola*

1936   Théâtre de la Madeleine: *Much Ado about Nothing*; Porte Saint-Martin: *Unparalleled Napoleon (Napoléon Unique)*; Comédie Française: *The Misanthrope*

1937   Porte Saint-Martin: *The Impostor of Seville (Le Trompeur de Seville)*; Comédie Française: *Bajazet; Asmodie (Asmodée)*

1938   Boboli Gardens, Florence: *As You Like It*; Comédie Française: *The Testament of Father Leleu*

1940   assumes directorship of Comédie Française: *The Misanthrope; A Caprice; The Steamship Tenacity; The Coach of the Holy Sacrament; The Cid (Le Cid); Twelfth Night*

1941   resigns directorship following conflict with German High Command

1943   Hospices de Beaune, Burgundy: *The Miracle of the Golden Bread (Le Miracle du Pain Doré)*

1949   dies in Burgundy

Bertolt Brecht

(1898–1956)

Few will doubt that the plays of Bertolt Brecht are the outstanding achievement of twentieth-century German drama. Even had Brecht never written a line of dialogue, however, his work as a theatrical theorist and director would have established him as one of the foremost figures in the history of the theatre. Taken as a whole, Brecht's theatrical career displays a decided unity, a continual give-and-take between his frequently revised and sometimes contradictory theoretical conceptions and their practical enactment in writing and directing. He always considered his plays as mere outlines for production; in his own stagings the merger of his directorial and playwriting genius produced the definitive aesthetic and intellectual statement on what the plays were intended to convey.

EARLY YEARS

Eugen Berthold (later changed to Bertolt) Friedrich Brecht, son of a Protestant mother and Catholic father, was born and raised in the Bavarian city of Augsburg. His father was employed in a paper factory and, in 1914, became its director. That same year the sixteen-year-old Brecht had his first experience in directing when he and some friends purchased a secondhand puppet theatre using stick puppets; under Brecht's direction, the group produced scenes from famous plays at the home of a friend. Brecht was already having his writings published in a local newspaper and was also gaining popularity in certain circles for the songs he wrote and compellingly sang as he accompanied himself on the guitar. As a way of avoiding the draft, Brecht enrolled in medical school at the University of Munich in 1917, but spent most of his time in the curricular pursuit of drama and the extracurricular pursuit of Munich's cabaret life. He was eventually drafted, though, and served very briefly as an orderly at an Augsburg clinic for venereal disease. After the war he returned to Munich where he very quickly began to gain a reputation as an ostentatiously bohemian poet, critic, and playwright, despite his clinging to most of the perquisites of a comfortable bourgeois existence.

Brecht did not direct a play until 1922, when he worked on Arnolt Bronnen's *Patricide* for the Junge Bühne. The Junge Bühne was a group that staged new plays for morning or matinee performances at various Munich theatres. Most productions were given only once and rehearsal conditions were often extremely trying. Here his rebellious nature and unconventional theatre views soon became visible. In Brecht's eyes, much German theatre during this time was weighted down by overproduced dramas with ranting, hollow performances and an emotional, sentimental naturalism which infuriated him. The theory of cool, objectivized acting for which Brecht later became famous was a reaction to this perceived bombastic approach in which actors indulged in "hysterical outbursts and paroxysms of uncontrolled roaring and inarticulate anguish."[1]

Patricide's author, never having had a play produced before, was amazed at how Brecht reduced the cast to a shambles and almost destroyed the production with the zealous ferocity with which he set about reforming the stage through this one production. The play had been cast before Brecht began to direct it, and Brecht was seriously perturbed by the choices that had been made. Especially annoying to him was the work of Agnes Straub (who later worked with Brecht in more amenable circumstances), the gigantic Heinrich George, and Hanns Heinrich von Tardowsky. All were well-known actors who had agreed to work gratis. Brecht's directions to Straub and Tardowsky, couched in biting invective, served only to diminish them by intimidation, but George grew more and more exasperated. Rehearsals were a series of disputes until George finally erupted and walked out, leaving Straub in hysterics and Tardowsky in confused despair. Brecht, however, satanic young rebel that he was, went right on, calling out, " 'The rehearsal continues,' rolling his 'r' a little more sharply than usual." Seeing how disheartened his remaining actors were, "Brecht grasped that this was his chance. He cleared his throat loudly, slammed shut his rehearsal book, loudly switched off the rehearsal light, said 'Good day,' and looked for Bronnen. . . . [Finding him, he said] 'Congratulations. With that bunch it would never have turned out right.' "[2] Brecht was released from his assignment, and the direction was assumed by Berthold Viertel.

Several months after the *Patricide* disaster, Brecht made his presence felt so insistently at Otto Falckenberg's Munich Kammerspiele rehearsals of the former's *Drums in the Night* that he practically took over the direction. He is supposed to have interrupted the actors, ridiculing their work by calling it "shit," and showing them how to act. Such was his influence, however, that Falckenberg and the cast actually acceded to his demands, and Falckenberg even gave Brecht a job at the Kammerspiele as dramaturge. (In 1924 he also worked for Max Reinhardt in Berlin as a dramaturge.) When the play was produced in Berlin at the end of 1922, Falckenberg was again the director of record, while Brecht continued to strongly influence the rehearsal work. *Drums in the Night*—in which Brecht himself appeared to sing and play the guitar—was a critical success and won for the young playwright the 1922 Kleist Prize, Germany's most coveted drama award.

In 1923 Brecht and Arnolt Bronnen codirected the barely noticed *Pastor Ephraim Magnus* by Hans Henny Jahn, and took an active part in the production of his *In the Jungle of the Cities,* directed at Munich's Residenztheater by Erich Engel. When Brecht's controversial *Baal* was staged by Alwin Kronacher in Leipzig, the former was uncredited for his considerable participation in the play's direction. Throughout much of his career, Brecht was—for a variety of reasons, often political—to have a powerful influence on productions for which he received no directing credit. Moreover, productions on which he received sole directing credit rather than as a member (admittedly the most influential member) of a collaborative team were the exception rather than the rule. Even when he received sole credit, he was likely to have had the collaborative help of others.

Brecht's first independent directing job was to be *Macbeth,* at the Kammerspiele, but he and Lion Feuchtwanger decided to substitute their own adaptation (based on an earlier German translation) of Marlowe's *The Life of Edward II* instead. Not only was this the first time Brecht had complete and unobstructed control over a production, with full casting powers and an unrestricted rehearsal schedule (which took two months), but he was also permitted to have all technical resources, from props to lighting, available from the very start of rehearsals. *Edward II* was Brecht's earliest attempt at his famous "epic" style of production (which he later preferred to call "dialectical theatre," although epic is better known); it featured an impersonal, detached approach to acting in contrast to the overly emotional histrionics of contemporary German stagings of the classics. The play, however, was not politically motivated, and Brecht had not yet formulated his notion of using the theatre to provoke social change. He asked the actors (among them Erwin Faber as Edward and Oscar Homolka as Mortimer) to perform such things as eating, drinking, and fencing in realistic and specific terms, rather than in the conventionally casual and suggestive way with which they were familiar. He wanted things done not only with great specificity, but with enormous polish and skill. He made a great fuss, for example, about the way the soldiers had to hang Gaveston, stopping them over and over until the execution seemed thoroughly professional. "The audience had to get pleasure from seeing them put the noose around the fellow's neck!"[3]

One of the oft-noted elements of *Edward II* was the chalk-white makeup of the soldiers, which was devised to suggest their feelings of fear and weariness; it was also an important early epic device related to Brecht's desire to put a cap on the audience's emotional identification with the performance.

In considering this production, it is important to notice that Brecht's position as playwright-director allowed him to adapt the play as necessary in terms of what rehearsals revealed about both his writing and the talents of his cast. The actors were continually being fed new lines, cuts, and other revisions, a practice Brecht had begun with the Leipzig *Baal* and continued throughout his career.

Caspar Neher, a boyhood friend of Brecht's designed *Edward II*; he soon became the quintessential Brechtian designer. He provided a set that incorporated a half-curtain slung across the stage on a wire, only partially obscuring the scene shifts going on behind it. The half-curtain eventually became a Brechtian trademark. Another soon familiar signature was projections, which introduced the scenes by giving information on their time and locale. The remainder of the setting was highly simplified, and given a rough-edged, homemade look. Similarly, the costumes, although fundamentally based on historical models, were unusually coarse in style, some of them being made from sacks.

Shifting in 1926 to Berlin, where his career was to be concentrated, he co-directed with Oscar Homolka, who also starred in, a revised version of *Baal* (now retitled *The Life of the Man Baal*); it was put on by the Junge Bühne for a single matinee and caused a scandal when a rowdy audience of supporters and detractors vociferously expressed their opinions. Helene Weigel, Brecht's future wife and chief representative of his acting methods, was in the cast.

During this period Brecht took the opportunity to direct two plays for the Junge Bühne by Marieluise Fleisser, *Purgatory in Ingolstadt* (1926) and *The Pioneers of Ingolstadt* (1929), but for neither did he accept the directorial credit, preferring to remain in the background. These were among the very few plays he ever staged of which he was not the official author or adapter.

In 1927 Brecht collaborated with composer Kurt Weill on the forty-five-minute operatic cantata, *The Little Mahagonny*, produced in a boxing ring at an annual music festival at the Stadttheater in Baden-Baden, with sets, projections, and costumes by Neher; it was later expanded into the opera *The Rise and Fall of the City of Mahagonny*, which had an extremely controversial production in Leipzig in 1930 under Walter Brugmann's direction. Weill's wife Lotte Lenya was a prominent member of the cast. Lenya starred as the whore Pirate Jenny in Brecht's next production, *The Threepenny Opera* (1928), with a memorable score by Weill. Although Erich Engel was credited with direction, Brecht collaborated on the staging, as did Neher and Weill.

The Threepenny Opera, a non-didactic satire on capitalism and on the Weimar Republic based on John Gay's 1728 English ballad opera, *The Beggar's Opera*, was produced at Berlin's Theater am Schiffbauerdamm; it eventually became an international success and remains the most widely popular of Brecht's works. Neher's set combined a huge upstage circus calliope and projections of titles in a childlike handwriting on upstage screens and on the white half-curtain.

Around this time, Brecht was deeply influenced by two powerful forces. One was Marxism, the serious study of which he undertook in 1926, and which was to have a profound effect on his plays and aesthetic theories. Brecht's interpretation of Marxism was often in conflict with the ideology espoused by the strict party line; he never actually joined the Communist party, even after settling in his own East German subsidized theatre in the late 1940s. The other influence was left-wing playwright-director Erwin Piscator, the founder of the term "epic theatre" (albeit with a somewhat different definition from Brecht's). In 1927

Brecht joined Piscator's "dramaturgical collective" at Berlin's Theater am Nollendorfplatz, and here he worked on a number of projects. (Piscator's effect on Brecht is discussed below.)

Brecht came more and more to the conclusion that the theatre could be profitably used as a classroom for Marxism; consequently he wrote a number of strictly didactic plays called *Lehrstück,* or "teaching plays"; they were intended primarily for performance by amateurs. Two of these, *The Flight of the Lindberghs* (music, Paul Hindemith and Kurt Weill) and *The Baden Didactic Play about Acquiescence* (music, Hindemith), were produced under his direction at Baden-Baden's music festival in the summer of 1929. For these he stripped the productions to the barest essentials, providing works which were little more than theatricalized lectures that insisted on a particular point of view. It is important to remember that Brecht's left-oriented aesthetics were prompted by his hatred for the rising Nazi powers and his burning desire to use the theatre as a weapon for combatting these insidious new forces.

That same summer Brecht and Erich Engel codirected his and Elisabeth Hauptmann's *Happy End* (score by Weill), an unsuccessful work about Chicago gangsters and the Salvation Army (Brecht soon disassociated himself from the writing credits). Carola Neher, Oscar Homolka, and Peter Lorre were its stars. The following year, Brecht and Weill codirected another of his *Lehrstück, He Who Says Yes,* at an educational institution in Berlin.

In 1931, Brecht was responsible for one of the most important of his prewar directing assignments, a revival at Berlin's Staatstheater of his 1926 Kiplingesque satire (written with the collaboration of several others), *Man Is Man* (score by Weill), revised to reflect a Marxist attitude. Peter Lorre was cast as the antihero, Galy Gay, and Weigel was the Widow Begbick.

Man Is Man was Brecht's most successful early application of epic techniques. In this version, Neher provided the half-curtain for expository projections. Props and scenic pieces were sparse and looked crude and well-used. Two of the actors playing the British soldiers, who convince the timid but pliable porter Galy Gay to replace a missing member of their company, wore stilts to make them seem grotesquely oversized; a third soldier was of normal stature but bizarrely padded. Giant hands and noses further emphasized the soldiers' unusual appearance. Galy Gay, who in the course of the play, undergoes a radical transformation from a meek little man to a ferocious killer, appeared in the latter guise with his face chalk-white (like the soldiers in *Edward II*), his waist encircled by grenades, a pistol strapped to his breast, and a bayonet in his teeth. In keeping with Brecht's desire for an "alienated," nonempathetic acting style, he spoke in strange rhythms, emphasizing unexpected words and phrases and understressing those normally stressed; Brecht hoped this would further clarify the socially relevant ideas beneath his dialogue, but most critics were confused and unhappy with the effect.

When, late in 1931, the Berlin production of *The Rise and Fall of the City of Mahagonny* began rehearsals, Brecht shared the direction with Neher, but

Brecht and composer Weill had such a stormy relationship that the show's producer wedged Brecht out of the picture by giving him funds and a space in which to rehearse another of his plays. Thus, Brecht's final production in Germany, before fear for his own and his family's well-being in the face of Hitler's rising power forced him to leave the country, was the powerfully staged *The Mother* (1932), based on Maxim Gorky's 1907 novel, written as a *Lehrstück*, and starring Weigel as Pelageya Vlassova and Ernst Busch as Pavel. Neher was responsible for the impressionistic, universalized sets and costumes, and Hanns Eisler for the music. It was produced at the Schiffbauerdamm, but the tension in the city between communists and Nazis convinced Brecht to remove it from that prominent theatre and produce it on temporary stages set up in various working-class neighborhoods, with sparse scenic resources capable of being packed immediately in case of visits by Nazi troublemakers. The adaptation itself was the result of a collaboration of Brecht and several others, including Eisler. Emil Burri received formal credit for the direction, but it is well known that he was Brecht's partner in the work. This tale of a poverty-stricken Russian mother's gradual awakening to a revolutionary consciousness was staged forthrightly in a manner suggestive of agit-prop, including projections of scene titles, exposition, photographs, and communist slogans. Because of its characters' fundamental humanity, however, it did not become two-dimensional poster-art theatre and is considered one of the most complete realizations of Brecht's epic theatre theories.

PERIOD OF EXILE

As a well-known left-winger, Brecht's name was prominent on the Nazi blacklist when Hitler came to power. In 1933 Brecht and his family left Hitler's Germany for what turned out to be a period of exile lasting fourteen years. During this time he resided in Denmark, Sweden, Finland, the United States, and Switzerland, and did little directing. He did participate, however, in the rehearsals of a number of his own plays directed by other people; these include his participation in some rehearsals of the 1933 Paris production of his *The Seven Deadly Sins*; assistance on Ruth Berlau's 1935 Copenhagen staging of *The Mother*; advisory work (largely unwelcome) on the 1935 Theatre Union production of *The Mother* in New York; involvement in Per Knutzon's 1936 Copenhagen presentation of his *The Roundheads and the Peakheads*; work on the 1936 showing of *The Seven Deadly Sins* in Copenhagen; attendance at rehearsals in 1937 Paris of Francesco von Mendelsohn's direction of *The Threepenny Opera*; presence at rehearsals of Slatan Dudow's 1937 premiere production of Brecht's *Senora Carrar's Rifles* in Paris, starring Weigel; visits to rehearsals of Berlau's 1937 Copenhagen mounting of the same play; presence at rehearsals of Slatan Dudow's direction of eight scenes from Brecht's *Fear and Misery of the Third Reich* (then titled *99%*) in Paris, 1938; codirection with Berlau of two one-acts, *What Price Iron?*, in Stockholm; brief participation in Berthold Viertel's Off-

Broadway staging of *Fear and Misery of the Third Reich*, 1945; conducting of some rehearsals of his and W. H. Auden's adaptation of *The Duchess of Malfi* in New York after the show already had opened and the director, George Rylands, had returned to England; and work with Charles Laughton and Joseph Losey (the credited director) on the direction of Brecht's *The Life of Galileo Galilei* in Los Angeles and New York, 1947.

In *Galileo*, the most important of these projects, Brecht explained the scenes to the actors and did much of the blocking; he actually seems to have done as much directing on this famous project as Losey. During the earlier collaborative work on the script with Laughton, Brecht and the actor made many of the choices regarding acting and decor that eventually were used in the production. However, during rehearsals Brecht constantly butted heads with the production team and actors, who he thought had no idea of what he was talking about; at one point, in fact, Losey walked out on the show for a time. Moreover, Brecht made life hell for the producers, because he was rarely satisfied with the props, costumes, lighting, sets, or blocking, and insisted on frequent changes, which added uncomfortable financial, emotional, and physical burdens to the production.

Brecht's irascibility was demonstrated on at least two other occasions in America. The first was when he erupted after seeing that his presence was merely being tolerated as he watched the Theatre Union mishandle *The Mother*; the second came when he disagreed with Erwin Piscator's 1945 treatment of his *Fear and Misery*; he actually fired his old mentor and replaced him with Berthold Viertel, but to little effect.

Galileo, Brecht's single most important theatrical endeavor during his American residency, opened in Beverly Hills in July 1947 at the small Coronet Theatre. Eisler wrote the music and Robert Davison did the designs. In December 1947 it opened, somewhat altered, for a three-week run on Broadway at the Maxine Elliott; Brecht already had returned to Europe. The production combined satirical background cartoons, projections borrowed from Da Vinci, Brueghelesque costumes and groupings, and a simplified set suggesting the period through furniture and props.

THEATRE AS SCHOOL

Simply stated, Brecht's directing career falls into two periods, preexile and postexile. The years of exile were decidedly barren for him as a director, but he could hardly have been more productive as a dramatist. It was during this painful period that he wrote such masterpieces as *Mother Courage; The Caucasian Chalk Circle; Mr. Puntila and His Man, Matti; Galileo; The Good Person of Setzuan; The Resistible Rise of Arturo Ui*, and several other important works. By the time he went into exile, however, his production style had evolved certain definitive features. A firm believer in the use of theatre as an instructional medium, Brecht, as has been mentioned, sought to prevent audiences from becoming too involved emotionally with the events portrayed on the stage. He considered it a shameful waste of the theatre's resources to mesmerize an audience and purge its emotions through an identification with the characters and situations. All such empathic theatrical experiences he identified as "Aristotelian." He called theatre that existed solely to give sensual pleasure without provoking socially meaningful thought "culinary." Theatre should inform the spectator; it should make him ponder the drama's Marxist implications—the need for societal change.

In the Brechtian notion of theatre, the old illusionary effects must be avoided by making everything clearly theatrical, so that what is acted does not seem to be occurring in the present but in the past—that it is a depiction of what *has* occurred. Whatever can be used to keep the audience aware of this "historical" essence must be employed so that identification does not occur. Consequently, the events were "distanced" or "made strange" in Brecht's productions. He devised a methodology he came to call *Verfremdung,* which has been translated as "estrangement," "distantiation," "alienation" (as in the "A effect"), or "defamiliarization"—techniques aimed at objectifying the theatrical experience so that its meanings could be clarified and made apparent. "The habitual ways of looking at a thing" are destroyed, says Brecht's disciple Manfred Wekwerth, "in order to reveal the contradictions within it, so that its reality may be perceived." As a result, the audience is allowed "to exercise fruitful social criticism."[4]

Although the playwright can aid this process considerably, Brecht postulated, by the use of various literary devices such as the chorus and the narrator, and by the proper structuring of scenes, narrative monologues, direct exposition, and so forth, the director, too, has a wealth of techniques he can use for similar ends. Lighting, music, projected and painted slogans, graphs, charts, acting style, masks and costumes, and various scenic devices—all can be used imaginatively to foster deliberation rather than intoxication. As a playwright-director, Brecht could achieve his ends more readily than might otherwise have been the case.

Brecht's early writings stressed the value of cool rationalism over emotional identification, but his practical theatre work constantly affected the feelings of his audiences; he came to see this contradiction and his postwar work presents a surprising rapprochement with the emotional expectations of traditional theatre and even with Aristotelian dramaturgy. Similarly, Brecht's later period placed an increasing emphasis on the importance for the spectator of having "fun" in the theatre, both on a sensual and an intellectual level. He saw the necessity of producing a balanced response to his work through a dialectical arrangement of emotional and rational effects.

The postwar Brecht was always quick to advise his actors and other personnel to ignore his theoretical scribblings and to attend instead to the needs of the work at hand. Recent commentators have noted clear distinctions between the Brecht pronouncements of the 1924–33 period, when his aesthetics were being formed by the pressure of the Nazi threat, and those of the postwar period, when he wrote *The Short Organum for the Theatre,* which sums up the revisions in his thinking. There is little evidence that audiences at any major Brecht production from either period were truly "distanced" emotionally from the action, no matter how many Brechtian "alienation devices" were thrust at them, but there is considerable support for the notion that audiences were often deeply affected emotionally, especially by such later plays as *The Life of Galileo Galilei* and *The Caucasian Chalk Circle.* The purely contemplative and rational audience Brecht originally said he was seeking seems never to have existed. Brecht never abandoned his desire for a thinking audience, of course; his later theories simply allowed for the combined exercise of both the rational and sensory-emotional faculties, and not one to the exclusion of the other.

PISCATOR'S INFLUENCE

As we have seen, Brecht worked intensively for a time at Piscator's Berlin theatre, where he came into direct contact with that director's politically oriented productions. Piscator used the stage as a propaganda platform, devising many innovative technical means, such as films, projections, movable stages, and treadmills, for providing his audiences with the information they needed to accept his tendentious messages.

Brecht, of course, used some Piscatorian elements himself; projections and (later in his career) the revolving stage, for example, became familiar staples of his stage techniques. However, unlike Piscator, Brecht recognized that the best way to make his point was to allow the audience to discover it themselves from the dialectical give-and-take inherent in his dialogue and situations; thus, in the main, his theatrical means were technically simpler than those of his mentor.

Brecht felt that Piscator's propaganda productions tended to draw the spectator into their world on a noncritical level of emotional absorption. Brecht wanted the theatre to demonstrate that the events depicted were not fixed but capable of alteration. He therefore used only those nonatmospheric techniques (such as the half-curtain) that would stimulate critical faculties and make the paradoxes and contradictions in the play apparent.

Perhaps the element that most clearly points up the contrast between Brecht's stripped-down effects and the more elaborate ones of Piscator was the former's frequent use of the plain half-curtain. This was placed so as to only partially hide the scene changes going on behind it, thereby reminding the spectator of the artificial trappings in which the play was being produced. The actors could use the curtain as an item of scenery (hiding behind it, for example), a simple background to play against, or even a screen for the projection of pictures or information. In many ways it recalled the type of naive background used in folk theatre or fairground performances.

POSTEXILE CAREER BEGINS

Brecht's postexile career began in a dilapidated theatre in the small town of Chur, Switzerland, in 1948, with his staging of his own adaptation (based on a nineteenth-century German translation) of Sophocles' *Antigone*. His version melodramatized the conflict by setting the action in the ruins of 1945 Berlin with Creon (called Kreon and played by Hans Gaugler) presented as a Hitlerian clone who had hanged Antigone's brother for his work with the resistance. The work—given a total of only five showings in Chur and Zurich—reunited Brecht with Neher (who had remained in Nazi Germany). Weigel—who played Antigone—acted again after an absence from the stage that, apart from a few performances in Copenhagen and Zurich, went back to 1932.

The audience viewed a semicircle of screens before which the actors sat on a low bench as they waited to enter their scenes. The chorus carried poles to which were attached abstract square masks that they placed before their faces as required. Framing the acting area was a set of four posts on each of which was mounted a real horse's skull painted blood-red, giving the space a feeling of barbarism. In place of the rather primitive look of Brecht's 1920s productions, *Antigone* aimed instead for what he called "the Grand Style." Even the half-curtain was gone—but not for long, as it reappeared in later works. Instead, Neher and Brecht now sought to make full use of the wide spaces of the open stage. The actors sped through the text at a very rapid pace and performed in an effectively stylized manner.

Brecht staged one other play in Switzerland in 1948, his folk comedy (cowritten with Hella Wuolijoki and Margarete Steffin) set in Finland and dealing with the class structure, *Mr. Puntila and His Man, Matti,* seen at the Zurich Schauspielhaus with Leonard Steckel, Therese Giehse, and Regine Lutz in the cast. Both Teo Otto and Caspar Neher worked on the designs. Brecht directed but, because he was an alien and did not have the proper working papers, had to relinquish all credit to Kurt Hirschfeld. The much admired production reintroduced the half-curtain; there were also projections of titles and action interrupted by musical interludes (score by Paul Dessau) that clarified the meaning of the story. Naive signboard-like representations of clouds, moon, and sun were hung on a birchwood scenic backing.

MODEL BOOKS

During Brecht's exile in Denmark, Ruth Berlau, a Danish theatre artist who became one of Brecht's closest collaborators as well as one of his mistresses, began to make photographic records of several of his productions, including *Senora Carrar's Rifles* and *What Price Iron?* Later, when *The Life of Galileo Galilei* was being prepared in America, she convinced Brecht that she should snap hundreds of photographs commemorating the moment-by-moment action of the play (her picture-taking supposedly drove Charles Laughton to distraction).

These were then assembled as a record of the production. Similarly when he finished staging *Antigone,* Brecht once more had hundreds of pictures taken, now with the aim of publication as a permanent record, with text and notes included, for others to read and study. These volumes were called model books and were to be used as references for productions by other directors, as well as by his own company, when preparing a revival. The taking of many photographs during rehearsal also became a standard practice, as Brecht liked to have them to refer to during his staging, particularly at the run-throughs.

Brecht believed the use of model books could be a highly creative task in staging a revival. The new director would not slavishly copy every detail, but would seek to understand the reasons behind the choices made in the original; in so doing, many new and even more effective treatments would be devised. The original served, then, as a starting point for new discoveries. A Brecht play, like any other, was not a finished product in its script form, but required fulfillment through theatrical production. Brecht's productions—expressions in time and space of the human actions only suggested by the text—were developed with intense attention paid to their reflection of carefully observed human behavior. They were quite unlike the type of productions Brecht loathed, where actors found inspiration not in their environment but in themselves, and where directors were more concerned with personal expression than with confronting society's problems. If these points were understood, Brecht felt, his models would serve as inspiration. Unfortunately, as has often been remarked, too many directors did just what Brecht hoped they wouldn't, and perpetuated his productions not as living artworks but as soulless historical artifacts.[5]

In January 1949 East Berlin's Deutsches Theater produced Brecht's *Mother Courage* (it had premiered in Zurich in 1941), starring Weigel in the title role. The work, which had only about four weeks of rehearsal, was a huge hit and ultimately toured abroad; it became the ideal example of Brecht's mature production style and helped to influence a whole generation of European directors, actors, and writers. Brecht shared directing honors with Engel, and Weigel shared the acting plaudits with Angelika Hurwicz as Kattrin and Paul Bildt as the cook, among others. The production was designed after Teo Otto's 1941 Zurich designs, which—through Brecht's reliance on photos of the Zurich mounting— influenced the staging in many ways, and Paul Dessau composed the music. Using his new model book, Brecht also staged another, somewhat different, production for Munich's Kammerspiele in October 1950, with Therese Giehse (who had played the role in the 1941 premiere) as Mother Courage. The first official Berliner Ensemble version of the play was in January 1951, with set by Neher and Kathe Reichel as Kattrin.

Among the various epic devices in *Mother Courage* were projections to provide the audience with important information. In addition, large, roughly hewn signs were hung above the stage noting the names of the countries in which the action was occurring. The projections were beamed onto another old Brecht device, the half-curtain. The recruiting officers wore masks. For the most part, however, the work's most powerful images stem from the practically bare stage seen against a cyclorama and the great revolve set into its floor. Moving slowly (in the direction opposite to that taken by the revolve) across this vast landscape representing the devastated domain of the Thirty Years War was Mother Courage and her progressively shabby sutler's wagon, pulled at first by her two sons, and then, at the devastating conclusion after her offspring are dead, by the ravaged, ragged figure of Courage herself. When needed, solid, realistic, but only partly built scenic pieces were brought on to localize scenes. Set changes were not swiftly Shakespearean but deliberate enough to clearly separate one scene from the other and thus give the audience time to ponder what they had just seen. The movement of the actors was sparse, coming only when absolutely necessary to define or clarify a dramatic issue that had arisen. Moment after moment in the staging was worked out with painstaking detail to express the socially and dramatically meaningful essence of each scene. The result was a richly textured, surprisingly realistic, acting tapestry in which each choice could be seen to contain multiple perspectives.

Brecht wanted the audience to assume an unsentimental, critical attitude toward Mother Courage for what he deemed her greedy bourgeois survivalism in trying to make a living out of war and for her inability to learn from her experiences. Still, he was aware that she was a complex figure with whom audiences would invariably empathize as a near-tragic figure. He and Weigel found means for allowing audience identification while simultaneously expressing underlying criticism. Weigel created many pieces of business to suggest how deeply, despite the character's more admirable qualities, Courage was fundamentally a mercenary creature. Furthermore, certain scenes in Brecht's staging, such as that of Courage's reaction to the offstage sound of her son Swiss Cheese being shot, of her response to Kattrin's heroic death, or—having learned nothing—of her stubbornly going about her business at the end by pulling the wagon alone in several revolutions of the acting area, are considered among the most memorable of any in modern theatre. Afraid to give her feelings away and thus reveal her relationship to the dead man, Weigel uttered an agonizing "silent scream" (an effect, by the way, that she created sometime during the run, not during the play's rehearsal period). The impact of the moment, tragically moving as it was, was undercut by the fact that Courage's son's death was linked to her own insistence on driving a hard bargain for his life.

BERLINER ENSEMBLE

The same month that saw the opening of *Mother Courage* witnessed the cofounding by Brecht, Helene Weigel, and Erich Engel of the Berliner Ensemble in East Berlin, an extremely well-subsidized repertory company which they cultivated until it became one of the world's leading theatrical institutions. Weigel was made artistic director, a post she held with distinction; many credit her managerial and performing efforts with being responsible for the ultimate success of the troupe. Actors were gathered from Brecht and Engel's earlier work together, and new young members were added as well. The Ensemble's official opening did not come until later in the year, when a highly praised new staging of *Mr. Puntila* (sets, Neher; music, Dessau) was given at the Deutsches in November with Brecht and Engel codirecting.

The next play Brecht staged for the Ensemble was his (and others') adaptation of J. M. R. Lenz's 1774 work, *The Tutor,* produced in April 1950 at the Deutsches Theater with designs by Neher, who codirected. Brecht revived his 1932 *Lehrstück, The Mother,* in January 1951, with Weigel repeating her great performance in the eponymous role, and Neher designing. In 1953 Brecht directed *Katzgraben,* Erwin Strittmatter's propagandistic play in favor of collective farming.

The final masterpiece of Brecht's direction that he lived to see was his great folk-parable play, *The Caucasian Chalk Circle,* produced in June 1954. Brecht's masterstroke of casting had Ernst Busch playing both the musical narrator and Azdak, the scoundrel who becomes a judge following a palace revolution; Weigel, wearing a half-mask (as did the other noble characters and the Ironshirts), was Natella Abashvili, the wickedly selfish governor's wife who abandons her baby during the revolutionary turmoil; and Angelika Hurwicz was Grusha, the peasant servant who risks her life to save the baby and raise it in the mountains. The music was by Dessau but it proved problematic for the actors and musicians and much of it had to be cut, to the detriment of the production.

Brecht and von Appen conducted extensive research into the costumes and props appropriate to the play's setting in the Russian province of Georgia, but the spirit of their work was conceived in the style of Brueghel. One of their chief Brueghel-like effects was the cramming together of a crowd of peasant neighbors into a very small space during the wedding party scene. The highly formalized painted backgrounds suggested Chinese watercolors. The backgrounds were combined with freestanding scenic units that were both representational and impressionistic. A notable example of the latter was the miniaturized but thoroughly detailed rope bridge, slung between two small rock outcroppings, for Grusha to cross in her mountain flight. The scenic pieces were brought on via the movement of the revolve, which would, in the play's first half, meet the escaping Grusha, who was running in the opposite direction, stop for the scene, and then move off again to be struck behind an upstage masking device. Gone, however, was the half-curtain, with its tightly drawn wires horizontally bisecting the stage opening. There were many distinguished performances, with a cast of approximately fifty playing three times that number of roles.

The Caucasian Chalk Circle was seen at the company's new and permanent theatre, the Theatre am Schiffbauerdamm, in June 1954 (the company had played mainly at the Deutsches in the interim); it was in this 727-seat playhouse that

The Threepenny Opera was originally staged. (The company actually had opened the theatre several reveal months earlier with Benno Besson's production of Molière's *Don Juan*.)

Johannes R. Becher's *The Winter Battle,* a 1941 work about a Nazi soldier whose conscience prevents him from killing Soviet partisans, was codirected by Brecht and Manfred Wekwerth (who had been Brecht's assistant on several recent works and who eventually took over the company's directorship) in January 1955. Brecht then undertook rehearsals of his third version of *Galileo* with Erich Engel, Neher providing the designs, and Ernst Busch playing the scientist. The physical side of the production was patterned closely on the 1947 version, and the model book was a significant factor in the staging. The play was in the midst of rehearsals—fifty-nine had been held—when Brecht died in August 1956. It opened in January 1957.

Brecht's reputation as a director stems chiefly from this period, since the world's attention was drawn to his productions through tours and the frequent visitation of foreigners to his well-subsidized theatre in East Berlin. The fact that Brecht used a conventional proscenium stage here (with a short forestage capable of being added on) accords well with his idea that the audience can contemplate the ideas of a drama better when looking down onto the stage from a raked auditorium than when made a part of the action, as in theatres employing the open stage.

Brecht's final decade saw the culmination of his practical theatre work as he continued to evolve a unique and exciting production style. While his work often coincided with his theories, many times it did not. Actors at the Berliner Ensemble rarely studied Brecht's theoretical writings, and he made little overt effort to implement the theory other than when it coincided with the practical process of achieving desired results. In this regard, actors found him not vastly different to work with than other directors.

SCENIC STYLE

"Estrangement" techniques continued to be a hallmark of Brecht's productions. Collaborative achievements in the realm of sets and music helped to further these effects. Brecht and his favorite designers, Caspar Neher, Teo Otto, and Karl von Appen, evolved a basic scenic technique in which realism and symbolism coexisted harmoniously. Certain essential features of the scenic background were shown in naturalistic detail while others, impossible to duplicate believably, were shown symbolically. Symbolic moons and suns, for instance, were always clearly artificial; instead of being hidden, even their chains were hung in aesthetically pleasing arrangements. Partial scenic elements, such as fragments of a wall or house, were often used to suggest the whole. Brecht called his designers "stage builders," and scenery was "stage construction." His functional attitude toward scenery, says designer Wolfgang Roth, who worked with Brecht from 1929 to 1933, was geared toward telling "the spectator that he was in the theatre and not in England, Greece, Scotland, etc." According to Roth, Brecht told his designers:

Don't try to put everything into something where it doesn't belong. You only do that to cover up your inability. You substitute things for essence. The performers should be the greatest part of our scenery: when the setting becomes a comfortable place for actors to walk around in, only then is it meaningful. No effects. They're not necessary. No false moods.[6]

A designer's work in a Brecht production was expected to comment on the action, not merely to decorate it. Martin Esslin describes how Neher provided an individual point of view for *The Life of Galileo Galilei* by "projections of maps, documents, and works of art of the Renaissance," and how, in *Mahagonny,* the action was shown from two different angles—that of the actor and that of the designer; the scene in which "Jakob eats himself to death was played in front of a backdrop showing a large portrait of Jakob eating."[7] Brecht himself wrote about how the set for *The Mother* "quoted, narrated, prepared and recorded. Its spare indication of furniture, doors, etc. was limited to objects that had a part in the play, i.e. those without which the action would have been altered or halted." The set consisted of iron pipe scaffolding, practical doors set into the pipes, and a large canvas screen for projections. "Thus the stage not only used allusions to show actual rooms but also texts and pictures to show the great movement of ideas in which the events were taking place."[8]

Wolfgang Roth remembers that designing for Brecht was always a pleasure as well as a challenge, as Brecht rejected all dogmatism in design and insisted on each problem being solved by an open, human, and flexible attitude. Brecht wanted designers who were aware of all current events in every sphere—political, scientific, and artistic—so they could reveal through their work an attitude toward events. He told his designers to enjoy their work, "to have fun with it, creatively and physically. . . . Our goal was to be part of a 'whole,' " writes Roth, "which should entertain audiences by its own qualities—beautiful materials, colours, clarity and cleanliness."[9]

The actual sets and furniture of a Brecht production were often praised for their simple, almost artless beauty, since the workmanship was always highly sophisticated and well crafted. Sets were suggestive and imaginative, but props and furnishings were always actual, never abstract. Brecht proudly claimed that some props were worthy of a museum.

In 1956, after viewing several productions of the Berliner Ensemble brought to London, critic Kenneth Tynan succinctly summed up the visual impression made by these works:

No steps or rostra encumber the platform; the dominant colours are browns and greys; and against a high, encircling, off-white backcloth we see nothing but solid, selected objects—the twin gates in *The Caucasian Chalk Circle* or *Mother Courage*'s covered wagon. The beauty of Brechtian settings is not of the dazzling kind that begs for applause. It is the more durable beauty of *use*.[10]

USE OF TECHNICAL RESOURCES

Brecht employed the technical resources of the theatre to create beauty where it might least be expected. There was, for example, a simple scene change in *The Caucasian Chalk Circle* whereby an immense white backdrop with a painting of a Georgian mountain village on it was lowered into position before the audience's eyes. As the cloth billowed slowly and settled into place, it created a charming picture which, besides being interesting to watch in its own right, helped enhance the theatricality of the moment so as to remind the audience it was watching a play.

As part of the design scheme, lighting played a crucial role. Through much of his career Brecht wanted the lighting instruments exposed to show the audience he had nothing up his sleeves and was not out to fool them into thinking stage light derived from "natural" sources. At the Berliner Ensemble, though, the lights were conventionally hidden, Brecht having come to think that their visible presence had become a disturbing aesthetic factor. Following in the tradition established by Piscator, Brecht was a proponent of white, ungelled light, often startlingly bright in its application. His intention was to prevent atmospheric effects and to reveal and illuminate the meanings of the action. This white light was not uniform, however, but carefully sculptured and an occasional use of blue provided some variety.

Brecht made it his business to know a good deal about the technical side of theatre and claimed he could do most technical jobs himself if called on. He had close relationships with his tech people, who respected him greatly, and usually included them at every rehearsal to call upon if an emergency arose.

MUSIC

Music also was a salient contributor to the process of "making strange." Eric Bentley notes that for *Mother Courage*

Paul Dessau composed his most delicate and lovely music for "The Song of Fraternization," which is what its title suggests, and is sung by a whore. The tune seems to embody the pure love that the text reports the fall of. Such music constitutes a kind of criticism of the text.[11]

Brecht carefully avoided music which could weave an emotional spell over the spectator, feeling this interfered with the rational processes he wished to foster. Music

was not to intensify the effect of the text but to interpret it, it was not to illustrate but to give a commentary, not to "serve-up" but to transmit. Music as commentary meant that the music had to avail itself of such means which, without abandoning their emotional content, allowed mental processes to take place, and even stimulated them.[12]

A specific instance of the musical "A effect," or "Alienation effect" as Kenneth Tynan calls it, came in *Mother Courage* when the orchestra played the national anthem in a satiric arrangement. "The melody is backed by a trumpet obbligato so feeble and pompous that it suggests a boy bugler on a rapidly sinking ship."[13]

To counteract any tendency the audience might have toward accepting even such self-conscious music as emotionally supportive, Brecht often had the musicians appear onstage, as in the Asian theatre, or partly visible in a stage box, where their presence served to remind the audience of the music's true function.

Brecht created the music for his earliest plays, and was an active collaborator in the musical composition for his post-1926 works, although he had no formal musical training. Music is a prominent feature of almost all his plays, and his collaborative endeavors with composers were of vital import to production. Often he would draft rough versions of the songs and give these to the composer to elaborate and refine. Kurt Weill, Paul Hindemith, Hanns Eisler, and Paul Dessau were major composers who willingly followed Brecht's musical dictation. Dessau wrote of how Brecht would work with him in various ways to attain the desired ends. In addition to improvising tunes and asking Dessau to build upon them, Brecht would also read to him the verses to be set to music, reciting "quietly, delicately, and in a manner wholly dedicated to the meaning, as musically as any poet had ever read aloud before."[14]

At times Brecht would plagiarize a melody from some other, older source, and ask the composer to build a new piece from it. Or the composer would create the music while involved in the progress of rehearsals. One such example was when, during the 1948 rehearsals for *Mother Courage,* Paul Dessau had to write half-a-dozen versions of the "Eilif Song" before Brecht was satisfied.

In the detailed notes he prepared for his productions, Brecht would write precise instructions for the type of music he desired. For example, his notes for *The Caucasian Chalk Circle* prescribe a "cold beauty" for the narrative music, which, he specified, should be easy to sing—even monotonous. Variety should appear in the stylistic alternations from one act to the other. Thus, whereas the first song of Act I should be "barbaric," the last song should "be cold, to make it possible for Grusha to act against it."[15]

THE GESTUS

Central to the performance style of a Brechtian actor was what Brecht called the *gestus,* a word suggestive of "gesture" but with richer overtones. A frequently used translation is "gest." A gestus was a total physical realization by the actor, developed in rehearsals, which summarized the relationship of the character to his own unique social circumstances. This gestus had to be capable of signifying the core or kernel of a scene; as such, it could be summed up in a simple sentence, phrase, or paragraph like those flashed on screens in many Brecht productions. An example might be ''Pierpont Mauler Humbles Himself and Is Exalted'' from *St. Joan of the Stockyards*.

Brecht wanted his actors to determine accurately how their characters would behave in a given set of circumstances; the actor's specific choice of posture, vocal and physical expression, and gesture were to reveal, almost as if in quotation marks, the character's social response to the particular circumstances. A properly selected gestus would illustrate for the audience the actor's personal comment on his character. Elisabeth Hauptmann, long one of Brecht's collaborators, recalled how, during the Frankfurt production of *Mother Courage,* the actress playing the title role spoke the words ''Let the war be damned!'' as a rebuttal to the remark of the pastor that the day would long be remembered because of a hero who had died on it. Courage believes she will remember it because, on the same day, her daughter was disfigured and lost her chance of finding a husband. According to Hauptmann,

at this point the actress playing Mother Courage took center stage and looking out at the audience said, ''Let the war be damned!'' *In the Brecht production as directed by Brecht, Mother Courage says the line as her hands are going over the merchandise that the daughter has brought from the town. Her grief is real, but she is still the merchant. . . .* Mother Courage, with her heart may say ''Let the war be damned!'' but with her hands she is the tradeswoman. (her italics)[16]

Hauptmann presents a clear picture of how Weigel, the actress, discovered a truthful and illustrative gestus based on the reaction of the character to her social circumstances. Through the elaboration of such stage business, Brecht the director was able to say far more effectively what Brecht the playwright could not.

Many months of rehearsal allowed Brecht's actors the time to discover methods for revealing, through characteristic behavior, the meaning behind the play's events. In rehearsing *Mother Courage* Brecht wanted to suggest that the emotional reaction of the peasant woman—whose son is taken away by the soldiers and on whose farm the dumb Kattrin beats the warning drum—is a response dulled by the long and futile war. In Brecht's words, ''Lamenting, begging and informing have become rigid forms; this is the way to behave when the soldiery appears.'' It was more important that the peasant show the long-range effects of war on human emotions than the immediate response to her son's loss. The scene, therefore, had to be played on a ''ceremonial'' level in which all reactions become those of someone numbed by constant hardship into repeating the gestures of ritual. The kneeling, whining, and praying of the old peasant were done in a routinelike fashion. In his model, Brecht comments that ''while praying, she had to strike a pose . . . to her as comfortable as possible—putting one knee on the ground first (careful not to chafe it), then the other one, and then the hands folded over her belly.''[17]

These examples picture a performance method in which the relationship of character to environment is seen in the acting choices dictated by the player's understanding of the character's position within a set of given social circumstances; the circumstances themselves are illuminated by the character's behavior—i.e., choice of *gestus*.

However, Brecht could call on a full panoply of spectacular theatrical effects to bring a point across when necessary. In the Berlin production of *The Life of Galileo Galilei*, which was completed by Engel after Brecht's death, the idea "that all living thought is sooner or later social thought," as Tynan describes it, was conveyed in the following staging for the play's second half:

A Florentine ballad singer hails Galileo's triumph over the church, and a symbolic procession is held, echoing Bosch and Breughel at their most lurid; garishly masked figures, jangling saucepans and brass bed-heads, toss a cardinal in a blanket; and finally a giant-figure, twenty feet high, clumps in on stilts, surmounted by a huge adorned head, representing Galileo. Into a moment the social repercussions of a scientific discovery are perfectly compressed.[18]

VOCAL DELIVERY

As mentioned earlier, a Brecht play usually employs music and song as essential production ingredients. Brecht had specific advice to offer his actors on the presentation of their songs as, indeed, he had for the speaking of dialogue. At all costs he wanted to avoid the effect of the actor not noticing that he has stopped speaking and started singing. The actor, he felt, must make each type of vocal delivery distinct, for each implies a different theatrical function. There must be no confusion by the actor of straightforward speech, rhetoric, and song, nor must the latter two be delivered as mere emotional intensifications of the previous level. The actor should never act as if he were unaware of the change in function he has assumed by moving from one level to another. As he sings, he should be "showing" that he is singing. He may demonstrate the pleasure he takes in singing by performing some sort of business, such as straightening a piece of furniture, which is designed to reveal that he relishes preparing for his task. If he can, the actor may also sing against the music, thus operating as an independent component in the orchestration and producing an interesting effect "from an obstinate matter-of-factness, independent of and uninfluenced by music or rhythm."[19]

As far as straight dialogue was concerned, Brecht looked for a rather realistic type of speech, devoid of bombast, and believably conversational. In the 1931 *Man Is Man* he had failed at creating a more stylized "gestic" type of speech and realized that the ideas of the play would be better transmitted if the dialogue sounded actual. To get his actors to sound natural, their speeches would be broken into small units to make them sound as much as possible like remarks the actor might make in the give-and-take of normal conversation.

Another device he employed was to have the actor speak in his own native dialect rather than the stage German in which the script was written. The ease with which an actor could say his lines in a familiar dialect restored the sense of reality brought out by the formal stage language. This reality could then be transferred to the actual dialogue.

DEMONSTRATING THE ROLE

Because Brecht believed human nature could be altered, he wrote and directed in such a way as to demonstrate that what the audience sees is a *picture* of people behaving in ways which reflect the influence on them of social, political, and economic conditions. It should be clear to the audience that, were these circumstances changed, the behavior of the people would likewise be changed. If the spectator is to consider the many factors that affect human behavior, it is essential that the actor "show" his character or "act in quotation marks." Never should the actor lose himself in his role by too completely identifying with it; if he does, the actor sacrifices his objectivity and ability to comment on the role through his performance. A Brechtian actor must demonstrate his character as if the character were someone outside himself, someone about whom one might suggest "*he* did or said that." Nevertheless, Brecht sought at all costs to avoid mechanical, "stylized," or abstract acting; he aimed for truth to life, naturalness, and close observation of actual behavior. Every relevant aspect of a dramatic situation affecting a character was studied, so that what was valid and true within the given circumstances would be enacted in the truest manner.

Ronald Gray provides a fine example of the actor Ekkehard Schall "showing" the character of Eilif in *Mother Courage* as he performed a war dance with "exultant savagery":

The dancer leaps high in the air, his sabre clasped between both hands above his head; but the head leans to one side and the lips are pursed as though in an effort to recall the next movement. Eilif is "shown" here as a young man who dances the wardance because he believes it is the right thing to do, but who is not wholly at home in it. The denial of a part of his humanity becomes evident and the contemporary relevance of the action dawns.[20]

TRUTH IN ACTING

There are, in fact, many places in which Brecht's ideas come close to those of his theoretical adversary in the art of acting—Stanislavsky. Actually, Brecht never insisted on any specific technique for his actors, providing they achieved his results. An outstanding Brecht actress. Angelika Hurwicz, relates that "it was irrelevant to him whether the actor was cold or hot in the process."[21] He even regarded as a "prerequisite" the kind of exercises which would ensure truth to life and the warmth of the role's presentation. "Brecht simply starts

with what Stanislavsky called the 'super-task' or superobjective of the actor,''
Hurwitz reports, and goes on to relate that Brecht's admonition about not becoming possessed by a role was ''aimed against actors who forget about their
super-task, who only see their own parts, and who offend against the content
of the play as a whole, even when they give their parts interesting details and
great acting ability.''[22]

It is thus understandable that Brecht should so loudly have insisted that his
was a realistic theatre, despite his pronouncements on the need for ''distance''
in the presentation. A realistic theatre such as his, he said, must employ fully
believable, completely rounded characters, with all their feelings and authentic
behavior intact. Brecht was proud of the totally convincing performances of his
actors. He was annoyed by those who accused his theatre of being devoid of
emotion, claiming that epic theatre did, indeed, employ emotional effects, but
that it clarified emotions and did not seek to probe psychological depths. Brechtian acting, as Norman Marshall observed in 1949, was ''very like the best kind
of naturalistic acting in the English theatre. It was controlled, economic in the
use of gesture, devoid of any suggestion of over-playing, but vividly effective.''[23]

A principal feature of the acting in Brecht's productions was the simplicity and
''rightness'' of effect, the effortless ease with which his actors carried out their
tasks. Brecht wanted the theatre experience to be enjoyable for both audiences and
performers; the latter should work easily and relaxed, as does a good athlete in a
tournament, for ''*a man who strains himself on the stage is bound, if he is any
good, to strain all the people sitting in the stalls.*''[24] Aesthetic pleasure could be
derived when the acting choices were so well selected and executed that they were
comparable to the ''rightness'' displayed in the work of a laborer who was expert
at his job. Even the proper carrying of a sack could thus be a source of aesthetic
delight. Brecht strove for this appropriateness in his actors' physicalizations and,
as a director, had the secret ability to make stage reality create so indelible an
impression that everyday reality seemed pale in comparison.

Clichéd acting, of course, was anathema to Brecht, and when he saw such
acting at a rehearsal he would shout, ''Wrong, quite wrong.'' For unless the
actor could grasp that which was unique in the character and circumstances the
performance would be false and without meaning. Still, Brecht was well aware
that acting is a heightened form of reality and not simply an imitation of life.
He wanted his actors to recognize that their presence onstage required a performance somewhat larger than offstage behavior. In these larger-than-life scenes,
he would call out to the actor, ''This is your moment. . . . Don't let it get away.
Now it's your turn, and to hell with the play.''[25]

COLLABORATIVE METHOD

As has been observed, Brecht was fascinated by the collaborative process.
Through much of his career he allowed visitors to attend rehearsals and often
asked for advice, accepting suggestions from almost everyone, including the

technicians. Rehearsals were never a source of ego-thumping for Brecht; he often threw off his own ideas in favor of those profferred by others whom he respected. A day's rehearsal typically was followed by a meeting with his assistants to discuss in detail what had been accomplished and to map out the following day's work plan. It was at these meetings—and not at rehearsals—that any theoretical ideas Brecht may have wished to explore were aired. The fact that so many of his productions list others as directorial collaborators is evidence of his openness to other creative minds. He tried to play down the autocratic nature of his role, even preferring the term "rehearsal manager" (*probenleiter*) to that of director.

The avowedly democratic nature of Brecht's rehearsals stemmed from his own theoretical concerns regarding the nature of the theatre event. He wanted to avoid the single, unified vision of a monarchical director who creates a fusion of all theatre arts in a Wagnerian *gesamtkunstwerk*; instead, he favored a confrontation between the audience and all the theatre's artists, each working to express his vision of the playwright's meaning. The audience's appreciation and understanding of the issues were derived from the multiple viewpoints represented by the creative staff; if only one man's ideas were represented, the ultimate impact would be relatively weak. This view of what A. D. White calls "disjunctive theatre"[26]—in which the spectator is forced to create, by his own intellectual response, the harmony apparently slighted by giving each theatre art freedom of self-expression—extends to the individual actors as well. Each was free to experiment and find his own answers to the problems of performing his role. Yet, as always, Brecht's practice could not bear the burden of his theories. No matter how he tried to democratize the rehearsal process, he could not avoid imposing his personal viewpoint on the production. He was revered as the "Boss" by his colleagues at the Berliner Ensemble, and could barely escape being the authoritarian leader. The Brechtolators were simply too insistent in their worship of him to achieve a truly democratic system. Still, Brecht began a practice of team-directing which continued at the Ensemble after his death, and which was, perhaps, more truly democratic than was possible while he was still alive.

PREPARATION FOR PRODUCTION

In preparing for a production, Brecht's first step would be to thoroughly study the work for its social insights. The story would be condensed to a few well-chosen sentences and then broken up into its separate episodes, those events that move the story along to the next stage. The director next determines how each episode is related to the others. These small episodes or "events," much like the "beats" or units into which Stanislavsky often divided his scripts, were worked on and polished to perfection in rehearsal as independent sections. Their actions were so thoroughly worked out and developed that they might have been played as independent pieces.

Brecht's model book for *Mother Courage* breaks the eleventh scene down into the following components:

The city of Halle is to be taken by surprise. Soldiers force a young peasant to show them the way.

• • •

Peasant and wife ask Kattrin to pray with them for the city of Halle.

• • •

The dumb girl climbs onto the roof of the stable and beats the drum in order to awaken the city of Halle.

• • •

Neither the offer to spare her mother in the city, nor the threat to smash the wagon keeps Kattrin from going on drumming.

• • •

Death of Dumb Kattrin.[27]

WORKING WITH THE DESIGNER

Step number two was the director's development of a scenic embodiment, developed in collaboration with the designer. Brecht often allowed his company to rehearse with no specifics of the design prearranged, especially when his designer was Caspar Neher. Neher preferred to design a play after familiarizing himself with the company's rehearsal progress, so that the sets and costumes could fit the actors' needs. He did, however, influence the course of rehearsal by sketching key episodes in which character groupings were vividly depicted. When staged, these scenes were often strikingly similar to Neher's original sketches. The actors and director would discover the actual physical placement of such scenes, and these would be incorporated into the final design. Similarly, preplanned designs also incorporated the designer's notions as to grouping; often the designer indicated specific aspects of the characters that helped to differentiate one from the other.

Neher, who designed the great majority of sets, and even participated in the direction on several occasions, was a genius at selecting furniture and props which, through their use, would help the actor assume a specific attitude. Thus, according to Brecht,

one chair will have short legs, and the height of the accompanying table will also be calculated, so that whoever eats at it has to take up a quite specific attitude, and the conversation of these people as they bend more than usual when eating takes on a particular character, which makes the episode clearer.[28]

CASTING

The third step in producing a Brecht show was the casting. Early in his career Brecht used such actors as Oscar Homolka, Lotte Lenya, Ernst Busch, Carola

Neher, Helene Weigel, and Paul Bildt over and over, creating in a sense an informal repertory company. In his postwar years he sought out as many of his former players as he could for the true repertory company at the Berliner Ensemble, forcing him to cast from a limited group of actors. Actually, the limitations of his casting suited his theoretical ideals quite well. Since he was primarily concerned with characters who could change their social conditions, he could cast against type and use actors who were able to embody the social gestures of their roles rather than the ideal physical embodiment of them. As a result, his actors got to play a wide variety of parts that other directors might not have allotted them. A good example of his unconventional tastes in casting would be his ideal of Hamlet, Peter Lorre, whom he even tried to talk into coming to Berlin to play the role. His casting methods were geared to the idea that the actor should be given the chance to stretch his talents. Indeed, he opposed typecasting on principle, since he did not believe in stereotypes. Still, he claimed, the actor should have basic characteristics in common with the role, though not necessarily the conventional ones. "It is pure folly to allot parts according to physical characteristics," he said, nor is temperament always a reliable guide.

True there are gentle people and noisy, violent ones. But it is also true that every man has every variety of temperament. And those varieties which he is repressing may be particularly effective when brought out. . . . It is most dangerous to cast a major part on the strength of a single characteristic.[29]

This is a key remark, because one of Brecht's greatest preoccupations in rehearsal was the process of developing contradictory elements in every character. No character was to be deemed entirely positive or entirely negative, but was to be composed of both the pluses and minuses of human temperament. The contradictions were to be consciously selected but so smoothly ingrained into the performance that several viewings of a production might be necessary before they became apparent to a spectator. This process of discovering contradictions in order to enrich characterizations has been cited as a principal reason for the lengthy rehearsal periods at the Berliner Ensemble.

Because of the long rehearsal process, casting was often revised when Brecht decided that someone was more appropriate for a role than the original actor. Another reason for switching actors might stem from Brecht's propensity for having affairs with various actresses in his company; when an actress cast as the Governor's Wife in *The Caucasian Chalk Circle* attempted suicide after Brecht switched his affections during the rehearsal period, she had to be replaced by another performer.

Another of Brecht's casting methods was to choose less experienced actors who could not bring to their performances the tricks associated with the smooth professional. He liked actors who had the unpolished vivacity of amateurs and who looked like average people, not stage personalities. The ordinariness of Brecht's actors struck Kenneth Tynan forcibly, as did the apparent artlessness of their style. He remarked how "they neither bludgeon us with personality nor woo us with charm; they look shockingly like people, real potato-faced people."[30]

REHEARSAL PROCESS

Following the completion of casting, rehearsals began with the reading of the play by the company; during this reading, excessive "acting" was frowned on as the purpose was simply to get a basic familiarity with the play. An analysis of the play was usually presented to the actors at this time. The blocking followed, without intervening roundtable discussions, which were part of Brecht's preparatory period with his collaborators and designers. In rehearsal he dealt with practicalities, not abstractions. Since the Berliner Ensemble was a state-subsidized theatre, rehearsals were unhurried and stretched over several months, sometimes, as in *The Caucasian Chalk Circle,* taking the better part of a year. Normally they were conducted six days a week from ten in the morning to two in the afternoon, interrupted only by a coffee break. Three or four months of blocking was not unusual. Everything remained loose and was subject to frequent revision, even at dress rehearsals. Carl Weber, who worked with Brecht, relates that Brecht felt

the blocking should be able to tell the main story of the play—and its contradictions—by itself, so that a person watching through a glass wall, unable to hear what was being said, would be able to understand the main elements and conflicts of the stage.[31]

Blocking was rough at first, the actors being given the freedom to improvise and experiment, but gradually the appropriate form and characterizations developed, and scenic units and props were added to aid in the rehearsal process. "The results of this blocking," says Bentley, "could be called stylized, almost mannered, definitely pictorial and formal. Brecht would go through a scene like a movie director noting every 'frame' in a sequence. Every 'frame' had to please him as a piece of visual art."[32] These "frames," of course, were preserved in the published model books of Brecht's productions.

There was a definite Brecht look to the staging, writes Bentley, as the director appeared to consistently break up any straight lines or symmetrical arrangements. "His preference was, for example, a solitary figure in one corner, and a clump of figures at a distance (a clump, not a row)."[33] Brecht also enjoined his actors to elicit dramatic interest from their way of walking, which should always be done silently so that the walk became a suspense-filled pause as the audience heard nothing but the sound of the actor's footsteps.

WORKING WITH ACTORS

Brecht's intense and minutely detailed work with the actors followed the blocking period. Turning to every helpful source available, including pictorial aids, especially the paintings of Bosch and Brueghel, he worked on clarity and precision, making absolutely certain his actors knew what was happening in a scene—what the chain of events was. In *Edward II*, where a character, Judas-like, signals to the authorities that the man they seek is the one with a blue handkerchief, Brecht repeated the scene over and over until the actor grasped the idea that the character was one who betrays and that the core of the scene was betrayal.

Brecht practiced several specific techniques to get his actors to "show" their characters rather than to identify with them. Often he would have the actor speak his lines in the third person and past tense, and also speak aloud the stage directions and authorial comments. Martin Esslin provides an example of how this sounded. If the script said (the quote is from *The Tutor*):

(Enter Count Wermuth. After a few silent compliments he sits down on the sofa.)

COUNT: Has your excellency seen the new dancing master who has arrived from Dresden? He is a Marchese from Florence. His name is. . . . On all my travels I have only met two dancers I would put above him . . .

the actor would say:

Then Count Wermuth entered. After a few silent compliments he sat down on the sofa and asked whether Madame had seen the new dancing master, who had arrived from Dresden. He was a Marchese from Florence. . . . The Count made a slight pause, as his memory failed him. He nimbly added that on all his travels he had only met two dancers whom he would put above him . . . etc.[34]

This technique was not employed arbitrarily, but always to make clear the underlying social meaning of the scene. In *Mother Courage* Brecht wanted a group of peasants to talk excitedly about their reaction to a surprise attack, but sought to avoid eliciting audience sympathy for them. His point was to stress the characters' inevitable decision; they avoided taking an active role in dealing with the attack by assuring "each other of the necessity of doing nothing—so that the only 'action' possible is prayer." Thus he told the actors to add "said the man" and "said the woman" after their lines. For instance:

"The watchman will give warning," said the woman.

"They must have killed the watchman," said the man.

"If only there were more of us," said the woman.[35]

Brecht was more concerned with how his actors responded to these techniques than he was with the ultimate *Verfremdung* effect on his audiences. After the actor had thoroughly absorbed the lesson learned from the rehearsal method, the effect became a seamless part of what preceded and succeeded it and in no way was meant to draw attention to itself in performance.

Brecht, by nature, was well suited to the role of director. Although generally quiet and unobtrusive at rehearsals (Bentley says, "He was the quietest director I've ever seen at work"),[36] he could be clearly assertive when necessary. Lotte Eisner remembered watching him from a seat in the theatre where she followed "his patient and ardent manner. How he balanced the value of every sentence, adapting gesture to it, shaping the counterpoint of facial and bodily expression, modulating at one and the same time the bearing and diction of his interpreters."[37] He would sit on a chair in the auditorium, dressed in his usual "workman's garb"—workshirt, leather tie, jacket, leather or cloth cap, and corduroy pants— with a smelly cigar stuck in his mouth, and, during run-throughs, interrupt as infrequently as possible, giving the actors a great deal of freedom and restraining himself from manipulating them as puppets. Yet he knew the value of directorial temperament, and on occasion—despite his good nature—would flare up excitedly to get results if all else failed. Indeed, he once declared that the rehearsal of every play should have at least two ringing displays of fiery anger. The most usual victims of his occasional wrath, in fact, were the technicians whom he would not cavil at calling "Nazis" when they didn't give him enough white light (he used a light meter) or ran a scene too slowly (a stopwatch was always by him). He was extremely pragmatic in his methods and did whatever he could to help his actors, even laughing audibly at their humorous lines no matter how often he had heard them. His rehearsal mood was usually light, rarely morose. When an actor was stuck for a solution to a problem, Brecht always had something to suggest, even if he realized later that his solution was far from brilliant and would have to be revised. Rehearsals ran smoothly because he never let them bog down every time a problem arose.

Brecht preferred his actors not to work with scripts in hand but to allow the prompters to feed them their lines, and even encouraged their improvising the words when they didn't remember them exactly; what he wanted them to emphasize was the progression of the story. The paraphrased lines often became part of the standard performance script (which differs from the approved published version) when Brecht felt that his own dialogue had been clarified and improved upon. Someone else took notes for Brecht, though in his last period he began to use a tape recorder to perform the function.

Rehearsals were conducted in an open, relaxed, enjoyable framework. Lotte Lenya noted that the public was generally unaware of

the fun we all had, the free-and-easy atmosphere in which we would always be free to make our suggestions, laugh and joke, and generally work together as a happy company should. No-one was ever less rigid in his interpretations of his works than was Brecht, and the works we produced together were always in a sense collaborative efforts.[38]

Pragmatist that he was, Brecht was not averse to demonstrating for his actors the results he sought. He was particularly skillful in showing them the correct way to do a piece of business or read a line of dialogue, and might have been a good actor if he desired. His demonstrations were always sufficiently exaggerated to suggest what he wanted while discouraging direct imitation. Restricting such directorial acting to brief moments, he never completed an extended passage but would always stop in the middle. Brecht preferred merely to stimulate the actor to use his own imagination, because he was sensitive to his actors' moods and talents. With his awareness of their strengths and weaknesses, and knowing how to exploit them, he was able to achieve excellent results. Lotte Lenya confirms this in telling of her rehearsal as Pirate Jenny in *The Threepenny Opera*. When, during a song, she used an overly balletic gesture he stopped her and said,

"Lenya, darling, don't let's be so Egyptian," and with a slight touch he just turned my hand round, and it became a famous gesture of mine which I have kept all my life. This was his way of just touching you and, while without taking away anything of your personality, he brought out whatever was there.[39]

Brecht hated long-winded rehearsal discussions and preferred to do things, not talk about them, especially when they pertained to the psychological problems of a character. A quarter of an hour's discussion sufficed during the two hundred hours spent rehearsing *The Tutor*. If someone had an interesting idea, he was free to try it out rather than talk about it. Good ideas were kept, poor ones discarded. Rationales, however, were of no use whatsoever.

Brecht took a tabula rasa attitude at rehearsals, waiting to see what the actors would show him before he attempted to suggest any of his own ideas. His was so wide-open an attitude that one observer felt that

you get the impression that Brecht does not know his own play. . . . And he does not want to know what is written, but rather how the written text is to be shown by the actor on the stage. If an actor asks, "Should I stand up at this point?," the reply is often typically Brecht: "I don't know!" Brecht really does not know; he only discovers at rehearsal.[40]

He would begin the rehearsal by rapping on the cover of the script, announcing, "Right, we'll forget what's in there!" and proceed to treat the text as "a theoretical guide for the performance that first had to be made, and was consulted as sparingly as possible; one was dealing with the realities of the stage now."[41]

Being both playwright and director, Brecht would rewrite the script endlessly, if necessary, to guarantee that the intended point was conveyed. Dress rehearsals were still not too late for new speeches to be written or business to be changed. Nor did a production become permanently set even after opening, for changes were likely to come whenever Brecht felt they were called for. He was extremely objective about his work; according to Weber, Brecht once watched a rehearsal of a scene in *The Caucasian Chalk Circle* which he had not seen in three weeks and forced the rehearsal to stop when he was seriously disturbed by an actor's move. When told that he himself had not only blocked the move but written a line which motivated it, he was startled. He was unable to accept his own creation and undertook to rewrite it and make it more acceptable in his own eyes.[42] Often he would react to a performer's reading of a line as if he had never heard the words before. He would have the actor repeat the line and then say, "Remarkable!" meaning either that the intonations had revealed new meanings for him in the line or that he had failed when writing it to consider the specifics of performance in the midst of which the line would be delivered. The latter might lead to a revision in the writing.

POLISHING

Once the blocking and basic characterizations were fairly well set, polishing began. Pacing was the least of Brecht's concerns here. He was more attentive to clarifying the action in the episodes and the ways in which they were linked. Run-throughs came in as he worked for a sense of progression and stability. Costumes and masks also entered the picture at this point. Just as the actor's blocking was needed for a scenic design to be created, the actor's characterizations were needed for the conception of costumes and masks. However, difficult features such as high heels, long skirts, beards, and so forth were introduced for the actor's practice early in the rehearsal period.

While he watched the run-throughs, Brecht observed how well the social points were being made and how completely and with what polish the performance was being presented. Next came costume rehearsals, during which pacing was attended to; about a week of technical rehearsals, with stand-ins for the actors; and then full dress rehearsals. Finally Brecht liked to run what he termed a "marking" or "indicating" rehearsal. In it, the actors spoke and moved rapidly through the play, not acting, but maintaining the play's basic rhythm, producing—for those watching in the house—an effect like that of a silent film. This exercise served to relax the cast, to remember all the details, and to impress upon them the rhythmic basis of the production.

Five to eight previews were now presented to check audience reactions, Brecht being the first to provide previews for East German audiences. Rehearsals to adjust to preview reactions were held when needed, and finally the opening night arrived. Brecht pointedly stayed away from this performance to give his company freedom from the feeling that they were under his rigid surveillance.

CONCLUSION

Thus did the greatest German playwright of the twentieth century succeed in providing for his own plays their truest means of expression—that of actual performance by a highly skilled corps of actors in a subsidized theatre wherein his every directorial whim could, without objection, become artistic reality. He brought to the theatre an entirely new way of presenting reality by his insistence on staging everything in terms of a dialectical awareness of social behavior. One might say that he was one of the few great theatre artists who were capable of finding an appropriate blend between art and politics. An entire generation of theatre workers fell under his influence; "Brechtian" productions, not only of his plays, but of other modern works and the classics, especially Shakespeare, were seen on stages all over the world. That he was able to accomplish all this while dodging the clutches of groups as diverse as the Gestapo and the CIA, and while spending his peak years in exile, barely able to practice his craft, makes his impact all the more remarkable. Brecht's iconoclastic plays and ideas will continue to fuel discussion (and inspire production) well into the future, and his model books will continue to remind us of what he actually achieved in the crucible of the theatre.

NOTES

1. Martin Esslin, *Brecht: The Man and His Work* (Garden City, N.Y.: Doubleday, 1961), p. 65.

2. Arnolt Bronnen, "Brecht Directs," in *Brecht, As They Knew Him,* ed. Hubert Witt, trans. John Peet (New York: International Publishers, 1974), p. 34.

3. Bernard Reich, quoted in Klaus Volker, *Brecht, a Biography,* trans. John Nowell (New York: Seabury Press, 1978), p. 72.

4. Manfred Wekwerth, "Brecht Today," *The Drama Review* 12 (Fall 1967): 119–20.

5. Carl Weber, "Brecht in Eclipse?" *The Drama Review,* 24 (March 1980): 123–24. An excellent analysis of the *Mother Courage* model book, together with a description of Brecht's production, is in David R. Jones, *Great Directors at Work: Stanislavsky, Brecht, Kazan, Brook* (Berkeley: University of California Press, 1986), pp. 78ff.

6. Wolfgang Roth, "A Designer Works with Brecht," *Theatre Quarterly* 2 (April-June 1972): 15.

7. Esslin, *Brecht,* pp. 128–29.

8. Bertolt Brecht, "Indirect Impact of the Epic Theatre," in *Brecht on Theatre,* trans. and ed. John Willett (New York: Hill and Wang, 1964), pp. 57–58.

9. Roth, "A Designer Works with Brecht," p. 15.

10. Kenneth Tynan, "Braw and Brecht," *Observer,* 2 September 1956.

11. Eric Bentley, *In Search of Theatre* (New York: Vintage Books, 1957), p. 146.

12. Fritz Hennenberg, "Brecht and Music," *Enact* 24 (December 1968): n.p.

13. Tynan, "Braw and Brecht."

14. Paul Dessau, "Composing for B.B.: Some Comments," *The Drama Review* 12 (Winter 1967): 153.

15. Bertolt Brecht, "On the *Caucasian Chalk Circle,*" *The Drama Review* 12 (Fall 1967): 100–101.

16. Quoted by John D. Mitchell, "Brecht's Theatre: The Berliner Ensemble," *Players* 39 (May 1963): 234.

17. Bertolt Brecht, "Model for *Mother Courage and Her Children,* Scenes XI and XII," trans. Eric Bentley and Hugo Schmidt, in *Directors on Directing,* ed. Toby Cole and Helen Krich Chinoy (Indianapolis: Bobbs-Merrill, 1963), pp. 337–38.

18. Kenneth Tynan, "German Measles," *Observer,* 20 January 1957.

19. Bertolt Brecht, "Production Notes for *The Threepenny Opera,*" trans. Eric Bentley, in *The Modern Theatre: Readings and Documents,* ed. Daniel Seltzer (Boston: Little, Brown, 1967), p. 302.

20. Ronald Gray, *Bertolt Brecht* (New York: Grove Press, 1961), p. 66.

21. Angelika Hurwicz, "Brecht's Work with Actors," in *Brecht, As They Knew Him,* ed. Witt, p. 132.

22. Ibid.

23. Norman Marshall, *The Producer and the Play* (London: David-Poynter, 1975), p. 90.

24. Bertolt Brecht, "Emphasis on Sport," in *Brecht on Theatre,* ed. Willett, p. 8.

25. Anonymous, "Bertolt Brecht the Director," in *Brecht, As They Knew Him,* ed. Witt, p. 128.

26. A. D. White, "Brecht's Quest for a Democratic Theatre," *Theatre Quarterly* 2 (January-March 1972): 66.

27. Brecht, "Model for *Mother Courage,*" in *Directors on Directing,* ed. Cole and Chinoy, pp. 334–35.

28. Brecht, "Stage Design for the Epic Theatre," in *Brecht on Theatre,* ed. Willett, p. 231.

29. Quoted by John Willett in *The Theatre of Bertolt Brecht: A Study from Eight Aspects* (London: Methuen, 1959), p. 155.

30. Tynan, "Braw and Brecht."

31. Carl Weber, "Brecht as Director," *The Drama Review* 12 (Fall 1967): 103.

32. Eric Bentley, *The Brecht Memoir* (New York: PAJ Publications, 1985), p. 61.

33. Ibid., p. 62.

34. Esslin, *Brecht,* p. 137.

35. Brecht, "Model for *Mother Courage,*" p. 336.

36. Bentley, *The Brecht Memoir,* p. 60.

37. Quoted in Frederick Ewen, *Bertolt Brecht: His Life, His Art, and His Times* (New York: Citadel Press, 1967), p. 159.

38. Quoted by Irving Wardle, "Brecht and I: Lotte Lenya Talks to Irving Wardle," *Observer,* 9 September 1962.

39. Ibid.

40. "Bertolt Brecht the Director," p. 126.

41. Erwin Strittmatter, "Brecht at Work," *Enact* 24 (December 1968): n.p.

42. Weber, "Brecht as Director," p. 103.

CHRONOLOGY

Brecht "participated in the direction of" various plays listed below. The degree of participation varied from his attendance at selected rehearsals—which usually involved his providing advice, sometimes unwanted—to his actually working with actors and even taking part in their casting. Plays not written or adapted by Brecht—alone or in collaboration—are indicated by an asterisk.

1898   born in Augsburg, Germany

1918   medical orderly in Augsburg military hospital

1921   attends rehearsals of leading Berlin directors

1922   Junge Bühne, Munich: fired from direction of *Patricide**; Kammerspiele, Munich: participates in direction of his *Drums in the Night* (credited director: Otto Falckenberg); marries opera singer Marianne Zoff; wins prestigious Kleist Prize

1923   Residenztheater, Munich: participates in direction of his *In the Jungle of Cities* (credited director: Erich Engel, with collaboration of Jacob Geis); Schwechtensal auditorium, Berlin: *Pastor Ephraim Magnus** (codirected with Arnolt Bronnen); Altes Theater, Leipzig: participates in direction of his *Baal* (credited director: Alwin Kronacher)

1924   Kammerspiele, Munich: *The Life of Edward II*

1926   Junge Bühne, Berlin: *The Life of the Man Baal* (codirected with Oskar Homolka); participates in direction of *Purgatory in Ingolstadt** (credited director: Paul Bildt); begins study of Marxism

1927   joins "dramaturgical collective" under Erwin Piscator; Baden-Baden Festival of Modern Music: *The Little Mahagonny*

1928   Theater am Schiffbauerdamm, Berlin: *The Threepenny Opera* (credited director: Erich Engel, with collaboration of Caspar Neher, Kurt Weill, and Brecht); second marriage, Helene Weigel

1929   Baden-Baden Festival of Modern Music: *The Flight of the Lindberghs; The Baden Didactic Play about Acquiescence*; Theater am Schiffbauerdamm: *The Pioneers of Ingolstadt** (codirected with Jacob Geis); *Happy End* (codirected with Erich Engel); Central Institute for Training, Berlin: *He Who Says Yes; He Who Says No*

1931   Staatstheater, Berlin: *Man Is Man*; Theater am Schiffbauerdamm: *The Rise and Fall of the City of Mahagonny* (codirected with Caspar Neher)

1932   Wallner Theater, Berlin: *The Mother* (private showing; public premiere at Komodienhaus am Schiffbauerdamm; codirected with Emil Burri)

1933   Brecht and family flee Germany, settle in Denmark; Paris; participates in rehearsals of ballet *The Seven Deadly Sins* (credited director [choreographer]: George Balanchine)

1935   Theatre Union, New York: observes rehearsals of *The Mother*; Copenhagen: assists Ruth Berlau in direction of *The Mother*

1936   Ridersalen, Copenhagen: participates in direction of *The Roundheads and the Peakheads* (credited director: Per Knutzon); Copenhagen: several scenes from *99% (Fear and Misery of the Third Reich)*; Royal Theatre, Copenhagen: participates in direction of *The Seven Deadly Sins*

1937   Paris: participates in direction of his *Senora Carrar's Rifles* (credited director: Slatan Dudow); Workers' Theatre, Copenhagen: participates in direction of *Senora Carrar's Rifles* (credited director: Ruth Berlau, who begins practice of taking numerous photographs of Brecht productions)

1938   Paris: participates in direction of *Fear and Misery of the Third Reich* (credited director: Slatan Dudow); moves to Sweden

1939   Stockholm: *What Price Iron?* (codirected with Ruth Berlau)

1940   moves to Finland

1941   moves to Santa Monica, California

1945   City College Pauline Edwards Theatre, New York: participates in direction of *Fear and Misery of the Third Reich* (credited director: Berthold Viertel)

1946   Ethel Barrymore Theatre, New York: participates in direction of *The Duchess of Malfi*, especially after play opens (credited director: George Rylands)

1947   Coronet Theatre, Hollywood: participates in direction of *Galileo*; then Maxine Elliott's Theatre, New York (credited director: Joseph Losey); appears before House Un-American Activities Committee

1948   moves to Switzerland; Stadttheater, Chur: *Antigone*; first published "model book" based on it; Schauspielhaus, Zurich: *Mr. Puntila and His Man, Matti* (credited director: Kurt Hirschfeld)

1949   Deutsches Theater, East Berlin: *Mother Courage* (codirected with Erich Engel); founding of Berliner Ensemble, East Berlin, at Deutsches: *Mr. Puntila and His Man, Matti*

1950   Deutsches: *The Tutor* (codirected with Caspar Neher); Munich, Kammerspiel: *Mother Courage* (with Theresa Grehse)

1951   Deutsches: *The Mother*

1953   Deutsches: *Katzgraben**

1954   Berliner Ensemble moves into permanent quarters at Theater am Schiffbauerdamm; company plays at Théâtre des Nations, Paris, and *Mother Courage* wins first prize; Theater am Schiffbauerdamm: participates in direction of *Don Juan** (credited director: Benno Besson); *The Caucasian Chalk Circle*

1955   Theater am Schiffbauerdamm: *The Winter Battle** (codirected with Manfred Wekwerth); *Caucasian Chalk Circle* tours to Paris

1956   *Caucasian Chalk Circle* tours to London; dies, East Berlin, during rehearsals for *Galileo*

Jean-Louis Barrault

(1910–)

Jean-Louis Barrault has dedicated much of his professional life to perfecting a unique vision of "total theatre," strikingly different from the presentations of the conventional theatre world. A total man of the theatre himself, Barrault is not only France's leading actor and director, but an accomplished producer, choreographer, designer, writer, and theorist. Today, Barrault's ideas are no longer startling; as always has been the case with the most gifted artists of the avant-garde, their experimental and path-breaking conceptions are either absorbed into the mainstream of contemporary practice or else become the inspiration for yet another avant-garde.

EARLY YEARS

Barrault, born at Vesinet, near Paris, in 1910, was a student of painting at the École du Louvre before turning to the stage at the age of twenty-one. His education had also given him a good background in philosophy and mathematics. He chose to join the Atelier school of Charles Dullin, under whom he studied and performed from 1931 to 1935. Dullin was one of the famous Cartel des Quatre, composed of Paris' four most idealistic and talented directors. The other three were Georges Pitoëff, Gaston Baty, and Louis Jouvet, men who continued, in their own ways, traditions established by the work of Jacques Copeau. Under Dullin, Barrault encountered the most refreshing ideas of the contemporary theatre, particularly those of Konstantin Stanislavsky, Gordon Craig, and Copeau, each of whom greatly influenced his life's work. Here, too, Barrault developed an appreciation for the Oriental theatre, especially the *nō*,[1] as well as the *commedia dell'arte* and classical mime. Dullin enthusiastically employed these forms in the training of his company.

Among his contemporaries, the strongest impressions made upon Barrault were from the work of his close friend and colleague at the Atelier, Étienne

Decroux, the famous mime under and with whom he studied this ancient art, and from Antonin Artaud, former Atelier member destined to be the prophet of the new theatre. Decroux sought a stripped-down form of theatre in which the actor's dance-like physical expressiveness replaced the need for decor and text. Decroux found in Barrault a completely devoted pupil who was willing to undergo the master's extremely rigorous training demands concerning diet, exercise, breathing, and the techniques of movement and balance.

With Artaud, whom he first met in 1932, Barrault shared many ideas. Barrault's occasional use of incantatory speech, unusual audience-actor relationships, masks, and symbolic gestures and movement paralleled many of the conceptions about which Artaud theorized but could not put into practice. Although Artaud recognized certain differences between his ideas and those of Barrault, he did declare that Barrault was the sole contemporary who comprehended his fundamental principles for a theatre of cruelty, especially as represented by Barrault's staging of *As I Lay Dying* (described below).

Other outstanding inspirations to Barrault were Paul Claudel, the brilliant symbolist playwright, a man much older than Barrault, but one with whom he had a long-lasting spiritual and emotionally profound relationship, and Charles Granval, the Comédie Française director under whom Barrault, in 1939, first acted Hamlet. Granval, too, conceived of a total theatre form, being himself capable of arranging music, designing scenery, and directing. Stanislavsky also played a role in Barrault's development, particularly through his stress on "sincerity" and "honesty" in acting.

Barrault's earliest directing assignment was in 1935 with his own version of William Faulkner's novel *As I Lay Dying,* which was rehearsed for almost half a year. As was often the case with plays he staged, Barrault played a major role. *As I Lay Dying* (*Autour d'une Mère* in Barrault's version) was also the first of a number of productions in which Barrault personally adapted a well-known literary work for the stage, attempting to discover a theatrical format which could convey the interior quality of the original. As Barbara Gordon puts it, he sought a "form able to recapture a life as complex as that of the dramatist and as immediate as that of the mime: a language of theatrical symbols created through the total utilization of the human instrument."[2] He transferred Faulkner's 1930 novel of Mississippi life into symbolic patterns of physical rhythms and movements, gestures, and incantatory vocalizations. The verbal text was absolutely minimal, occupying about one half hour of the two hours of performance, and much of it was sung or chanted by a chorus. There was no "dialogue" as such, but the central character, a mother who dies, delivered two lyrical speeches after her death. The fourteen actors represented not only human characters, but everything in the environment, from objects to natural forces, through a wide range of vocal and bodily methods, including chanting, strange vocal effects, a variety of sounds produced by the actors' bare feet, dance and mime movement, use of actual masks and improvisational techniques. One of the most striking moments came in the death scene when Barrault, dressed in a mask and flared skirt—he was substituting for the actress cast as the mother who withdrew from the production just before it opened—created the sound of a saw by breathing raspily in time to the movements of the son who was preparing the coffin. As his raised arm and then his body gradually stiffened, he conveyed the mother's death with memorable effect. All was done within the simplest possible means with little reliance on technical resources which might detract from the actor's performance. A tomtom provided the only musical accompaniment. This first production gave clear indications of the path much of Barrault's later work would take. In a way, As I Lay Dying was his "first manifesto" in its attempt to formulate a technique by which the actor can reach beyond the merely external surface of naturalism to enact both human beings and elements from the nonhuman animate and inanimate world, making numerous transformations in the process.

In the 1960s Barrault, looking back on this production, declared how modern it would look in a theatre which viewed Julian Beck and Jerzy Grotowski as its newest gods. In As I Lay Dying he appeared almost in the nude, wearing only a dance strap; years later he told an interviewer:

My theory was that muscles have human expression. The muscles of my belly house a human expression, and my conviction was to express myself with the muscles of my belly. While the production lasted two hours, there were only 30 or 40 minutes of text. We sang; we cried; we shouted.[3]

Dedicated to the concept of ensemble theatre, Barrault spent much of his early career valiantly attempting to found a company of his own. He left Dullin in 1936 to form an ensemble group with a company which shared his ideas, but unfortunately, his attempt at a collective in the Grenier des Augustins failed to mature. He had hoped to produce an ambitious program with himself and four other directors, including Jean Dasté and Jean Vilar, in which a training program could be run concurrently with the production activity. The group disbanded, however, before any plays were staged. He had to wait until 1946 when he and his wife, the outstanding actress Madeleine Renaud, formed the Compagnie Madeleine Renaud–Jean-Louis Barrault for his dreams to fructify. In the meantime he was extremely busy as an actor and director, in films and on the stage.

The money he earned from his cinema appearances was usually funnelled into the work he wanted to do in the theatre. With these earnings he offered in the late thirties two more notable examples of avant-garde theatre, his adaptation of Cervantes' late sixteenth-century Senecan tragedy, *The Siege of Numantia*, called *La Numantia* in Barrault's 1937 adaptation, and Norwegian author Knut Hamsun's *Hunger* (*La Faim*) (1939), derived from the latter's 1890 novel. Although Barrault's choice of plays, by and large, has been apolitical (he has forcibly expressed his distaste for tendentious theatre), *La Numantia* was politically motivated, being an act of support for the Spanish Republicans, then involved in civil war. The play, in which the hero is the populace of the Spanish town of Numancia and no single individual, concerns the second century B.C. attack on the town of the Roman general Scipio Africanus; rather than permit the general the taste of victory, the people of the town destroy both it and themselves. Barrault took this often brutal but too rambling and unfocused work, combining both epic and allegorical features, and imbued it with topical relevance. The culture of eternal Spain was beautifully evoked, while the invading Romans, marching in goosestep formations, had about them the unmistakable air of fascists. To mock the ridiculous pomposity of the invaders, Barrault included such touches as having Scipio use a child's play shovel when he ritualistically began the act of digging the trench designed to isolate the townspeople. The presentation was so stylized some critics felt it bordered on ballet. *New York Times* correspondent Philip Carr observed that "vigor and movement and a certain gymnastic frenzy of sincere passion are . . . characteristic of the whole production."[4] Ironically, the production, inspired by the Spanish civil war, was to be vividly recalled a few years later when France suffered German occupation.

THE COMÉDIE FRANÇAISE

He joined the Comédie Française as an actor under Copeau in 1940 and was elected a permanent member, or *sociétaire,* in 1942. In 1941 he directed two massive outdoor daylight productions at the Roland-Garros Stadium, one being André Obey's *800 Meters* (*800 Mètres*) (which included Barrault running an 800-meter race around the stadium) and the other Aeschylus' *Suppliants.* In 1942 at the Comédie Française he staged Racine's *Phèdre,* his first French classic.

With *Phèdre* his practice began of preparing for a classic revival by minutely studying the text, annotating it in great detail, and writing down his creative aims for the total production in terms of color, sound, lights, gestures, decor, vocalization, and movement. He viewed *Phèdre* as a symphonic composition, its every moment capable of orchestration in musical terms. It contained movements, duets, motifs, recitatifs, trios, rhythms, and so forth, with even the roles viewed in terms of their musical qualities. Thésée was a baritone, Phèdre a mezzo-soprano, Hippolyte a tenor, and so on. He sought in the movement a physical counterpart to the vocal music, hoping to achieve a truly classical tragic style to meet the demand of Racine's dramaturgy. A simplified decor employed no furniture other than that called for by the script, a solitary chair.

A year later he realized many of his ideas regarding total theatre in his spectacular version of Claudel's verse drama, *The Satin Slipper* (*Le Soulier de Satin*). Barrault had to put up a fight to be allowed to stage this so-called unproducible symbolist closet drama (published in 1924) set in Spain at the turn of the seventeenth century. The play, which ran in Barrault's heavily pared-down version between four and a half and five hours, runs from tableau to tableau—against a background of the Spanish Golden Age, Christian saints, dream scenes, international conquest, guardian angels, magical visions, political success and defeat, sin, suffering, heroism, imprisonment, faith, renunciation, death, and salvation—as it presents a tale of hopeless love between the conquistador Don Rodrigue and the married Doña Prouhèze. It was considered baffling because of its kaleidoscopic playing with time and space, comedy and tragedy, poetry, romance, religion, and mysticism. Claudel, himself reluctant about the project because of the need to make heavy cuts, ultimately found himself taking an active part in the final rehearsals. Barrault discovered the key to this seminal work mainly through the effective use of mime; physical objects were often represented by actors, thereby heightening the theatrical atmosphere and allowing the play to move swiftly from locale to locale.

The Satin Slipper was his first Claudel production. From 1943 to 1970 Barrault directed six Claudel works, some of them several times. One was an evening of Claudel selections. As Christopher Innes points out, "Claudel's plays, with their multiplicity of short scenes and characters, their marvelously baroque, incantatory language, and their shifting transformations of visual imagery,"[5] were ideal objects for Barrault's radical staging ideas. Much of their unique flavor comes from Claudel's exposure to the drama of the Orient, especially the Japanese *nō* theatre, a genre for which Barrault already had a predisposition (although he was not to see an authentic *nō* performance until 1957). Moreover, their spiritual themes, which often concern the cosmic meaning of love, the goal of which Claudel believed to be salvation (Claudel was a devout Catholic who infused all his plays with religious ideas), were deeply appealing to the mystically inclined Barrault, who has even declared his belief that Claudel was the century's greatest playwright. Whatever reputation Claudel holds as a notable dramatist, says David Whitton, is largely owing to Barrault's influence: "Their partnership is the most spectacular example of a director literally rescuing a major playwright, converting his universally admired but unperformed texts into a living dramatic force."[6]

Barrault's close collaboration with Claudel was not purely literary; the older man made numerous useful suggestions regarding all aspects of production, from casting and the selection of designers and composers to rehearsal notes on the staging and acting. He provided his ideas in both verbal and written form, occasionally even demonstrating his ideas for an actor. Normally, though, his thoughts on acting were conveyed through Barrault.

In 1945, his last full year at the Comédie Française, Barrault directed André Gide's translation of Shakespeare's *Antony and Cleopatra* and François Mauriac's *The Unloved* (*Les Mal Aimés*). The first was an unusual production in which, according to Dorothy Knowles,

He introduced three mimed scenes, making of the carousel at sea a silent ballet which worked up to a striking crescendo of movement, of the battle of the galleys a mime executed by three figures at the prow of a ship, and three "dancers" (Barrault, Decroux, and Jacques Charron), who suggested the unhurried movement of the galleys by their slow-motion twists and turns and the sound of waves against the ship's sides by their glissades; and of the land battle a sort of Pyrrhic dance by two soldiers using stylized cuts and thrusts and circling movements.[7]

THE COMPAGNIE RENAUD-BARRAULT

Barrault and his wife left the Comédie Française in 1946 to found the Renaud-Barrault company, mentioned above. Their opening bill, on October 17, 1946, at the Théâtre Marigny, which the company was to call home for a decade, was Gide's translation of *Hamlet,* directed by and starring Barrault. *Hamlet* became a permanent part of Barrault's repertory and was staged numerous times in France and around the world. Barrault found the title role a never-ending source of revelation and made it the principal role in his repertory. His *Hamlet* was an acrobatic and vigorous portrayal, played with savage energy and irony, unpredictable in the extreme. He introduced exciting new business, such as toying with his "bare bodkin" in the "To be or not to be" scene as though it were a street tough's stiletto, touching the First Player's face to verify the reality of his tears, and grasping Horatio after seeing the ghost to insure himself of his friend's corporeal presence. Especially exciting was the opening scene on the battlements. The ghost scenes were accentuated by an accompaniment of a high-pitched whistle and ominous drumbeats. This *Hamlet* also displayed a marked sexuality, as seen, for example in the prince's scene with Ophelia as Claudius and Polonius eavesdrop. As Whitney Bolton described it during its 1952 New York showing, Hamlet "caresses Ophelia with lordly purpose and the scene dazes the audience when, with slow deliberation, he seizes the front of her skirt and lifts it, takes his fill of a candid look, then contemptuously drops it."[8]

REPERTORY

The work of the new repertory company, which existed without subsidy, doing three or four new productions annually, was the crowning achievement of Barrault's career. This group presented both classics and new plays, a great many of them directed by Barrault, with outside directors called in for the others. Operating on a self-sustaining basis, the outstanding company produced fifty-four plays during a life of thirteen seasons. During their decade at the Marigny, the total number of revivals was eleven, in addition to twenty new works and eight classics—in all, a total of forty-one productions. Of the new plays, most were by untried playwrights, an accomplishment of which Barrault was extremely proud. These years also saw him experimenting in the discovery of wide-ranging approaches to genre and style, from the melodrama of the *The Hunchback* (*Le Bossu*) to the vaudeville of *Keep an Eye on Amélie!* (*Occupe-toi d'Amélie!*) to the total theatre of spectacular productions and the simplicity of almost one-man plays, like Jean Vauthier's *The Fighting Character* (*Le Personnage Combattant*). From 1959 to 1960 the company toured and played at diverse Paris theatres. In 1959 they became the Théâtre de France under the terms of a state subsidy.

Barrault's aim with this company had been to run it along the lines of a model farm, "the elders supplying the grafts, the adults the bulk of the crops, the younger ones the seeds for the new crops,''[9] an analogy Barrault drew to express his idea that a good company needs three generations of performers.

Operating on a true repertory system, the Renaud-Barrault company was France's first success in this vein since Copeau's Vieux Colombier. Despite the presence in the repertory of works by Shakespeare, Lope de Vega, and Aeschylus, the bulk of the plays staged were French, since the company toured frequently and was expected to represent the cream of French drama in the international arena.

Repertory is a crucial factor in Barrault's theatre thinking. He strongly believes an actor can grow in his art only through playing the wide range of roles afforded by this system. Actors in his company have been more concerned, on the whole, with the seriousness of their art than the size of their bank accounts, for the economics of repertory prevent a company from earning the sizable profits available to more commercially minded managements when they produce a hit.

To give his actors and audience a variety of choices, Barrault selected a well-balanced repertory. He knew that the repertory system allowed him to fail with a play, as it could always be replaced immediately with a proven success. Freedom to experiment is crucial to a theatre man like Barrault. He balanced his repertory between the classics, which he considers the best laboratory for teaching an actor and director his craft, and modern plays, to help keep the company a living part of its times.

At the Marigny the company's 1946 productions included Pierre de Marivaux's *The False Confessions (Les Fausses Confidences)*; Jacques Prévert's *Baptiste*, based on Barrault's great role in the film *Children of Paradise*; and Armand Salacrou's *Nights of Fury (Les Nuits de la Colère)*. The following season saw Franz Kafka's *The Trial (Le Procès)*. Other Barrault-directed productions of the season were Anton Chekhov's *The Bear*, Molière's *Amphitryon*, and Boris Kochno's mime-play, *The Fountain of Youth (La Fontaine de Jouvence)*. He staged Georges Feydeau's *Keep an Eye on Amélie!* in 1948, followed by Albert Camus's *State of Siege (L'État de Siège)* and Claudel's *Break of Noon (Partage de Midi)*. Outstanding in 1949 were Marivaux's *Love's Second Surprise (La Seconde Surprise de l'Amour)*, Ferdinand Bruckner's *Elizabeth of England*, and Paul Fevel and Anicet Bourgeois' *The Hunchback*. In 1950 Feydeau was again represented by *Going to Pot (On Purge Bébé)*. Marcel Achard's *Marlborough Off to War (Marlborough s'en va-t-en Guerre)*, Jean-Paul Sartre's *Dirty Hands (Les Mains Sales)*, Jean Anouilh's *The Rehearsal (La Répétition)*, and Henri de Montherlant's *Malatesta* were also staged by Barrault. There was more Marivaux in 1951 with *The Test (L'Épreuve)*, and a play by Alfred de Musset, *No Trifling with Love (On ne Badine pas avec L'Amour)*. Barrault put together an evening of Claudel selections in 1952, *Cognizance of Paul Claudel (Connaissance de Paul Claudel)*, his only directorial creation of the year. Claudel's *Christopher Colombus (Christophe Colomb*, described below) was presented in 1953, as was Jean Giraudoux's *Duel of Angels (Pour Lucrèce)*. Barrault inaugurated a new intimate theatre, the Petite Marigny, in 1954, a year with a number of new productions, including Molière's *The Misanthrope,* Fernand Crommelynck's *The Magnificent Cuckold (Le Cocu Magnifique)*, and Chekhov's *The Cherry Orchard.* Christopher Fry's *A Sleep of Prisoners* joined the repertory in 1955 along with *Volpone* by Ben Jonson, *Intermezzo* by Giraudoux, *The Oresteia* (described below), *The Gardener's Dog (Le Chien du Jardinier)* by de Vega, and *Sequels to a Race (Les Suites d'un Course)* by Jules Supervielle. The last Marigny season, 1956, saw Barrault's presentation of *The Fighting Character* and Georges Schéhadé's *The Story of Vasco (Vasco)*. It must be remembered that the repertory was further enriched during these years by the productions of other exciting directors, including Louis Jouvet, Roger Planchon, Jean Desailly, Jean Vilar, Jean Cocteau, Jorge Lavelli, Pierre Bertin, and Jean-Pierre Granval.

The next few years saw Barrault's stagings of Kafka's *The Castle* (1957), coadapted by Barrault and Pol Quentin, and a revival of *The Satin Slipper* (1958).

THÉÂTRE DE FRANCE

When the company's title was changed in 1959 to Théâtre de France, they were housed by André Malraux, minister of culture, at the Odéon-Théâtre de France, one of Paris' three state-subsidized playhouses. Here they remained until 1968. It was hoped that, despite an insufficient subsidy, Barrault could somehow wring a profit out of this run-down theatre, whose history goes back to 1782. Barrault approached the goal with enormous energy and imagination, and his productions here of the more advanced contemporary French playwrights in an abundant repertory shared with national and international classics made the Odéon-Théâtre de France a highly successful progressive counterbalance to the staid traditions of the Comédie Française. The playhouse was restored and, to suit the needs of some of the new plays for a more intimate environment, an arrangement was devised whereby the auditorium was made smaller by the use of a canopy uniting the orchestra and first balcony. This arrangement eventually was superseded by the creation of a small theatre space, the Petit Odéon, out of a foyer area. Major new Barrault productions included Claudel's *Head of Gold (Tête d'Or,* 1959), Anouilh and Roland Landonbach's *The Little Molière (Le Petit Molière,* 1959), Eugène Ionesco's *Rhinocéros* (1960), Shakespeare's *Julius Caesar* (1960), André Obey's *The Rape of Lucrece (Le Viol de Lucrèce,* 1961), Feydeau's *But Don't Run Around in the Nude (Mais n'te Promene donc pas Toute Nue,* 1961), Schéhadé's *The Voyage (Le Voyage,* 1961), Gilles Segal's *Penny Pantomimes (Pantomimes d'un Sou,* 1961), Giraudoux's *Judith* (1961), René-Jean Clot's *The Revelation (La Révélation,* 1962), Fry's *The First Born* (1962), Racine's *Andromache* (1962), Ionesco's *The Pedestrian in the Air (Le Pieton de l'Air,* 1963), Marivaux's *Double Inconstancy (La Double Inconstance,* 1963), François Billetdoux's *You Must Pass through the Clouds (Il Faut Passer par les Nuages,* 1964), Marguerite Duras' *Days in the Trees (Des Journées Entières dans les Arbres,* 1965), Ionesco's *The Lagoon (La Lagon)* and *Frenzy for Two (Le Délire à Deux,* 1966), an adaptation from Ruzzante, *Ruzzante*

Returns to the War (1966), Shakespeare's *Henry VI* (1966), adapted by Barrault, Seneca's *Medea* (1967), Nathalie Sarraute's *Silence, Lie* (*Le Silence, Le Mensonge*, 1967), and Edward Albee's *A Delicate Balance* (1967). At the Odéon, Barrault brought in a series of major directors, many of them leaders of the avant-garde, to stage new productions. Also, many of his old successes were restaged and brought back into the repertory.

In May 1968 radical student uprisings in Paris included the occupation of various establishment institutions, among them the Sorbonne. For some reason, never adequately explained, Barrault's theatre was taken over by the students, and Barrault, ever sympathetic to the problems of youth, engaged in an open discussion with them. Infuriated by his behavior, the conservative Malraux dismissed the company from the Odéon, removing its comfortable subvention. Once more, the large and versatile company had to fend for itself. The minister of culture had been seething, apparently, ever since the Odéon had allowed Roger Blin to stage Jean Genet's drama *The Screens* (*Les Paravents*), a controversial work dealing with French rule in Algeria. Its production, in which Barrault had played the role of Si Slamane, had been a political cause célèbre, with frequent disruptions in the theatre inspired by rabid right-wingers.

LATEST PRODUCTIONS

Barrault turned what might have been a catastrophe into a triumph. Being forced out of the Odéon led him to forgo his reliance on the proscenium stage, with which he had been growing increasingly uncomfortable for certain plays. Much of his work henceforth was to be in flexible environments that originally had been designed for other than theatrical purposes. This new direction began with the now unsubsidized company's move to the Élysée-Montmartre, a converted boxing arena, where Barrault staged his renowned adaptation of *Rabelais* (1968), based on the life and work of the famed iconoclastic French writer. It has been suggested that this production—with its multiple, if simplistic, acknowledgments of such hippie culture trademarks as nudity, marijuana, rock music, and a disgust with formal education—was conceived as an act of revenge on the narrow-mindedness which could provoke the stupid repression of the arts represented by Malraux's action. Despite the lack of subsidy following Malraux's decision, the company's success in *Rabelais* allowed it to stay alive. Though he continued to direct other plays for his company, Barrault's *Rabelais* remained the high-water mark of his latest period of activity. Here again was evidence of Barrault's consistent avant-gardism. *Rabelais*—originally intended for the Odéon—expressed Barrault's new interest in the idea of environmental theatre. The production was staged at the center of the former arena with the audience surrounding the cruciform-shaped acting area. The only scenery was a clever arrangement of ropes, disposed during the first half to suggest the outlines of a circus tent, and during the second half to stand for the riggings of a ship. The exceedingly episodic three-hour work was lauded for its theatrical ingenuity, but it was also widely acknowledged to be dramaturgically clumsy and unfocused. Barrault's success with the show led him to take the company on a world tour with another of their productions, Samuel Beckett's *Happy Days*. Soon after, Barrault staged an English version of *Rabelais* in England and America.

A 1970 montage of works by Alfred Jarry, *Jarry on the Mound* (*Jarry sur la Butte*), adapted by Barrault, was, like *Rabelais*, a spectacular theatre piece with elements of circus, vaudeville, and choreography presented in arena fashion, and with some of the action taking place on platforms placed in the audience's midst. Like *Rabelais,* it was conceived around the figure of a man (the late nineteenth-century dramatist, Alfred Jarry) who held strikingly anti-establishment beliefs. Several years later (1972), Barrault returned to a "found" location with Claudel's *Before the Wind of the Balearic Islands* (*Sous le Vent des Îles Baléares*, part of *The Satin Slipper* not produced before), presented in a tent in a splendid out-of-use nineteenth-century train station, on the left bank of the Seine across from the Louvre. The same year a tent setup in the Tuileries Gardens was the locale for *The Bourgeois Gentleman* (*Le Bourgeois Gentilhomme*).

From 1970 to 1974 Barrault and company played at the Théâtre Recamier. Here they successfully housed many visiting foreign companies, several revivals, and a number of new productions, including Barrault's unusually popular staging of British playwright Colin Higgins' *Harold and Maude* (premiered in Bordeaux in 1973, and seen in Paris in 1974), with Madeleine Renaud giving a luminous performance in the part of the octogenarian who has a love affair with a boy. The company then took over the disused train station, the Gare d'Orsay, where *Before the Wind of the Balearic Islands* was produced, and converted it to the Théâtre d'Orsay, a twin theatre complex with a restaurant. Here were produced such works as *Thus Spake Zarathustra* (*Ainsi Parlait Zarathustra*, 1974), adapted by Barrault from Nietzsche's writings with music by Pierre Boulez; *The Nights of Paris* (*Les Nuits de Paris*, 1975), adapted from the works of the eighteenth-century writer Restif de la Bretonne; *The New World* (*La Nouvelle Monde*), and a little known 1875 play by Villiers de l'Isle-Adam (1977); a reworked interpretation of *Harold and Maude* and a new work by Georges Coulonges, the *Candide*-like *Zadig,* based on a story by Voltaire (1978). Thomas S. Turgeon's description of the latter reminds us that Barrault's approach to the theatre remained undimmed by time:

The short story is told in the theatrical shorthand of cabaret comedy. Short scenes run by briskly, like black-out sketches, and many are orchestrated around a piece of deft performing technique. Barrault himself, as well as directing the piece, exemplified this convention in the many roles he joined his company to play.[10]

In 1981 Barrault took over a new venue, the Théâtre du Rond-Point, on the site of a former ice-skating rink near the Champs-Élysées. Here, a 930-seat theatre was accompanied by one with 190 seats (Le Petit Rond-Point). He opened the larger space with *The Love of Love,* a montage production inspired by the Psyche legend and based on numerous writings about love. This establishment was home to all his productions of the eighties. These included *The Strausses* (*Les Strausses*) (1982), by Georges Coulonges, about the Viennese composers; a new version of Sophocles' *Antigone* (1982); Paul Valéry's *The Soul and the Dance* (*L'Âme et la Danse*) (1983); Victor Hugo's rarely seen *Angelo, Tyrant of Padua* (*Angelo, Tyran de Padoue*) (1984); a spectacular, circus-like presentation of Aristophanes' *The Birds* (1985), with a 1927 score by Georges Auric; and Barrault's final production to date, a spectacle entitled *Théâtre Fair* (1986).

Barrault had been restored to government favor in 1971 when he was reappointed head of the international program the Théâtre des Nations, designed to bring foreign companies to Paris. He had held the post until his dismissal from the Odéon.

The company's frequent tours to major cities around the globe have brought it tremendous acclaim. Barrault's tours even led him to conceive of an "international" theatre style. His cofounding of the International Theatre Research Center in Paris with Peter Brook in 1967 was a partial fulfillment of this dream.

PRODUCTION STYLE

As may be imagined from the vast range of genres represented by his productions, Barrault's directing style has been, on the whole, eclectic, shifting according to the demands of his material. It has ranged, according to Jacques Guicharnaud and June Beckelman, from "epico-lyrical symbolism for Claudel's works, expressionism for . . . *The Trial,* [to] sophisticated pantomime for Marivaux's comedies, etc."[11] Opera also has been staged by Barrault. His wide familiarity with theories of modern and classical staging has been of great value in choosing the best approach for each production. Pragmatism, rather than dogmatism, consistently has been a Barrault hallmark. Though he often has sought to produce works conducive to total-theatre staging, he has been limited by a lack of plays perfectly suited to its demands. Consequently, most of his productions are not in total theatre style, though parts of them may be.

Barrault, despite his being closely associated with total theatre, does not feel any particular identification with it. As an eclectic, he prefers to use total theatre only when appropriate. Thus, despite his avowed Artaudian preference for nonverbal, mimetic, and spectacular drama, the list of plays directed by Barrault reveals many which, for all their physical possibilities, are essentially works in which spoken language predominates. Even the term "total theatre" bothers him. "Personally I don't like this word. I am not the one who thought it up. For me it's all just theatre."[12] Each play requires a new method. He will therefore generalize, "When we do a classic play we try to be the most obedient, and when we do a new play we try to be the most audacious."[13] The artist can do no more than confront each new problem in isolation, using his instincts and theatrical knowledge to find a solution.

Like Copeau and those he influenced, Barrault claims great respect for the text of the play. The director's function is to find the author's point of view and to stage the play as its author might have envisioned it. He firmly believes that style must not be mere superficial gloss, but should be an integral part of the drama's nature. Each play, moreover, especially a classic, has a singular quality or tone which the director must grasp firmly and encapsulate in the production. This inner quality will dictate the proper style required to embody the reality of the world within the play. One cannot take a play and impose a style on it for the sake of cleverness alone. Fundamental to a production which has achieved a play's appropriate style is the sense of truth; no matter how "stylized" a work may be, it must always be true to the playwright's vision of reality. Style without truth is mere "stylization," an artificial encrustation of self-serving directorial ideas that betray the integrity of the original play. Yet, the style employed will always differ from one director to another because of differences in each director's outlook and the resources (actors, theatre, money, etc.) he has available. Likewise, the director must consider the audience for the production. A foreign play in French translation must be performed, for example, at a tempo appropriate to the French temperament rather than to that of the audience for which it originally was written.

As we have seen, the singular stylistic principle which informs his most applauded productions is that called "total theatre." Total theatre, as Barrault conceives it, springs from the fullest, most profound exploitation of the actor's resources—physical, spiritual, and emotional. As suggested, Barrault's ideas derive to a large extent from Artaud, who stimulated him to see the "simultaneity" of theatre art in which all theatrical elements form an orchestral unity at the heart of which is the actor, used as completely as possible. Finding serious drawbacks in the partial outlook of the theatre of psychological realism, Barrault seeks a holistic theatre where the spectator's perception of the totality of man's existence is embodied, an existence physical, spiritual, emotional, and instinctual. Appeals are made to all the spectator's senses to make him aware of the totality of life in and around him. Barrault believes that the spectator confronted by a work that allows him to experience the totality of existence, in its sensual, psychological, and metaphysical dimensions, will somehow be made more whole and will achieve a harmonious unity with the world.

Barrault employs visual taste, acting ability, directorial power, and literary craft to produce exceptionally unified theatre works. He strongly believes in the Craigian idea of a super theatre-artist who can write, act, and direct, as well as contribute to the design of a production. If writing is not the director's strength, then close collaboration with the playwright is essential. He realized early that to create theatre as he envisioned it, it would be necessary either to write or adapt his own dramas. Few playwrights wrote according to his personal vision of theatre. When he found one who did, Paul Claudel, he developed an intense symbiotic relationship with the man.

The Craigian ideal extended to the director's necessary capability in all the technical areas of theatre production. Design and musical talents were essential, and even management techniques, lighting, and props must come within the director's purview. Barrault's training as a painter prepared him to participate intimately in the design of his productions, especially in the art of lighting. A director must be thoroughly familiar with every aspect of his profession through extensive experience in each area. Only then can he claim the right to criticize and direct the work of specialists in these fields.

Gordon Craig's demands for an actor whose expressive faculties could be totally controlled blended with the ideals of Artaud, Decroux, and Claudel in Barrault's attempt "to establish a vocabulary and grammar of theatrical symbols, based on the actor's vocal intonations and rhythms, and on the gestures and relative positions of the body—in some ways a Western equivalent of Oriental theatre."[14] An early example of the Artaudian and Craigian influence in total theatre staging was Barrault's version of *The Trial*. Norman Marshall writes that of all the Barrault productions he witnessed, *The Trial* was the closest approximation of the total unity of conception envisioned by Craig. He found the production to be "symbolistic, both in decor and acting, a combination of pantomime, rhythmic movement, and shadow graphs, with speech used merely as an accessory to visual means of expression."[15] Eric Bentley viewed the production as Artaudian in its overt physicality and secondary reliance on the verbal. Bentley, however, disagreed with Barrault's conception of Kafka's dream world, feeling that the text required a visualization "full of natural movement and detail" and not a

stylized version of actuality . . . "alienated" by mystery. Voices come at you out of the dark. Figures emerge and recede in silhouette. Objects are a caricature of their real selves—too big or too small. Movements are reduced to a mechanical pattern so that men become as dolls. The environment runs away from the people . . . walls rise and fall. There are many broad, dark arches, many little dark rooms and eerie perspectives.[16]

Bentley was fascinated by the theatrical devices conceived by the director while disputing their thematic appropriateness. Among these he notes Barrault's emphasis on the Jewishness of the play's world, especially the creation of a "chorus of Jews, which moves as a *corps de ballet* and by its ordered movements and disorder expresses Joseph K.'s bewilderment and ours."[17] Barrault's imagination also helped overcome staging problems unsolvable by conventional means. In the concluding scene of the play, Joseph K.'s execution is enacted.

Joseph K. is led on by his guards. They enact a longish journey by foot. Supported . . . by his guards, Barrault mimes a fast walk with knees raised high. This first on one side of the stage, then on the other. There follows the preparation of his execution. . . . On the stage the lighting-up of a window in the distance and Joseph K.'s wondering if help is at hand does not "register"; what does register is Joseph K.'s nervous seeking of an attitude to die in. When one side of the block doesn't seem right he tries the other. Meanwhile the guards perform what Kafka calls the "odious ceremony of courtesy," the exchanging of the knife back and forth, until one of them sends it into Joseph K.'s breast with a twist and flourish. The simple mention of the ceremony in the text becomes on stage a complete pantomimic sequence.[18]

In Bentley's opinion Barrault's directorial style in *The Trial* represented the culmination of German expressionist tendencies, and was probably the best solution to the aesthetic ideals the expressionists dreamed of but did not fully realize. However, the Artaudian element, notes Bentley, is superficial in its failure to evoke the darker, subterranean, emotional currents of a play, a drawback stemming from Barrault's overly cerebral orientation.

Barrault's concentration on choreographic movement was quite radical within the context of the French theatre world where the stage was dominated by the spoken word and the movement of the human being through space was less valued aesthetically than the sound of the human voice.

According to Barrault, the actors in a total-theatre work play their environment as well as their characters: "the river, the fire, the rasping of the saw breaking down wood. The actor: a total instrument. The characters have a social behavior and a fundamental behavior. They are living on two planes, the man and his double."[19]

The actor must not be simply "framed" by the other ingredients in the theatrical performance, but these ingredients must themselves be necessary contributants to the whole; they must rise above being "interior decoration" and become "essential theatre." Craig's ideal of theatre—that it is an organic art form in which no single element dominates, but in which all elements are used by the creative director to compose the work of art—is clearly operative in Barrault's conception.

The most important point in a play consists . . . in finding the means of so raising the level of production (decor, props, lighting, sound effects, music) that it no longer contents itself with the secondary role of "frame" or mixture of the arts but succeeds, on the contrary, in humanizing itself to such an extent that it virtually becomes part of the action, that it succeeds, in short, in serving the theatre in its totality—at this moment, total-theatre finds its unity.[20]

Barrault's total-theatre actors, then, perform both as characters, and, to an extent, as the props and scenery of the play. They use their voices to create not only verbal meaning but sound effects and music, too. Thus, in Claudel's *Christopher Columbus*, the players,

alternatively spinning wool, playing the guitar, becoming waves, walking, running, undulating on the sea, receiving the wind, dead, living, assuming reality, becoming shade, bellowing as Indian gods, howling like the tempest, murmuring like the breeze, prattling like gossips, indignant as mutineers, singing their joy, shouting their enthusiasm . . . motionless as a picture, stamping like maniacs, . . . spectators, commentators, actors, . . . conjure up . . . our dream of complete theatre.[21]

Bill Wallis, an actor in Barrault's English production of *Rabelais*, found that the performers had to be

constantly ringing the changes on their identities. At different times within the same scene, they are miming objects or animals, speaking as themselves, acting as mouthpieces for some philosophical or religious movement. . . . The "total theatre" is not so much (for those in the play) the array of technical effects that are produced . . . but this constant ranging through all the forms of dramatic action of which an actor is capable.[22]

Even the costumes and scenery assume a multiplicity of functions. In *Christopher Columbus* they

humanize themselves: the chains grate with precision, the sail billows like a living creature. Does one need a court dress? Two flaps detach themselves from the dress one is wearing and become a hoop. . . . One rolls up one's trousers, and, barechested, becomes a sailor. . . . The lighting joins in, the projectors move, luminous intensity oscillates, shadows are cast, fade away, change shape. . . . As for the music . . . it proposes, it intervenes, it traces lines of joy or of distress.[23]

Barrault derives his theatrical ideas not only from his great French predecessors and contemporaries, but from the entire scope of the world theatre; whatever he believes can contribute to his theatre is grist to his mill. Thus, the highly formalized theatre of the East, especially that of Japan, has made a deep impression on his aesthetic.

Aware of theatre activity throughout the world, and largely responsible for the encouragement of outstanding theatrical experimentation in France and abroad, Barrault has a rich comprehension of theatrical styles. In 1969 he described what he saw as the seven main currents of contemporary theatre. All can be seen in his own work, thus clearly displaying his enormous breadth as a director. (The following is my summation of Barrault's comments to his interviewer.)

1. The documentary drama, a form based on the compilation of original source materials put together to form an evening's entertainment. He feels this form's major weakness is the selectivity of the adapter who is bound to arrange the source materials in a biased direction.

2. Political theatre, theatre with didactic intentions. This is a valid form, he asserts, for it makes theatre relevant; a serious flaw is its tendency to divide, rather than unite, its audiences. To Barrault a good performance should create harmony, not imbalance.

3. Psychological theatre, a current he finds springing from Molière and continued today by Harold Pinter and Edward Albee.

4. Theatre of the absurd, for which he then had a great fondness. The absurd has always been a side of the human condition, the other side of which is tragic. Modern times in particular make one responsive to the echoes of absurdity in drama.

5. Sacred theatre, a form often created by atheists, like Beckett and Genet. Man eternally is searching for something higher and more profound in life, and these playwrights represent that quest.

6. Total theatre based on pantomimic style, a form requiring total use of the human mechanism for its inherent aesthetic values.

7. The happening, a concept encouraged by the avant-garde. It is based on the premise that "our world is destroyed and we have to create from nothing."[24]

In addition, there is the classic theatre from which, states Barrault, we must be strong enough to learn, for it has much to offer modern man. "We don't become parrots of the classics; but we absorb them and find food in them."[25]

IMPORTANCE OF MOVEMENT

Barrault's importance stems, to a great degree, from his infusion into French theatre of skillful movement techniques, derived from all forms of theatre, including classical mime. Not only his total-theatre pieces but the standards of the French neoclassic stage have profited from his deep-felt need to employ the actor's vocal as well as physical resources. As he explains:

Very often we express in words only what we wish to show, while our smallest gestures reveal what we would like to hide. For the psychoanalyst, careful observation of someone's gestures is a valuable way of finding out what that person is concealing. In rehearsing *Phèdre*, a whole plastic language has therefore to be constructed bit by bit. This plastic language constitutes in some sort the secret, subterranean and subconscious revelation of the action. . . . Buried secrets, bad faith, dissimulation, involuntary compulsions, weaknesses, escapes, and so forth, will find themselves a place beneath the official behavior patterns.[26]

Mime, of course, is a quintessential technique for expressing concretely the ineffable. What would require many words to convey can be communicated physically through the appropriate selection and performance of symbolic movements. In the very first work he directed, *As I Lay Dying*, Barrault showed his own brilliant mime technique, particularly in the scene where he had to act Jewel taming a wild horse and then riding it, becoming both horse and rider. Barrault's command of physical expression also is revealed in the choreography of his productions. Always he employs mime and choreography for their ability to expose thematic values and not as mere ends in themselves.

The ability to fully exploit the actor's mimic resources has made Barrault a master at staging what others consider the "unstageable." Through his unique directorial conceptions and the light and easy naturalness and technical perfection of his actors, many plays which few would dare to touch have become outstanding successes.

SCENIC TECHNIQUES

Aside from what the actor contributes, scenic techniques, of course, are by no means slighted in a Barrault production. In conceptualizing a production, Barrault speaks of his search for some central object—a "catalyst object" or "signifying object"—to act as a metaphorical core for the presentation. This must be something that embodies the central thrust of the play. It might be the throne in *Hamlet*, the screens behind which people hide and eavesdrop in *The False Confessions*, the sail in *Christopher Columbus*, or the oversized phone in *The Trial*. In *Rhinoceros* Dudard used a walking stick with a handle shaped like a rhino's horn; when the actor stood in profile the horn could be made to look as though it were growing from his head.

Masks, too, are often seen in Barrault's work, as in *The Oresteia, The Satin Slipper, Christopher Columbus,* and *Rabelais*. His decision to use masks arrived after serious meditation on their appropriateness. In preparing for *The Oresteia* he considered that the characters are not merely totemic beings but as human as any in Shakespeare. Though the mask's original functions of heightening visibility and audibility were no longer primary within a conventional theatre, he chose to use them anyway. He believed that wearing masks was a potent force in drawing the audience into an awareness of "the inner and outer aspect of life, of the relative and of the absolute, of life and death."[27] In this case, the masks were made of leather, and decorated in the fashion of African tribal masks rather than copies of old Greek styles.

Barrault works intimately with his set and costume designers, who have been among the finest in the French theatre. Christian Bérard, Georges Wahkevitch, André Barsacq, Denis Macles, Christian Dior, Maurice Brianchon, and Pierre Delbée have been among the designers of Barrault productions. Barrault is fond of beautiful settings, but is always careful to pare down the scenery to a point where it will not distract from the interior life of the drama.

Costumes are painstakingly considered, and are often the sensitive products of scholarly research as well as aesthetic concerns. They must always be expressive of the play's life and never distracting. Barrault's research for *The Oresteia* revealed that the play took place in the eleventh century B.C. He therefore felt justified in having the costumes designed in terms of "archaic times." The scholarship of experts was employed in devising these garments, which bore the imprint of African, Eastern, and Greek motifs. The archaic quality was further heightened by sets made of wood only—stone and marble belonging to the later period of "decadence."

An expert lighting designer, Barrault makes light a living ingredient of the total theatre. Suzanne Dieckman points, for example, to his use of light in both realistic and symbolic terms in *Phèdre* "to visualize through contrasting light and shadow the characters' inner struggle with mysterious forces and their gradual immersion in darkness—death."[28]

Barrault's late work used the unusual staging arrangements of arenas and parks, though for most of his career he was perfectly happy with the proscenium theatre. As he once said, "All stages are good providing the play comes to life— and the characters begin living and breathing."[29] His reliance on the actor's tools often has obviated the need for unusual scenic devices, but he had known how to employ these when appropriate. Film mixed with live action, for instance, was used in *Christopher Columbus*. However, Barrault is cautious about such technical intrusions. Film must not be used simply to show what the technical resources of the theatre limit it from showing. It is only when film images blend with stage images to allow an artistic juxtaposition of simultaneous actions, and no other means can be found for creating this effect, that the use of film is justified.

SOUND AND MUSIC

Naturally, the auditory aspect of a Barrault production is as important as the visual. Music, unusual speech and breathing techniques, and special sound effects are carefully selected to balance that which can be seen. Barrault has worked with some of the major composers of his day to find the best musical background for his work. Pierre Boulez, Georges Auric, Honnegger, Arthur Milhaud, Francis Poulenc, and others have created original themes, often of a controversial sort, for Barrault's productions. Barrault does whatever he can to stimulate the composer's creativity, reading and performing the entire play while explaining what he wants the music to convey. His musical choices are always organic to his total production scheme. A six-track tape and nonmusical objects used to create musical effects for *Rhinoceros,* and a wealth of nonmusical sound effects like the banging of wooden spoons in *Rabelais* to suggest copulation, are typical of Barrault's auditory imagination as a director.

Like so many other elements, the music sometimes results from historical research, as when the music chosen for *The Oresteia* had a decidedly Oriental flavor, since Barrault viewed the play as representing a transitional phase between an ancient Orientalism and the more Western mode of the Hellenic period.

Voices are employed for effects from normal stage speech to incantatory cries and chants, with any number of novel effects introduced when required.

PREPARATION FOR PRODUCTION

In preparing a production, Barrault reads everything about the play and its author on which he can lay his hands. Extensive note-taking and meditation are concomitants of this studious period during which he becomes totally absorbed in thoughts of the work to be staged. As he delves more and more deeply into the intellectual side of the play, he gradually allows his imaginative faculties to take over, so the play takes on multidimensional aspects in his brain. Finally, he puts his ideas down on paper in a meticulous promptbook for use in rehearsal.

He sets down the entire mise-en-scène, including all gestures and movements. Believing that actors feel more secure when the director has worked everything out beforehand, Barrault realizes that needed changes can always be made during the later stages of rehearsal.

Barrault has written deeply and at length on his ideas for staging certain plays, and it is impossible to read these essays without marveling at the sincerity and profundity of his views. Too often, however, Barrault's writing tends to become pompous, mystical, and metaphysical. His description of his work on Aeschylus' *The Oresteia,* though, provides an illuminating account. In 1941 his outdoor daylight production of Aeschylus' *Suppliants* had failed, he thought, because the sun had robbed the staging of all its mystery. But his appetite for Aeschylus had been whetted, not impaired. A trip to Rio de Janeiro had revealed to him certain African ritual ceremonies involving "occult seances," and he undertook to investigate these rites to further comprehend them. He had been "struck" by "the way in which someone . . . finds himself struggling with a spirit, the way trances develop and the flat calm which follows the ritual of these nocturnal ceremonies." His vivid memory of the rituals played a valuable role in his preparations for *The Oresteia,* in which he detected traces of a similar world of magic. Within the shell that had grown over the play in the two-and-a-half millennia since it was created he found a vein of pulsing life that made present "the Greece of coloured statues, an archaic and magical Greece, which was in constant contact with the mystery of life."[30] He thus attempted to produce the play by evoking this "more humane and . . . more theatrical interpretation of Greece,"[31] incorporating what he had learned from the African rituals in Brazil.

In his account, Barrault delves into the historical moment when the drama was written, seeing it as the work of a creative renaissance, heralding a new age. He outlines the argument of the play, in which "we have fratricide, treason, injustices and cruelty. The gods are angry and the humans full of hate." He goes on to describe the plot of each play in the trilogy, which he sees arching from "anxiety" in the *Agamemnon* to "renewal" in the *Eumenides.* This is followed by a structural analysis of the work, "the problems concerning the text to use, the chorus, the characters, . . . the decor, the costume, the masks, the mime, techniques of the performance—song, diction." Using André Obey's translation, he worked with Paul Mazon to pare the work down to "a dramatic and concise text," aiming to reproduce in French the exact timing it seemed would be required to stage the work in Greek. "We felt that by so doing we should gain in intensity and density and we should avoid the sorrow of having to make cuts in the course of rehearsals and performances."[32]

For a year he worked with scholars from the Sorbonne to simulate precisely the incantatory effect of the choruses in French. He also attempted to employ the accepted conventions regarding the choral entrances and groupings, trusting to his own improvisations as he worked out the patterns of movement. The orchestra pit was converted to an acting area for the chorus. A curtain which could rise or fall through a slit onstage was installed between the forestage and proscenium. (In the latter instance, of course, Barrault was adapting a convention not from the Greeks but from the Romans.)

Barrault notes that, technical considerations of performance aside, the play appealed to him because of its abundance of meaningful ideas. As noted above, Barrault holds no brief with theatre used to purvey propaganda, and whatever social concerns may appear consistently in his productions are those that favor human freedom over dogma. *Rabelais,* for instance, was a "homage to today's young"[33] in which he attempted to make parallels between Rabelais' age and the modern world. One performance of *Rabelais* was given at the University of California, Berkeley, on the night in 1970 when several Kent State University students were killed by National Guardsmen during an antiwar protest. In a scene taking place at the Abbey of Thélème, where freedom from clerical regimentation was imagined by Rabelais, the theme of liberty from repression was enhanced by having the company don Berkeley T-shirts, thus effectively enlisting the sympathies of the student audience.

Barrault's description of the ideas in *The Oresteia* concludes his treatment of that play; he relates the ideas not in an abstract literary formulation but in terms of their direct application to performance, especially in light of the patterns and rhythms of the play. He sees the drama operating within a ternary rhythm which he likens to the act of love (a frequent image in Barrault's writing about the nature of the theatrical experience) or the action of a storm: "It seems to me that most acts of life follow this kind of pattern . . . the neutral element heavy and slow, the masculine element sharp and brief, the feminine element, slow and heavy."[34] But such a rhythm is unusual in the modern age of "agitation," he argues, and *The Oresteia,* being the work of a true master, brings us back to a more normal and lifelike rhythm unlike "the sterile, empty agitation of most plays which are offered for production now."[35]

A final section of Barrault's treatment of this play concerns itself with Aeschylus' concept of justice and destiny. He sees the "civilizing effect" of Athena's divine wisdom as making "harmonious life possible," a meaning which makes the play's production "worthwhile."[36] The ultimate purpose of the work, however, is to free man of his inherent anxiety, to soothe man's jangled nerves, and to pacify his soul. The progress from anxiety to renewal has been charted and the residue for mankind is hope.

REHEARSALS AND CASTING

Rehearsals begin with Barrault reading the entire play to the company, a practice fairly common among French directors. He checks the company's reactions to the play to gauge their interest in it. The reading allows him to determine script problems and the actors' responses permit him to surmise the potential reaction of an audience. His reading is very specific. Unlike Harley

Granville-Barker, who avoided a reading which his actors might want to copy, Barrault reads in a way which suggests to his company a model they should emulate in their own performances. A week of roundtable discussions follows, with Barrault expounding his views on the play and its production, and the company then examining the psychological subtleties of the play and characters. Only then does he cast the production, as he says, "basing my decision on the personality, temperament, voice, demeanor, ability, and penchant of the actor."[37]

Like many directors, Barrault is very finicky about his casting, aware that a great part of a director's burdens can be relieved by choosing the proper actors. He works mainly in a repertory framework so his casting choices are more limited than those of a commercial director; this is a charge he must bear with great sensitivity. He admits that the most difficult plays to cast are those with small companies because of the greater selectivity the director must exercise. Occasionally he will change his casting when he sees that a better choice is possible. This is a very difficult task, as an actor's feelings are easy to bruise in such a situation. He often has chosen to cast another player in a role which, by his position, he could have taken himself. Fortunately, his company has always contained superb players such as Jean Desailly whom he could trust with roles he might ordinarily have played. When necessary, Barrault has gone beyond the boundaries of his company to bring in actors for roles which could not be filled from within the ranks. The outside actors are welcomed by the company for the fresh stimuli they provide.

When he addressed the English company which was to do his *Rabelais,* he told them at the first session the results he wanted them to achieve, saying "I want style and precision within an appearance of improvisation." But in this production he did not get involved in long textual discussions, presumably because of time limitations and his own language problems. This method appears to have confused the cast, which was unable "to discuss and discover the meaning of scenes from puzzling over the text." The confusion was gradually dissipated once the actors began to realize how straightforward and unnuanced Barrault expected their work to be. As actor Bill Wallis recounted, "The changes of texture, the richness of the play, were to be found in the movement of its surface and sound rather than within the delicate indications of the inner workings of the individual actors."[38]

Barrault generally begins to block during the second week and works on developing the movement patterns for about two weeks. His production of *Rabelais* at London's Roundhouse followed a somewhat different schedule since he cut out the first week of reading and discussion in favor of roughing in the blocking of Part I. Wallis recalls that Barrault intensified in week two the work of week one, not getting to Part II until week three.

He works rapidly, according to his written mise-en-scène, though he is opposed to learning lines too soon. Doing so can disturb the creative instincts. Lines must be learned precisely, however, with no paraphrasing. The playwright's unique methods of expression, or his verbal music, are inherent in the specific words he has chosen.

WORKING WITH ACTORS

Blocking by Barrault is mechanical and is accepted without discussion. This, he believes, allows the actors time to concentrate on their characters without having to ponder the whys and wherefores of their movements. An active director who likes to work onstage amid his actors, Barrault often moves his people about physically. According to Maurice Schaded, "He prefers to be involved with each actor's work moment by moment, working out with him small and large problems of movement."[39] He constantly adjusts and readjusts positions and gestures, and is apt to demonstrate what he wants without the slightest reservation. When the actors in the English *Rabelais* were confused as to his intentions, he demonstrated for them. By the end of rehearsals he had acted every part. This overt participation partly resulted from Barrault's having staged the play before with French actors and his desire to simulate the effects of that production. The English version was approached almost totally as an externalization of the original, with the actor left on his own to fill in the internal elements. Barrault has himself written, however, that a good director

works on the stage at the side of the actors and shares equally in their efforts in order to help them to discover. He stands in front of them, nose to nose, in order to hypnotize them. He takes them by the arm, as if he were suddenly leading a blind man. He hides behind them, his mouth against their ear, as if he were their guardian angel—or some demon, after all![40]

As this quote makes clear, Barrault dominates his rehearsals no matter who his actors are. Jack Brooking observed Barrault's rehearsals at the Odéon in the early sixties and noted how precise Barrault was in showing what he wanted:

When Barrault directs he is constantly on the move, explaining, demonstrating, mimicking. As he demonstrates, one witnesses a finely wrought performance. He does not work step by step with his actors, but rather shows them the full complication of the finished product.[41]

But Barrault's demands would occasionally be tempered by an understanding of an actor's limits and he sometimes allowed the actor to give him a shadow of the demonstration in return.

Barrault worked under enormous pressure at the Odéon, preparing world tours and acting as business manager, leading actor, producer, and director for a large company, with nightly changes of repertory. It is natural for him to have imposed specific performances on his company members. He did not have the leisure, like Stanislavsky, to work for a year or two on a production. Thus, one can understand an approach in which, as Brooking says, he never draws "ideas *from* an actor; he always gives *to* the actor." Yet, as Brooking goes on to say, "the actor is quite free to bring to the character and the moment as much as he wishes, as long as it fits into the rather precise framework established by the director."[42]

With *Rabelais,* Wallis admits that Barrault was able to stir the company's creative instincts through his charismatic and energetic personal qualities. He brooked little interference from his large company and managed through his personal blend of benevolent despotism to keep them tightly under control, though he "appeared to lose his temper more often than he in fact did."[43]

Barrault's penchant for manipulating his actors is right in line with his belief in the director's responsibility for the entire production. Gordon Craig, one of the strongest influences on his career, would have agreed, as Craig considered the intrusion of the actor's personality a detriment to the totality of a production as conceived by its director. As is well known, Craig even thought of replacing the actors with super-marionettes so that the director's vision could be perfectly realized. It is therefore easier to understand Barrault's viewpoint as noted in a *New York Times* interview in which he disclosed that "from the very first his thoughts on directing were firmly rooted on the premise that to direct is to assume every role—to show how they are done—to maneuver the actor like a horse trainer."[44]

Naturally, actors must respect a director who acts out their roles for them or they will feel creatively frustrated. In Barrault's case, the director is himself so masterful an actor that few who wish to work with him will dispute his methodology. Wallis remarks that "the company's admiration for him as an actor was enormous; he occasionally demonstrated particular exercises and feats of muscular awareness and control that delighted everybody."[45] When the *Rabelais* company ran into difficulties with their vocal work in the huge barnlike environment of the Roundhouse,

Barrault's demonstration of how physical positions required conscious changes and compensations in vocal effort and intensity were of enormous value. He was constantly reminding the company that they were strolling players, performing in a circus. Their vocal level should be pitched at attracting the attention of passersby over the distractions of a busy street.[46]

Despite his tendency to demonstrate for his actors, Barrault has great understanding and respect for the people who act under him. He is sensitive to their natures and adjusts his manner to suit them. He believes that

the ideal actor is the one who can completely complement the character he portrays but the director knows his actor will set the part according to the actor's temperament. With Ophelia, for instance, if the actress playing her has a lovely voice, the director will capitalize on that quality.[47]

Barrault suggests that the director walks a fine line between being an autocrat and having an attitude of laissez-faire. He allows his actors much freedom in developing their characterizations, but is rather dictatorial in his demands for specific physical and vocal responses. He tries to be as sensitive as he can to the actor's explorations, helping him when he begins to make contact with the character and ensuring that he does not lose ground. Working with a permanent company allows him to develop a sixth sense in dealing with his actors, as familiarity makes him more aware of strengths, weaknesses, and needs.

One outgrowth of his familiarity with the actors in his company is his essentially arbitrary categorization of them into three groups in terms of age and experience. The "elders" are the true veterans, whose technical and career accomplishments entitle them to be handled with great sensitivity and respect. The "adults" are those who approximate the director's age and experience, and who can be treated more or less as equals because of the knowledge and technique they share with the director. With the third group, the "young," Barrault mingles teaching with direction, and may even assign such a player to an older one for personal guidance.

The Renaud-Barrault company, after years of intimate work together under Barrault's inspiriting leadership, became very much like a large, happy family. With Barrault's serious demeanor and intense way of working tempered by the light grace and charm of Mme. Renaud, the company's level of joy in the artistic process was consistently high. Describing the rehearsal atmosphere, Brooking observed:

There is a rare consideration for one another's problems and pressures; an understanding of the unharnessed ego. There exists among them a deep-seated realization that back-breaking work and a subjugation of personal ambitions is often necessary to achieve the goal of artistic quality and to preserve the familial rapport which the company enjoys.[48]

It is in the final stages of rehearsal—the last two weeks—that Barrault affords the greatest freedom to his players. This period is spent, he says,

"disobeying" the original mise-en-scène I created on paper. After more work, the play begins to speak to us, the play commands us. Our vision of the entire production changes little by little. . . . The characters have been created and the "mayonnaise," so to speak, has taken.[49]

This period is perhaps the toughest for the director and company, as they work to dig into the very lifeline of the play, to pump truth and vitality into it, and find its final form. The director must be ready to modify his original vision, to make concessions, to allow the actors to find what they need for inspiration, and to keep spirits high, while keeping the whole fragile enterprise on course and preventing it from becoming fragmented by the many new directions into which each new breakthrough threatens to lead it. As each act is set, it is run and timed, and each subsequent run-through aims for the same tempo. Then, as costumes and scenery arrive, the director must keep his actors confident despite the numerous distractions these elements can provide, especially when they do not satisfy whatever objectives it was for which they were originally designed. However, if the final dress rehearsal goes too smoothly, Barrault feels there is reason to worry, as he, like numerous others, believes a good dress rehearsal may lead to a weak opening because of the excessive confidence it inspires in the players. When the show opens it will normally have had six weeks of rehearsal.

CONCLUSION

Barrault is a short, wiry man with striking birdlike features topped by a tousled but thinning head of curly gray hair. He is a glowing affirmation of the artistic spirit in theatre, a man of the fiercest determination matched by the highest ideals. His religious devotion to his artistry has enabled him to achieve the rank of the foremost contemporary man of French theatre. Playing a leading role in a play he is directing allows his personal qualities to infect his players even more vividly than when he wears only the director's hat. Brooking writes, "He inspires spirit and ensemble by acting with his players, infusing both scene and actors with his enduring vivacity and creative energy. His troupe gives the maximum because he does."[50]

Yet acting and directing at the same time can have its drawbacks. Being the sole commander without an assistant director sometimes leads to sloppy blocking and masking which the director cannot see when he is onstage rehearsing. Brooking notes that what saves Barrault from floundering in the double capacity is his great ability to concentrate.

In the role of the director, he dons the shell-rimmed glasses and leans forward giving himself completely to the scene with hawk-like intensity. His eyes narrow and his face contorts, pulling the lips away from the teeth in a kind of grimace. He is then able to step into the scene and switch his [concentration to the role at hand].[51]

Jean-Louis Barrault is a man of deep humanity, with a probing philosophical view of life. He is a lover of life and art; a rebel against the falsely conventional; a searcher after truth. He has great Gallic charm and warmth as well as an abundance of good humor. As Schaded has said, "His regard for everyone with whom he works and his respect for each individual's capacity and art, indicates the humility and integrity within himself."[52]

NOTES

1. See John K. Gillespie, "Interior Action: The Impact of Noh on Jean-Louis Barrault," *Comparative Drama* 16 (Winter 1982–83).

2. Barbara Gordon, "Le Théâtre Total as Envisioned by Jean-Louis Barrault" (Ph.D. diss., Columbia University, 1973), p. 174.

3. Glenn Loney, "In the Words of Jean-Louis Barrault," *Cue Magazine*, 4 October 1969, p. 13.

4. Philip Carr, "Paris Looks at Spain," *New York Times*, 13 June 1937.

5. Christopher Innes, *Holy Theatre: Ritual and the Avant Garde* (Cambridge, Eng.: Cambridge University Press, 1981), p. 119.

6. David Whitton, *Stage Directors in Modern France* (Manchester, Eng.: Manchester University Press, 1987), p. 146.

7. Dorothy Knowles, *French Drama of the Inter-War Years, 1918–1939* (New York: Barnes and Noble, 1968), p. 44.

8. Whitney Bolton, review of *Hamlet, New York Morning Telegraph*, 3 December 1952. Despite the production's worldwide acclaim, it should be noted, its New York presentation raised considerable controversy. To some critics who otherwise were delighted with Barrault's repertory, *Hamlet* was a play that was better left to Americans than Frenchmen. Most outspoken among the disappointed was John Mason Brown, who cavilled at the crowded staging, the "shoddy" settings, the lack of a "driving idea," and the uncertain central performance (*Saturday Review*, 27 December 1952, p. 25). Among the minority who strongly supported the production was Margaret Marshall, for whom "it turned out to be one of the most exciting performances of the series and the one in which Barrault's range as an actor was conclusively demonstrated" (*Nation*, 13 December 1952, p. 562. Of course, similar controversy surrounded many of Barrault's other productions. For an excellent survey of contradictory critical responses to Barrault's work, see Suzanne Burgoyne Dieckman, "Theory and Practice in the Total Theatre of Jean-Louis Barrault" (Ph.D. diss., University of Michigan, 1975), ch. 4. Dieckman's study, although it concludes in the mid-1970s, remains the most thorough and balanced account of Barrault's work in English.

9. Jean-Louis Barrault, *The Theatre of Jean-Louis Barrault*, trans. Joseph Chiari (New York: Hill and Wang, 1961), p. 256.

10. Thomas S. Turgeon, "Theatre in Review: *Harold and Maude; Zadig*," *Theatre Journal* 32 (December 1980): 532.

11. Jacques Guicharnaud, with June Beckelman, *Modern French Theatre from Giraudoux to Beckett* (New Haven: Yale University Press, 1961), p. 256.

12. Quoted by Henry Hewes, "Total Theatre," *Saturday Review*, 26 January 1957, p. 22.

13. Charles R. Lyons, "Le Compagnie Madeleine Renaud–Jean-Louis Barrault: The Idea and the Aesthetic," *Educational Theatre Journal* 19 (December 1967): 416.

14. Guicharnaud and Beckelman, *Modern French Theatre*, p. 256.

15. Norman Marshall, *The Producer and the Play* (London: David-Poynter, 1975), p. 43.

16. Eric Bentley, *In Search of Theatre* (New York: Vintage Books, 1957), p. 186.

17. Ibid., p. 187.

18. Ibid., pp. 189–90.

19. Barrault, *The Theatre of Jean-Louis Barrault*, p. 67.

20. Jean-Louis Barrault, "Four Directors: I. Jean-Louis Barrault," *Theatre Quarterly* 3 (April-June 1973): 4.

21. Ibid.

22. Bill Wallis, "Jean-Louis Barrault's *Rabelais*," *Theatre Quarterly* 1 (July-September 1971): 92.

23. Barrault, "Four Directors," p. 4.

24. Loney, "In the Words of Jean-Louis Barrault," p. 13.

25. Ibid.

26. Jean-Louis Barrault, "Child of Silence," trans. Eric Bentley, *Theatre Arts Magazine* 33 (October 1949): 30.

27. Barrault, *The Theatre of Jean-Louis Barrault*, p. 65.

28. Dieckman, "Theory and Practice," p. 374.

29. Quoted by Bettina Knapp, *Offstage Voices: Interviews with Modern French Dramatists*, ed. Alba Amoia (Troy, N.Y.: Whitson, 1975), p. 44.

30. Barrault, *The Theatre of Jean-Louis Barrault*, p. 69.

31. Ibid.

32. Ibid., pp. 69, 71, 73, 74.

33. Quoted in John Gruen, "I've Taken Risks for 30 Years," *New York Times*, 17 May 1970.

34. Barrault, *The Theatre of Jean-Louis Barrault*, p. 80.

35. Ibid., p. 81.

36. Ibid., p. 82.

37. Knapp, *Offstage Voices*, p. 44.

38. Wallis, "Barrault's *Rabelais*," pp. 85, 93.

39. Maurice Schaded, "Remembering the Compagnie Renaud-Barrault," *Institute of International Education News Bulletin* 35 (December 1959): 23.

40. Quoted and translated from Jean-Louis Barrault, *Je Suis Homme de Théâtre*, by Dieckman, "Theory and Practice," p. 44.

41. Jack Brooking, "Four Bare Walls and a Touch of Joy," *Players* 41 (October 1964): 7.

42. Ibid.

43. Wallis, "Barrault's *Rabelais*," p. 93.

44. Gruen, "I've Taken Risks for 30 Years."

45. Wallis, "Barrault's *Rabelais*," p. 93.

46. Ibid.

47. Luce Klein and Arthur Klein, "Jean-Louis Barrault," *Theatre Arts Magazine* 31 (October 1947): 27.

48. Brooking, "Four Bare Walls and a Touch of Joy," p. 6.

49. Knapp, *Offstage Voices*, p. 45.

50. Brooking, "Four Bare Walls and a Touch of Joy," p. 7.

51. Ibid.

52. Schaded, "Remembering the Compagnie Renaud-Barrault," p. 21.

CHRONOLOGY

(All productions Paris, unless noted.)

1910   born in Le Vesinet, near Paris

1931–35   trains at Atelier Théâtre school of Charles Dullin

1931   professional acting debut at Atelier

1935   Atelier: *As I Lay Dying (Autour d'une Mère)*; begins film acting career

1936   establishes theatre collective with Jean Dasté in Grenier des Augustins

1937   Théâtre Antoine: *The Siege of Numantia (La Numantia)*

1939   Atelier: *Hunger (La Faim)*; participates in founding of periodical, *La Nouvelle Saison*

1940   joins Comédie Française; marries actress Madeleine Renaud

1941   Roland-Garros Stadium: *800 Meters (800 Mètres)*; *The Suppliants*

1942   Comédie Française: *Phaedra (Phèdre)*

1943   Comédie Française: *The Satin Slipper (Le Soulier de Satin)*

1945   Comédie Française: *Antony and Cleopatra*; *The Unloved (Les Mal Aimés)*

1946   leaves Comédie Française; cofounds La Compagnie Madeleine Renaud–Jean-Louis Barrault at Théâtre Marigny: all productions to 1954 at Marigny, except where noted: *Hamlet; The False Confessions (Les Fausses Confidences); Baptiste; Nights of Fury (Les Nuits de la Colère)*

1947   *The Trial (Le Procès); The Bear; Amphitryon; The Fountain of Youth (La Fontaine de Jouvence)*; company tours Belgium, Holland, Luxembourg

1948   *Keep an Eye on Amélie! (Occupe-toi d'Amélie!)*; *State of Siege (L'État de Siège)*; *Break of Noon (Partage de Midi)*; company invited to Edinburgh Festival

1949   *Love's Second Surprise (La Seconde Surprise de l'Amour); Elizabeth of England; The Hunchback (Le Bossu)*

1950   *Going to Pot (On Purge Bébé); Marlborough Off to War (Marlborough s'en va-t-en Guerre); The Rehearsal (La Répétition)*; South American tour; *Dirty Hands (Les Mains Sales)*, premieres Rio de Janeiro; *Malatesta*

1951   *Maqueleone; The Test (L'Epreuve); Lazarus (Lazare); The Exchange (L'E-change); No Trifling with Love (On ne Badine pas avec L'Amour)*; company tours to Italy, Belgium, London

1952   Lyon: *Cognizance of Paul Claudel (Connaissance de Paul Claudel)*; company tours to Belgium, Italy, Canada, and United States, including New York, with *Baptiste; The False Confidences; The Trial; Amphitryon; Keep an Eye on Amélie!; The Rehearsal; Hamlet*

1953   Festival of Bordeaux: *Christopher Columbus (Christophe Colomb); Duel of Angels (Pour Lucrèce)*; founds *Cahiers de la Compagnie Renaud-Barrault*, a literary periodical

1954   Petit Marigny opens; Petit Marigny: *Renard; The Party of the Proverbs (La Soirée des Proverbes)*; South American tour with *The Misanthrope (Le Misanthrope); The Magnificent Cuckold (Le Cocu Magnifique); The Cherry Orchard*; Marigny: *The Cherry Orchard*

1955   Marigny: *A Sleep of Prisoners; Volpone; Berenice; Intermezzo*; Festival of
            Bordeaux: *Oresteia*; Marigny: *The Gardener's Dog (Le Chien du Jardinier);
            Sequels to a Race (Les Suites d'une Course)*

1956   Petit Marigny: *The Fighting Character (Le Personnage Combattant)*; Schaus-
            pielhaus, Zurich: *Story of Vasco (Vasco)*

1957   leaves Theatre Marigny; Théâtre Sarah Bernhardt: *Story of Vasco; The Castle*;
            company tours Canadian and American university theatres; Winter Garden,
            New York: *Christopher Columbus; Volpone; The Misanthrope; Nights of
            Fury; Intermezzo; Farewells (Les Adieux); The Gardener's Dog; The Re-
            hearsal*

1958   Théâtre du Palais-Royal: *La Vie Parisienne; The Satin Slipper*

1959   appointed director of the Odéon-Théâtre de France; all productions to 1968
            at Odéon, except where noted; *Head of Gold (Tête d'Or); Little Molière (Le
            Petit Molière); The False Confidences; Baptiste*

1960   *Rhinocéros; The Cherry Orchard*; company tours to Japan, Israel, Greece,
            Yugoslavia; *Christopher Columbus; Julius Caesar; Keep an Eye on Amélie!*

1961   *The Rape of Lucrece (Le Viol de Lucrèce); But Don't Run Around in the Nude
            (Mais n'te Promene donc pas Toute Nue); The Voyage (Le Voyage); Penny
            Pantomimes (Pantomimes d'un Sou); War and Poetry (Guerre et Poésie)*;
            company tours to South America, Switzerland, and Belgium; *Break of Noon;
            The Trial; Amphitryon; Judith*

1962   *Oresteia; Hamlet; The Revelation (La Révélation); The First Born*; Essen,
            Germany: *Christopher Columbus*; company tours to Moscow and Leningrad;
            Andromache; La Vie Parisienne

1963   *The Pedestrian in the Air (Le Pieton de l'Air)*; company tours to Belgium,
            Italy, Switzerland; *The Satin Slipper; Double Inconstancy*

1964   tour to United States (including New York), Canada, Italy, Belgium, Switzer-
            land: *The Marriage of Figaro; Andromache; Salute to Molière; Pedestrian in
            the Air; La Vie Parisienne*; Odéon: *It Must Pass through the Clouds (Il Faut
            Passer par les Nuages); The Marriage of Figaro*

1965   company tours to Belgium, Switzerland, Germany, Roumania, Austria; *Nu-
            mantia; Days in the Trees (Des Journées Entières dans les Arbres)*

1966   *The Lagoon (La Lagon); Frenzy for Two (Délire à Deux)*; company tours to
            Italy and Switzerland; *Ruzzante Returns to the Wars; Henry VI*

1967   *Medea*; opens foyer area at Odéon as Petit Odéon with *Silence, Lie (Le Silence,
            Le Mensonge); Saint-Exupéry*; company tours to Montreal, New York, Berlin;
            A Delicate Balance

1968   *Head of Gold*; Odéon occupied by radical students; Barrault dismissed as
            director of Odéon; company, no longer subsidized, moves to Élysée-
            Montmartre: *Rabelais;* company on world tour: *Rabelais, Happy Days*

1970   company tours to Italy, Germany, Netherlands, and United States; Élysée-
            Montmartre: *Jarry on the Mound (Jarry sur la Butte)*

1971   Théâtre Recamier: *Fighting Character; Happy Days*

1972   circus tent theatre situated in Gare D'Orsay: *Before the Wind of the Balearic Islands (Sous les Vent des Îles Baléares)*; circus tent in Tuileries: *The Bourgeois Gentleman (Le Bourgeois Gentilhomme)*

1973   Théâtre d'Orsay (TO): *Harold and Maude*

1974   TO: *Thus Spake Zarathustra*; English version of 1972 autobiography, *Memories for Tomorrow*, published

1975   TO: *The Nights of Paris (Les Nuits de Paris)*

1977   TO: *The New World (La Nouvelle Monde)*

1978   TO: *Zadig; Harold and Maude*

1981   opens Théâtre du Rond-Point (RP) and its smaller playhouse, the Petit Rond-Point: *The Love of Love*

1982   RP: *The Strausses (Les Strausses); Antigone*

1983   RP: *The Soul and the Dance (L'Âme et la Danse)*

1984   RP: *Angelo, Tyrant of Padua (Angelo, Tyran de Padoue)*

1985   RP: *The Birds*

1986   RP: *Théâtre Fair*

1988   Théâtre du Rond-Pont renamed Théâtre Renaud Barrault

Select Bibliography

GENERAL

Many of the works listed here treat several of the directors discussed in the text. Works dealing primarily with one such director are listed under the director's name.

Bakshy, Alexander. *The Path of the Modern Russian Stage*. Boston: J. W. Luce, 1918.

Bentley, Eric. *In Search of Theatre*. New York: Vintage Books, 1957.

Bradby, David, and David Williams. *Directors' Theatre*. New York: St. Martin's Press, 1988.

Bradshaw, Martha. *Soviet Theatres 1917–1941*. New York: Research Program on the U.S.S.R., 1954.

Braun, Edward. *The Director and the Stage: From Naturalism to Grotowski*. London: Methuen, 1982.

Brockett, Oscar G., and Robert R. Findlay. *Century of Innovation: A History of European and American Theatre and Drama Since 1870*. Englewood Cliffs, N.J.: Prentice-Hall, 1973.

Brown, Frederick. *The Theatre and Revolution: The Culture of the French Stage*. New York: Viking, 1980.

Carter, Huntley. *The New Theatre and Cinema of Soviet Russia*. London: International Publishers, 1924.

———. *The New Spirit in Russian Theatre, 1917–1928*. London: Brentano's, 1928.

Cheney, Sheldon. *The New Movement in the Theatre*. New York: Benjamin Blom, 1971.

Clark, Barrett H., and George Freedley, eds. *A History of the Modern Drama*. New York and London: Appleton-Century, 1947.

Clurman, Harold. "Conversation with Two Masters." *Theatre Arts Monthly* 9 (November 1935).

Cole, Toby, and Helen Krich Chinoy, eds. *Directors on Directing: A Source Book of the Modern Theatre*. rev. ed. Indianapolis, Indiana: Bobbs-Merrill, 1963.

Dickinson, Thomas H. *The Theatre in a Changing Europe*. New York: Henry Holt, 1937.

Eaton, Katherine Bliss. *The Theatre of Meyerhold and Brecht*. Westport, Conn.: Greenwood Press, 1985.

Flanagan, Hallie. *Shifting Scenes of the European Theatre*. New York: Coward-McCann, 1928.

Fuerst, Walter René, and Samuel J. Hume. *Twentieth-Century Stage Decoration*. New York: Dover, 1967.

Gassner, John. *The Theatre in Our Times*. New York: Crown, 1954.

————. *Directions in Modern Theatre and Drama*. New York: Holt, Rinehart and Winston, 1967.

Gorchakov, Nikolai A. *The Theatre in Soviet Russia*. Translated by Edgar Lehrman. New York: Columbia University Press, 1957.

Gorelik, Mordecai. *New Theatres for Old*. New York: Samuel French, 1940.

Gregor, Joseph, and René Fulop-Miller. *The Russian Theatre*. Translated by Paul England. Philadelphia: Lippincott, 1930.

Guicharnaud, Jacques, and June Beckelman. *Modern French Theatre from Giraudoux to Beckett*. New Haven: Yale University Press, 1961.

Houghton, Norris. *Moscow Rehearsals*. New York: Harcourt Brace, 1936.

Innes, Christopher. *Holy Theatre: Ritual and the Avant Garde*. Cambridge, Eng.: Cambridge University Press, 1981.

Johnson, Albert, with Bertha Johnson. *Directing Methods*. South Brunswick, N.J.: A. S. Barnes, 1970.

Jones, David R. *Great Directors at Work: Stanislavsky, Brecht, Kazan, Brook*. Berkeley: University of California Press, 1986.

Kiebuzinska, Christine. *Revolutionaries in the Theater: Meyerhold, Brecht, and Witkiewicz*. Ann Arbor, Mich.: UMI Press, 1988.

Kirby, E. T., ed. *Total Theatre: A Critical Anthology*. New York: E. P. Dutton, 1969.

Knowles, Dorothy. *French Drama of the Inter-War Years, 1918–1939*. New York: Barnes and Noble, 1968.

Leiter, Samuel, ed. *Shakespeare Around the Globe: A Guide to Notable Postwar Revivals*. Westport, Conn.: Greenwood, 1985.

Macgowan, Kenneth. *The Theatre of Tomorrow*. New York: Boni and Liveright, 1921.

Macgowan, Kenneth, and Robert Edmond Jones. *Continental Stagecraft*. New York: Benjamin Blom, 1964.

Markov, Pavel. *The Soviet Theatre*. London: Victor Gollancz, 1934.

Marshall, Herbert. *Pictorial History of the Russian Theatre*. New York: Crown, 1977.

Marshall, Norman. *The Producer and the Play*. rev. ed. London: David-Poynter, 1975.

Miller, Anna Irene. *The Independent Theatre in Europe*. New York: Ray Long and Richard B. Smith, 1931.

Patterson, Michael. *The Revolution in German Theatre, 1900–1933*. London and Boston: Routledge and Kegan Paul, 1981.

Roose-Evans, James. *Experimental Theatre, From Stanislavsky to Today*. New York: Avon, 1971.

Sayler, Oliver M. *The Russian Theatre*. New York: Brentano's, 1922.

Slonim, Marc. *Russian Theatre from the Empire to the Soviets*. New York: Crowell-Collier, 1962.

Speaight, Robert. *Shakespeare on the Stage*. Boston and Toronto: Little, Brown, 1973.

Styan, J. L. *The Shakespeare Revolution*. Cambridge, Eng.: Cambridge University Press, 1977.

Van Gysegham, André. *The Theatre in Soviet Russia*. London: Faber and Faber, 1943.

Whitton, David. *Stage Directors in Modern France*. Manchester, Eng.: Manchester University Press, 1987.

Wiles, Timothy J. *The Theatre Event: Modern Theories of Performance*. Chicago: University of Chicago Press, 1980.

KONSTANTIN STANISLAVSKY

Balukhaty, S. D., ed. *"The Seagull" Produced by Stanislavsky*. Translated by David Magarshack. New York: Theatre Arts Books, 1952.

Benedetti, Jean. *Stanislavski: A Biography*. New York: Routledge, 1988.

Boleslavsky, Richard. "Stanislavsky—The Man and His Methods." *The Theatre Magazine* 37 (April 1923).

Brinton, Christian. "Idols of the Russian Masses." *The Cosmopolitan* 40 (April 1906).

Carter, Huntley. "The New Age of the Moscow Art Theatre: Ten Years Under Soviet Power." *Fortnightly Review* 123 (January-June 1928).

Cole, Toby, and Helen Krich Chinoy, eds. *Acting, A Handbook of the Stanislavsky Method*. New York: Crown, 1955.

Edwards, Christine. *The Stanislavsky Heritage*. New York: New York University Press, 1965.

Garfield, David. *A Player's Place*. New York: Macmillan, 1980.

Gorchakov, Nikolai A. *Stanislavsky Directs*. Translated by Miriam Goldina. New York: Grossett and Dunlap, 1962.

Gordon, Mel. *The Stanislavsky Technique: Russia, A Workbook for Actors*. New York: Applause, 1988.

Hewitt, Barnard, and Aristide d'Angelo. "The Stanislavsky System for Actors." *Quarterly Journal of Speech* 17 (June 1932).

Hirsch, Foster. *A Method to Their Madness*. New York: W. W. Norton, 1984.

Korneva, Oksana, comp. *Konstantin Stanislavsky: Selected Works*. Moscow: Raduga Publishers, 1984.

Logan, Joshua. "Rehearsal with Stanislavsky." *Vogue* 113 (June 1949).

Magarshack, David. *Stanislavsky, A Life*. New York: Chanticleer Press, 1951.

Melik-Zakharov, Sergei, and Soel Bogatryev, comps. and eds. *Konstantin Stanislavsky 1863–1963: Man and Actor*. Translated by Vic Schneirson. Moscow: Iskustvo Publishers, 1963.

Morgan, Joyce Vining. *Stanislavski's Encounter with Shakespeare*. Ann Arbor, Mich.: UMI Research Press, 1984.

Munk, Erika, ed. *Stanislavski and America*. Greenwich, Conn.: Fawcett, 1967.

Nemirovich-Danchenko, Vladimir. *My Life in the Russian Theatre*. Translated by John Cournos. New York: Theatre Arts Books, 1936.

Norelle, Lee. "Stanislavski Revisited." *Educational Theatre Journal* 14 (March 1962).

Polyakova, Elena. *Stanislavsky*. Moscow: Progress Publishers, 1982.

Press, David R. "Autocrat or Collaborator? The Stanislavsky Method of Directing." *Educational Theatre Journal* 18 (October 1966).

Sayler, Oliver. "Theory and Practice in Russian Theatre." *Theatre Arts Monthly* 4 (July 1920).

———. "The Moscow Art Theatre." *Theatre Arts Monthly* 4 (October 1920).

———. *Inside the Moscow Art Theatre*. New York: Brentano's, 1925.

Senelick, Laurence. *Gordon Craig's Moscow "Hamlet": A Reconstruction*. Westport, Conn.: Greenwood Press, 1982.

Stanislavski, Constantin. *My Life in Art*. Translated by J. J. Robbins. New York: Meridian Books, 1956.

————. *An Actor Prepares*. Translated by Elizabeth Reynolds Hapgood. New York: Theatre Arts Books, 1936.

————. *Building a Character*. Translated by Elizabeth Reynolds Hapgood. New York: Theatre Arts Books, 1949.

————.*Creating a Role*. Translated by Elizabeth Reynolds Hapgood. New York: Theatre Arts Books, 1961.

————. *Stanislavsky's Legacy: A Collection of Comments on a Variety of Aspects of an Actor's Life and Art*. Edited and translated by Elizabeth Reynolds Hapgood. New York: Theatre Arts Books, 1958.

Stanislavsky, Konstantin. *Stanislavsky on the Art of the Stage*. Translated and introduced by David Magarshack. New York: Hill and Wang, 1961.

Toporkov, Vasily Osopovich. *Stanislavski in Rehearsal: The Final Years*. Translated by Christine Edwards. New York: Theatre Arts Books, 1979.

VSEVOLOD MEYERHOLD

Barkhin, Mikhail, and Sergei Vakhtangov. "A Theatre for Meyerhold." *Theatre Quarterly* 2 (July-September 1972).

Biberman, Herbert. "Meirhold at Work." *Theatre Guild Magazine* (January 1929).

Braun, Edward, ed. and trans. *Meyerhold on Theatre*. New York: Hill and Wang, 1969.

————. *The Theatre of Meyerhold: Revolution on the Modern Stage*. New York: Drama Book Specialists, 1979.

Bristow, Eugene K. "The Making of a Regisseur: V. E. Meyerhold, the Early Years, 1874–1895." *The Theatre Annual* 25 (1969).

Deak, Frantisek. "Meyerhold's Staging of *Sister Beatrice* (1906)." *The Drama Review* 26 (Spring 1982).

Fagin, Bryllion. "Meyerhold Rehearses a Scene." *Theatre Arts Monthly* 16 (October 1932).

Gladkov, Alexander. "Meyerhold Speaks." Translated by Alma H. Law. *The Drama Review* 18 (September 1974).

————. "Meyerhold Rehearses." Translated by Alma H. Law. *Performing Arts Journal* 3 (Winter 1979).

Glover, Joseph Garrett. *The Cubist Theatre*. Ann Arbor, Mich.: UMI Research Press, 1983.

Gordon, Mel. "Biomechanics." *The Drama Review* 18 (September 1974).

Graham, Kenneth. "Meyerhold and Constructivism in the Russian Theatre." *Quarterly Journal of Speech* 29 (April 1943).

Hedgbeth, Llewelyn H. "Meyerhold's *D. E.*" *The Drama Review* 19 (June 1975).

Hoover, Marjorie L. "V. E. Meyerhold: A Russian Predecessor of Avant-Garde Theatre." *Comparative Literature* 27 (1965).

————. "A Mejerxol'd Method? *Love for Three Oranges* (1914–1916)." *Slavic and East European Journal* 13 (Spring 1969).

————. "The Meyerhold Centennial." *The Drama Review* 18 (September 1974).

————. *Meyerhold: The Art of Conscious Theatre*. Amherst: University of Massachusetts Press, 1974.

Houghton, Norris. "Theory into Practice: A Reappraisal of Meierhold." *Educational Theatre Journal* 20 (October 1968).

Jelagin, Yuri. *Taming of the Arts*. Translated by Nicholas Wreden. New York: E. P. Dutton, 1951.

Keeler, William. "Photographic Sources of the Productions of Vsevelod Emiliovich Meyerhold." *Theatre Documentation* 4 (1971–72).

Kommisarjevsky, Theodore. *Myself and the Theatre*. New York: E. P. Dutton, 1930.

Law, Alma H. "Meyerhold's *Woe to Wit* (1928)." *The Drama Review* 18 (September 1974).

————. "Meyerhold's *The Magnanimous Cuckold* (1922)." *The Drama Review* 26 (Spring 1982).

Leach, Robert. *Vsevolod Meyerhold*. Cambridge, Eng.: Cambridge University Press, 1989.

Lozowick, Louis. "V. E. Meyerhold and His Theatre." *Hound and Horn* 4 (October-December 1930).

Moore, Sonia. "Meyerhold: Innovator and Example." *Players* 48 (October-November 1972).

Rudnitski, Konstantin. *Meyerhold the Director*. Translated by George Petrov. Ann Arbor, Mich.: Ardis Publishers, 1981.

Schmidt, Paul. "A Director Works with a Playwright." *Educational Theatre Journal* 29 (May 1977).

————, ed. *Meyerhold at Work*. Austin: University of Texas Press, 1980.

Strasberg, Lee. "Magic of Meyerhold." *New Theatre* 1 (September 1934).

————. "Russian Notebook (1934)." *The Drama Review* 17 (March 1973).

Symons, James M. *Meyerhold's Theatre of the Grotesque: The Post-Revolutionary Productions, 1920–1932*. Coral Gables, Fla.: University of Miami Press, 1971.

Worrall, Nick. "Meyerhold's Production of *The Magnificent Cuckold*." *The Drama Review* 17 (March 1973).

————. "Meyerhold Directs Gogol's *Government Inspector*." *Theatre Quarterly* 2 (July-September 1972).

Zozulya, E. "Vsevolod Meyerhold." *International Theatre* (October 1934).

Unpublished Materials

Alpers, Boris. "The Theatre of the Social Mask." Translated by Mark Schmidt. New York: Group Theatre, 1934. Typescript of unpublished translation; copy in the collection of David Garfield.

Beeson, Nora. "Vsevolod Meyerhold and the Experimental Pre-Revolutionary Theatre in Russia (1900–1917)." Ph.D. dissertation, Columbia University, 1961.

Biely, Andrey. "Gogol and Meyerhold." Translated by Mark Schmidt. New York: Group Theatre, 1934. Typescript of unpublished translation; copy in the collection of David Garfield.

Schmidt, Paul. "The Theatre of V. E. Mejerxol'd." Ph.D. dissertation, Harvard University, 1974.

MAX REINHARDT

Appignanesi, Lisa. *The Cabaret*. New York: Universe Books, 1976.

Barker, Colgate. "Reinhardt." *New York Review,* 2 January 1912.

Bauland, Peter. *The Hooded Eagle: Modern German Drama on the New York Stage*. Syracuse: University of Syracuse Press, 1968.

Bechert, Paul. "Reinhardt—Supreme Master of Stagecraft." *Theatre Magazine* 37 (June 1923).

Bel Geddes, Norman. *Miracle in the Evening: An Autobiography*. Edited by William Kelley. Garden City, N.Y.: Doubleday, 1960.

Blank, Martin. "When Farce Isn't Funny: The Original Production of *The Merchant of Yonkers*." *Players* 50 (April-May 1975).

Brooks, Alfred G., and Freda Paris, eds. "Max Reinhardt 1973–1943: An Exhibition Commemorating the Hundredth Anniversary of his Birth." New York: New York Cultural Center, 1974.

Carter, Huntley. *The Theatre of Max Reinhardt*. New York: Benjamin Blom, 1964.

Davies, Cecil W. *Theatre for the People: The Story of the Volksbühne*. Austin, Tex.: University of Texas Press, 1977.

Dukes, Ashley. "The Scene in Europe." *Theatre Arts Monthly* 17 (October 1933).

Eisner, Lotte. *The Haunted Screen: Expressionism in the German Cinema and the Influence of Max Reinhardt*. Translated by Roger Greaves. Berkeley: University of California Press, 1969.

Esslin, Martin. "Max Reinhardt, High Priest of Theatricality." *The Drama Review* 21 (June 1977).

Eustis, Morton. "The Director Takes Command, II." *Theatre Arts Monthly* 20 (March 1936).

Fehl, Fred, William Stott, and Jane Stott. *On Broadway*. Austin: University of Texas Press, 1978.

Felton, Felix. "Max Reinhardt in England." *Theatre Research* 5 (1963).

Gabriel, Gilbert. "The Reinhardt in his Den." *Theatre Arts Monthly* 7 (January 1923).

Hadamowsky, Franz. "Max Reinhardt and Austria." Translated by Stanley Radcliffe. *Theatre Research* 5 (1963).

High, Veronica. "Max Reinhardt: An Appreciation." *Drama* 2 (July-September 1933).

Horner, Harry. "Harry Horner Talks About Max Reinhardt." *The Stage in Canada* 1 (May 1965).

Jackson, Alan S. "The Max Reinhardt Archive, New York." *Theatre Studies* 20 (1973–1974).

Jelavich, Peter. *Munich and Theatrical Modernism: Politics, Playwriting, and Performance, 1890–1914*. Cambridge, Mass.: Harvard University Press, 1985.

Kitchen, Karl. "Berlin's 'Great Playhouse.' " *Theatre Magazine* 32 (December 1920).

Knudsen, Hans. "Max Reinhardt in Berlin." Translated by Estelle Morgan and H. Winter. *Theatre Research* 5 (1963).

Kueppers, Brigitte. "Max Reinhardt's *Sumurun*." *The Drama Review* 24 (March 1980).

Laver, James. *Drama: Its Costume and Decor*. London: Studio Publications, 1951.

Lynn, Grace. "Patience Is Reinhardt's First Rule." *Boston Evening Transcript,* 3 March 1928.

———. "Max Reinhardt 1873–1943." *Theatre Arts Monthly* 28 (January 1944).

Melnitz, William. "Tribute to Max Reinhardt." *The Theatre Annual* 12 (1956).

Munro, George. "How Reinhardt Works." *The Scottish Stage* 1 (February 1932).

Nathan, George Jean. *The Magic Mirror*. Edited by Thomas Quinn Curtis. New York: Alfred A. Knopf, 1960.

Piliakian, Hovhannes I. "Max Reinhardt and Total Theatre." *Drama* 91 (Winter 1968).

Pinthus, Kurt. "Max Reinhardt and the U.S.A." *Theatre Research* 5 (1963).

Reinhardt, Gottfried. *The Genius: A Memoir of Max Reinhardt by His Son*. New York: Alfred A. Knopf, 1979.

Reinhardt, Max. "Of Actors." *Yale Review* 18 (September 1928).

Rorrison, Hugh. "Designing for Reinhardt: The Work of Ernst Stern." *New Theatre Quarterly* 2 (August 1986).

Savage, Richard. "A Chinese Fairy Tale." *Theatre Magazine* 12 (December 1912).

Sayler, Oliver M., ed. *Max Reinhardt and His Theatre*. New York and London: Benjamin Blom, 1968.

Scheffaur, Herman George. "A Festival Playhouse in the Alps." *Theatre Arts Monthly* 5 (1921).

Shewring, Margaret. "Reinhardt's *Miracle* at Olympia: A Record and a Reconstruction." *New Theatre Quarterly* 3 (February 1987).

Stern, Ernst. *My Life, My Stage*. Translated by Edward Fitzgerald. London: Victor Gollancz, 1951.

Sterne, Maurice. "Reinhardt in the Church." *Theatre Arts Monthly* 7 (January 1923).

Styan, J. L. *Max Reinhardt*. Cambridge, Eng.: Cambridge University Press, 1982.

Volbach, Walter R. "Reinhardt." *American German Review* 29 (August-September 1963).

———. "Memoirs of Max Reinhardt's Theatres, 1920–1922." *Theatre Survey* 13 (Fall 1972).

Vom Bauer, Eva Elise, "Max Reinhardt and His Famous Players." *Theatre Magazine* 11 (August 1911).

Warren, John. "Max Reinhardt and the Viennese Theatre of the Interwar Years." *Maske und Kothurn* 29 (1983).

Washburn-Freund, F. E. "Max Reinhardt's Evolution." *International Studies* (January 1924).

Wellwarth, George E., and Alfred G. Brooks, eds. *Max Reinhardt 1873–1973: A Centennial Festschrift*. Binghamton, N.Y.: Max Reinhardt Archives, 1973.

Unpublished Materials

Horner, Harry. "Epilogue: Notes on Max Reinhardt's Last Years." Typescript in Research Collection, Lincoln Center Library for the Performing Arts, n.d.

JACQUES COPEAU

Copeau, Jacques. "The True Spirit of the Art of the Stage, As It Is Being Interpreted at the Vieux Colombier." *Vanity Fair,* 19 April 1917.

———. "An Essay of Dramatic Renovation: The Théâtre du Vieux Colombier." Translated by Richard Hiatt. *Educational Theatre Journal* 19 (December 1967).

———. "Remembrances of the Vieux Colombier." Translated by Nanette Sue Flakes. *Educational Theatre Journal* 22 (March 1970).

Select Bibliography

Select Bibliography

d'Amico, Silvio. "The Play of St. Uliva." *Theatre Arts Monthly* 17 (September 1933).

Fletcher, John, ed. *Forces in Modern French Drama: Studies in Variations on the Permitted Lie*. New York: Frederick Ungar, 1972.

Fowlie, Wallace. *Dionysus in Paris*. New York: Meridian Books, 1960.

Frank, Waldo. *Salvos, An Informal Book About Books and Plays*. New York: Boni and Liveright, 1924.

———. "Copeau Begins Again." *Theatre Arts Monthly* 13 (September 1929).

Katz, Albert M. "The Genesis of the Vieux Colombier: The Aesthetic Background of Jacques Copeau." *Educational Theatre Journal* 19 (December 1967).

———. "Jacques Copeau: The American Reaction." *Players* 45 (February 1970).

———. "Copeau as Regisseur: An Analysis." *Educational Theatre Journal* 25 (May 1973).

Knapp, Bettina. *Louis Jouvet, Man of the Theatre*. New York: Columbia University Press, 1957.

———. *The Reign of the Theatrical Director: French Theatre, 1887–1924*. Troy, N.Y.: Whitson, 1988.

Littell, Phillip. "Books and Things." *New Republic* 26 (April 1918).

Paterson, Douglas. "Two Productions by Copeau: *The Tricks of Scapin* and *Twelfth Night*." *The Drama Review* 28 (Spring 1984).

Paul, Norman H. "Jacques Copeau Looks at the American Stage, 1917–1919" *Educational Theatre Journal* 29 (March 1977).

Pronko, Leonard. *Theatre East and West: Perspectives Toward a Total Theatre*. Berkeley: University of California Press, 1966.

Roeder, Ralph. "Copeau, 1921." *Theatre Arts Monthly* 5 (October 1921).

Rudlin, John. *Jacques Copeau*. Cambridge, Eng.: Cambridge University Press, 1986.

Saint-Denis, Michel. *Theatre: The Rediscovery of Style*. London: 1960.

———. *Training for the Theatre*. New York and London, 1982.

———. "Modern Theatre's Debt to Copeau." *The Listener,* 16 February 1950.

Sergeant, Elizabeth S. "A New French Theatre." *New Republic,* 21 April 1917.

Steell, Willis. "Jacques Copeau—Author, Actor and Producer." *Theatre Magazine* 25 (May 1917).

Volbach, Walter R. "Jacques Copeau, Appia's Finest Disciple." *Educational Theatre Journal* 17 (October 1965).

Unpublished Materials

Katz, Albert M. "A Historical Study of Jacques Copeau and the Vieux Colombier Company at the Garrick Theatre in New York City, 1917–1919." Ph.D. dissertation, University of Michigan, 1966.

Paterson, Douglas Lister. "Jacques Copeau's Theatrical Image." Ph.D. dissertation, Cornell University, 1972.

BERTOLT BRECHT

Baxendall, Lee. "Brecht in America, 1935." *The Drama Review* 12 (Fall 1967).

Bentley, Eric. "What Is Epic Theatre?" *Accent* 6 (Winter 1946).

———. "Epic Theatre Is Lyric Theatre." In *The German Theater Today*. Edited by Leroy R. Shaw. Austin: University of Texas Press, 1963.

———. "Are Stanislavski and Brecht Commensurable?" *The Drama Review* 9 (Fall 1964).

———. *The Brecht Commentaries*. New York: Grove Press, 1981.

———. *The Brecht Memoir*. New York: PAJ Publications, 1985.

Brecht, Bertolt. *Couragemodell 1949*. Berlin: Henschelverlag, 1958.

———. *Seven Plays by Bertolt Brecht*. Edited by Eric Bentley. New York: Grove Press, 1961.

———. "On the *Caucasian Chalk Circle*." *The Drama Review* 12 (Fall 1967).

Brecht, Bertolt, and Caspar Neher. *Antigonemodell 1948*. Edited by Ruth Berlau. Berlin: Bebruder Weiss, 1949.

Cook, Bruce. *Brecht in Exile*. New York: Holt, Rinehart and Winston, 1982.

Demetz, Peter, ed. *Brecht: A Collection of Critical Essays*. Englewood Cliffs, N.J.: Prentice-Hall, 1962.

Dessau, Paul. "Composing for B.B.: Some Comments." *The Drama Review* 12 (Winter 1967).

Esslin, Martin. *Brecht: The Man and His Work*. Garden City, N.Y.: Doubleday, 1961.

Ewen, Frederick. *Bertolt Brecht: His Life, His Art, and His Times*. New York: Citadel Press, 1967.

Fuegi, John. "*The Caucasian Chalk Circle* in Performance." *Brecht Heute/Brecht Today: Yearbook of the International Brecht Society*. Vol. 1. Edited by Eric Bentley, et al. Frankfurt: Athenaum, 1971.

———. *The Essential Brecht*. Los Angeles: Hennessey and Ingalls, 1972.

———. *Bertolt Brecht: Chaos According to Plan*. Cambridge, Eng.: Cambridge University Press, 1987.

Gray, Ronald. *Bertolt Brecht*. New York: Grove Press, 1961.

Haas, Willy. *Bert Brecht*. New York: Frederick Ungar, 1970.

Hayman, Ronald. *Brecht: A Biography*. New York: Oxford University Press, 1983.

Hecht, Werner. "The Characteristics of the Berliner Ensemble: Remarks on Brecht's Method." Translated by Eckhard O. Auberlen. *Theatre Research* 8 (1967).

———. "The Berliner Ensemble and the Spirit of Brecht." *World Theatre* 14 (July-August 1965).

Hennenberg, Fritz. "Brecht and Music." *Enact* 24 (December 1968).

Higham, Charles. *Charles Laughton: An Intimate Biography*. Garden City, N.Y.: Doubleday, 1976.

Lyon, James K. *Bertolt Brecht in America*. Princeton, N.J.: Princeton University Press, 1980.

Melchinger, Siegfried. "Neher and Brecht." *The Drama Review* 12 (Winter 1968).

Mitchell, John D. "Brecht's Theatre: The Berliner Ensemble." *Players* 39 (May 1963).

Needle, Jan, and Peter Thomson. *Brecht*. Chicago: University of Chicago Press, 1981.

Politzer, Heinz. "How Epic Is Brecht's Epic Theater?" *Modern Language Quarterly* 24 (June 1962).

Roth, Wolfgang. "A Designer Works with Brecht." *Theatre Quarterly* 2 (April-June 1972).

Sanders, Ronald. *The Days Grow Short: The Life and Music of Kurt Weill*. New York: Holt, Rinehart and Winston, 1980.

Schoeps, Karl H. *Bertolt Brecht*. New York: Frederick Unger, 1977.

Seltzer, Daniel, ed. *The Modern Theatre: Readings and Documents*. Boston: Little, Brown, 1967.

Strittmatter, Erwin. "Brecht at Work." *Enact* 24 (December 1968).

Tenschert, Joachim. "The Mask at the Berliner Ensemble." *World Theatre* 10 (Spring 1961).

Tynan, Kenneth. "Braw and Brecht." *Observer*, 2 September 1956.

———. "German Measles." *Observer*, 20 January 1957.

Volker, Klaus. *Brecht Chronicle*. Translated by Fred Wieck. New York: Seabury Press, 1975.

———. *Brecht, a Biography*. Translated by John Nowell. New York: Seabury Press, 1978.

Wandel, Joseph. "Brecht and His A-Effect." *Drama Critique* 10 (September 1967).

Wardle, Irving. "Brecht and I: Lotte Lenya Talks to Irving Wardle." *Observer*, 9 September 1962.

Weber, Carl. "Brecht as Director." *The Drama Review* 12 (Fall 1967).

———. "Brecht in Eclipse?" *The Drama Review* 24 (March 1980).

Wekwerth, Manfred. "Brecht Today." *The Drama Review* 12 (Fall 1967).

White, A. D. "Brecht's Quest for a Democratic Theatre." *Theatre Quarterly* 2 (January-March 1972).

Willett, John. *The Theatre of Bertolt Brecht: A Study from Eight Aspects*. London: Methuen, 1959.

———. *Caspar Neher: Brecht's Designer*. London: Methuen, 1986.

———, ed. *Brecht on Theatre*. New York: Hill and Wang, 1964.

Witt, Hubert, ed. *Brecht, As They Knew Him*. Translated by John Peet. New York: International Publishers, 1974.

JEAN-LOUIS BARRAULT

Ansorge, Peter. "Genet Avenged, or How to Survive in France: JLB Talks to Peter Ansorge." *Plays and Players* 18 (April 1971).

Barrault, Jean-Louis. "Child of Silence." Translated by Eric Bentley. *Theatre Arts Monthly* 33 (October 1949).

———. "My Doubts and My Beliefs." *World Theatre* 1 (1951).

———. *The Theatre of Jean-Louis Barrault*. Translated by Joseph Chiari. New York: Hill and Wang, 1961.

———. "Four Directors: I. Jean-Louis Barrault." *Theatre Quarterly* 3 (April-June 1973).

———. *Memories for Tomorrow*. Translated by Jonathan Griffin. New York: E. P. Dutton, 1974. .

Bradby, David. "A Chronology of Jean-Louis Barrault's Career." *Theatre Quarterly* 3 (April-June 1973).

———. *Modern French Drama 1940–1980*. Cambridge, Eng.: Cambridge University Press, 1981.

Brooking, Jack. "Four Bare Walls and a Touch of Joy." *Players* 41 (October 1964).

Gillespie, John K. "Interior Action: The Impact of Noh on Jean-Louis Barrault." *Comparative Drama* 16 (Winter 1982–1983).

Hewes, Henry. "Total Theatre." *Saturday Review*, 26 January 1957.

Klein, Luce, and Arthur Klein. "Jean-Louis Barrault." *Theatre Arts Monthly* 31 (October 1947).

Knapp, Bettina. *Offstage Voices: Interviews with Modern French Dramatists*. Edited by Alba Amoia. Troy, N.Y.: Whitson, 1975.

Loney, Glenn. "In the Words of Jean-Louis Barrault." *Cue Magazine,* 4 October 1969.

Lyons, Charles R. "Le Compagnie Madeleine Renaud–Jean-Louis Barrault: The Idea and the Aesthetic." *Educational Theatre Journal* 19 (December 1967).

O'Connor, Garry. *French Theatre Today.* London: Pitman, 1975.

Schaded, Maurice. "Remembering the Compagnie Renaud-Barrault." *Institute of International Education News Bulletin* 35 (December 1959).

Turgeon, Thomas S. "Theatre in Review: *Harold and Maude; Zadig.*" *Theatre Journal* 32 (December 1980).

Wallis, Bill. "Jean-Louis Barrault's *Rabelais.*" *Theatre Quarterly* 1 (July-September 1971).

Unpublished Materials

Dieckman, Suzanne Burgoyne. "Theory and Practice in the Total Theatre of Jean-Louis Barrault." Ph.D. dissertation, University of Michigan, 1975.

Gordon, Barbara. "Le Théâtre Total as Envisioned by Jean-Louis Barrault." Ph.D. dissertation, Columbia University, 1973.

Index

About the Author

SAMUEL L. LEITER is Professor of Theatre at Brooklyn College, City University of New York. His previously published books include *The Art of Kabuki: Famous Plays in Performance* (1979); *Ten Seasons: New York Theatre in the Seventies*; *The Encyclopedia of the New York Stage, 1920–1930*; *The Encyclopedia of the New York Stage, 1930–1940*; and *From Belasco to Brook: Representative Directors of the English-Speaking Stage* (Greenwood Press, 1986, 1985, 1989, and 1991). He also edited *Shakespeare Around the Globe: A Guide to Notable Postwar Revivals* (Greenwood, 1986). Professor Leiter is editor of the *Asian Theatre Journal*.